EGGSHE

ROY KEANE AT IPSWICH TOWN
2009-2011

Series editor: Clive Leatherdale

Ian Oxborrow

DESERT ISLAND BOOKS

First published in 2011
by
DESERT ISLAND BOOKS LIMITED
16 Imperial Park, Rawreth Lane, Rayleigh, Essex SS6 9RS
United Kingdom
www.desertislandbooks.com

© 2011 Ian Oxborrow

British Library Cataloguing-in-Publication Data
A catalogue record for this book is available from the British Library

ISBN 978-1-905328-89-5

Printed and bound in Great Britain by
4edge Limited, Hockley. www.4edge.co.uk

Contents

Author's Note & Acknowledgments

There was a time when I thought this book was going to be extremely short, when Roy Keane's tenure started in the most inglorious manner. His own mentor, Brian Clough, lasted just 44 days as manager of Leeds United, but Keane eventually hauled Ipswich Town away from the depths of the Championship and I, along with the thousands of Town fans, were forced to ride the rollercoaster for a few more laps yet. I have tried to give a balanced account of all that has happened since he arrived in Suffolk.

In the main, it has been a difficult period – for the club and its supporters. I could have ignored some of Keane's failings and painted him simply as the footballing legend who continued the club's trend of struggling to escape the Championship for grander surroundings.

There were, however, many well-documented controversies along the way and I believe I have been fair in presenting Keane's own views and retaliations to the criticisms and stories he was subjected to.

The author would like to thank Dan Thomas of Come Hither Design and TWTD.co.uk for the cover image, Keith Oxborrow for his reading, and all of the people who were interviewed for their contributions.

Bibliography: *The East Anglian Daily Times, Ipswich Evening Star, Colchester Gazette, The Sun, The Daily Mirror, The Daily Mail, The Guardian, The Daily Telegraph, TWTD.co.uk, Keane: The Autobiography.*

Copyright for image of Roy Keane's head on the cover: Mike Brown.

IAN OXBORROW
February 2011

Chapter One

Jim – A Man Scorned

'UNLIKE ROY KEANE I AM NOT GOING TO WALK AWAY. I AM HERE LONG TERM AND HAVE NO INTENTION OF LEAVING.'

In the words of Jim Magilton, Roy Keane was 'in the building'. But what went so wrong that Magilton be given his P45? Town were backed by a wealthy owner, they finished a point off the play-offs the previous season (2007-08), and they were not going to make it this time around either, but it could have been worse. They could have been Norwich City and heading for League One. This was Ipswich Town, though, the club of Sir Bobby Robson and Sir Alf Ramsey, of Mick Mills and Terry Butcher, of European and domestic glory.

After announcing his playing retirement at the end of the 2005-06 season, the tears were barely dry from Magilton's emotional farewell from Portman Road when he was appointed as the club's new manager in June. He was said to be 'the outstanding candidate', whose vision for the club far exceeded any of the other managers on the shortlist, which included Northern Ireland manager Lawrie Sanchez.

As a player, Magilton was popular with Town fans for his commitment, enthusiasm and constant berating of anyone in sight. Team-mates were bawled at if a pass went astray, or a move failed to include the Northern Irishman at some point. Lacking pace, but blessed with vision and weight of pass, he orchestrated Town's midfield as they won promotion to the Premier League in 1999-2000. His finest moment came in the play-off semi-final, second-leg, against Bolton when he scored a hat-trick in one of the most thrilling matches Portman Road has ever seen. As well as giving his team-mates an ear-bashing, Magilton was fortunate enough to have the ability to seemingly talk to the ball. Without this, he would never have made it past non-league football, for his rubbery-looking legs moved far slower than his mouth. He never hid, always demanding the ball from defenders, wanting to receive every throw-in and take every set-piece. His enthusiasm spilled over in an ugly confrontation with Town striker David Johnson at West Bromwich Albion in a televised match, but otherwise, his career as a Town player was remembered for all of the right reasons.

His appointment was a shock. Not a shock on the same scale as Keane's appointment – a big name at the centre of the footballing circus – but a shock because he had no managerial experience and the man he was replacing, Joe Royle, a manager with many miles on the clock, was quite the opposite. Chairman David Sheepshanks admitted at the press conference called to unveil Magilton that the club's choice was a gamble. He said the board, however, could not ignore Magilton's passion for the club, knowledge of the staff and players and vision for restoring the club's fortunes and leading them back to the Premier League. Magilton, at 37, was the youngest manager in the Championship at the time. He expressed his desire to win in style – music to the ears of Town fans, who had become none too impressed with the style of play adopted by Royle since the team's fortunes under the former FA Cup winning boss dwindled. 'I've always had the ability to pass it to someone else in my shirt, so our players have got to get used to that,' was Magilton's message. Bryan Klug was appointed first-team coach and both were handed two-year contracts.

Magilton's first season was expected to be a work-in progress, as he sorted the dead wood – for which there was plenty – left to him by Royle. Three defeats in the first three games of the season set the alarm bells ringing, but a final finish of 14th – 13 points off the play-offs was no disgrace. The loan market was used astutely to bring in Francis Jeffers from Blackburn Rovers and Mark Noble from West Ham United, while Jon Walters was a bargain buy from Chester and was proof Magilton could work satisfactorily with little money to spend. Satisfactory would not do, however.

A summer of free transfers, such as the returning Pablo Counago and Tommy Miller, saw Town turn on the kind of style Magilton spoke of when he was appointed. He now had the players in his squad to do so – at Portman Road anyway. They failed to win away from home until February, despite steamrollering all before them in front of their own fans. A 6-0 blitz over Bristol City was reminiscent of the late 1990s under George Burley when it was a question of how many Town were going to score. But away from home, the story was a complete contrast and it was this that cost Town a place in the play-offs as they missed out by one point. Magilton was halfway there.

He created a side which could beat anyone at Portman Road and all they needed to do was pick up more points away from home. It was a mystery as to why they struggled so badly on their travels. In front of the home crowd, the combination of Jon Walters and David Wright on the right-hand side was as good as any in the division, while Owen Garvan and Counago gave Town fluency and flair. The ball was largely kept on the floor, except when Walters was used as an effective diagonal outlet, like the one used by George Burley with James Scowcroft, and John Lyall with Steve Whitton in the early 1990s. Town set out with a method and knew how to win. Away from home, though, the method vanished. Like the England team of the era, Town developed a lop-sided issue, with no left-footer to give the side balance. Gary Roberts's Town career faded after a promising start and Magilton needed to find a replacement. It would take more than a year and would be one of Magilton's biggest downfalls.

The face of the club changed massively at the end of 2007 when Marcus Evans became the new owner. Saddled with £32 million of debt, Magilton and predecessor Joe Royle were left scraping the bottom of the transfer market bucket, and the only way Town were going to experience a brighter future was if the club was either sold to a wealthy new owner, or they won promotion – an unlikely outcome given the lack of progress on the pitch. Fans stood in hope rather than expectation that Magilton was going to mastermind a storming run to the top of the table.

Elusive and reclusive, no picture of Evans existed in the public domain. For Town fans, their international man of mystery could stay anonymous for ever as long as he continued ploughing in the £12 million he handed Magilton, who was given a two-and-half-year extension to his contract when the takeover was finalised, and the end result was promotion. The enigmatic money-man made his millions from conferencing, hospitality and training across the globe. The early beginnings of his empire saw him serve champagne lunches and strawberries and cream from a marquee in the garden of his home in Somerset Road, London during Wimbledon. By 2004 he was making an unsuccessful £700 million bid for *The Daily Mirror*. A well-known organisation around the City, The Marcus Evans Group employed more than 3,500 people around the world, and while his wealth was in a separate bracket to Chelsea's Roman Abramovich, he was certainly the sugar-daddy that Town were seeking.

Evans was expecting to recoup his money by bankrolling Town back to the Premier League. It was not beyond the realms of reality, provided his funds were spent wisely and Town continued to improve. Funding of £12 million went a long way in the Championship. It is more than enough to buy the spine of a team – a centre-half, midfielder and striker on decent wages. Magilton set his sights on Premier League players, whose extra quality would, he hoped, be the defining factor in hauling Town out of the wilderness.

However, with Premier League wages spiraling, persuading players to drop down a division was a problem, particularly to a club in mid-table and not assured of a quick return to the top flight. Portsmouth striker David Nugent was a prime example.

Magilton had a habit of revealing his transfer targets, and when the January 2008 transfer window opened, it was a well-known fact that Plymouth's David Norris was on his wanted list. The midfielder cost £2 million, with a sell-on fee to Norris's previous club Bolton Wanderers dragging the transfer out as the clubs haggled over the price. Norris was not a typical Town midfield player. Dogged and terrier-like, Magilton wanted more bite than he was getting from Owen Garvan and Tommy Miller to end Town's desperate away form. Gareth McAuley was another player Magilton was openly trying to sign, but Leicester City would not budge until the summer. Goalkeepers Stephen Bywater and Nick Colgan arrived, with Neil Alexander heading back to Scotland to join Rangers, while Macedonian Veliche Shumulikoski and Alan Quinn also signed for Town, who were now overloaded with midfield players. Fans expecting big names were left disappointed. Shumulikoski, signed from Turkish side Bursaspor for around £500,000, was an unknown quantity, but came with 46 international caps to his name. A holding midfielder, he was expected to step straight into the squad, which included Norris and Quinn – also central midfielders who were able to play out wide, but less effectively. Added to those were Garvan and Miller, plus Sylvain Legwinski and Gavin Williams, who were still at the club, leaving Magilton spoilt for choice.

The policy of revealing the identity of Town's targets received mixed reaction among Town followers. Some appreciated Magilton letting the press know whom the club was trying to sign. Others saw it that he should be keeping his lips sealed to avoid letting rival clubs know who may be available, and subsequently sparking a bidding war. The Evans investment predictably increased the value of any player Town chased. They had the money, so they would have to pay the inflated price.

Town's away form picked up though, with two victories on their travels in February, but too many defeats meant they were always playing catch up and they could not rely solely on home form. The equilibrium of the team was affected by the January arrivals, as Norris was played on the right side of midfield, leaving Magilton to find somewhere else for Walters. He was either played wide on the left or up front where he was less suited. Otherwise, Magilton went with either Norris, Danny Haynes or Alan Quinn on the left, as Town's system was crying out for a left-winger.

Evans was patient with the situation, as Town missed out on the play-offs by a point. He backed Magilton to come good in 2008-09, with money still left over from the £12 million invested when he took over. It was not a huge amount by footballing standards but it gave Magilton room to manoeuvre. The left-hand side of the team desperately needed rebuilding, with Dan Harding, Matt Richards, Billy Clarke and Gary Roberts all shipped out, either on loan or permanently. The popular Sito Castro, comfortable on the left or right was also released – a controversial decision among fans.

A quiet summer followed, with only the return of Richard Wright making a marked improvement on the side. The quest for the '20-goal a season' striker brought in Kevin Lisbie, but Magilton could not depend on a player who had enjoyed one fruitful season in more than a decade of professional football, though he had scored regularly in a relegated Colchester United side. Gareth McAuley finally signed as a replacement for the retiring Jason De Vos, but on paper, Town were little stronger than when they finished the previous season.

Magilton sprung a surprise on the first day of the season when young defender Tommy Smith was given his debut in the back four alongside summer signing Pim Balkestein. The Dutchman was said to have all the attributes needed to be a top centre-half, but the term 'raw' was also used. Town were beaten 1-2 by Preston at Portman Road and the locals were growing restless. With Evans's money all but spent, Town had gone backwards.

Spanish international Ivan Campo was signed on a free transfer after his release by Bolton. Having missed pre-season training, it would be weeks before he was involved. Magilton was quick to add to his team's depleted left side by signing free agent Ben Thatcher, although he was clearly past his best and came with a reputation for ill-discipline. Right-back Moritz Volz arrived on loan from Fulham, as Magilton began a game of mix and match. It was anyone's guess as to who was going to play, and where. The inclusion of Volz saw David Wright moved to left-back, while Walters was employed on the left, sometimes on the right, and also up front. Norris, his best position being in the centre of midfield, was mostly used on the right, while Alan Quinn was in and out on the left. McAuley and Richard Wright overcame dodgy starts to the season and Town's away form proved superior than their home form. But in creating a side which was harder to beat on their travels, Magilton removed all the flair and creativity which had seen Town entertain the fans at Portman Road in 2007-08.

Alan Lee was sold as Jon Stead came in from Sheffield United. Stead scored a beauty on his debut at home to Reading, but his form suffered, as Town began to go through the motions. Magilton preferred a 4-5-1 formation away from home which nullified their opponents, but Town, unable to keep the ball grounded, failed to pass their way through teams when it came to playing at Portman Road. The (David) Wright, Walters, Garvan, Counago quartet was rarely seen together and defenders resorted to playing long balls, with neither Alex Bruce or McAuley adept at carrying the ball out from the back. Campo's role as playmaker was short-lived and he was quickly dumped by Magilton after a 2-2 draw with Swansea in October before reappearing later in the season at centre-half – the position he was expected to fill when he signed.

By the time Town went to Norwich for the East Anglian derby in December, Magilton was under severe pressure. The money was spent, his side playing unattractive football, and all the talk of the team 'gelling' was nothing more than an excuse. Magilton and the players continued to ask for patience from the fans. They insisted the new signings needed time to bed in and would eventually come good. The problem, however, was Magilton changed the team week after week, trying to find combinations which worked. Some would, though only for 45 minutes or 90 at the most. Two wins would be followed by three games without a victory and there were no signs of a run up the table arriving any time soon. Lisbie and Stead were in the team one week and out the next, as was Counago, who suffered most from the long balls pelted at his head. Darren Ambrose's signing on loan from Charlton seemed like shrewd business. Originally sold to Newcastle when Town were strapped for cash, and a talented wide man with a vicious shot and cross in his armoury, Ambrose was played in the troublesome left-wing position but was so ineffective he returned to Charlton in January.

The news that Town would listen to offers for defender Alex Bruce filtered out before the clash at Carrow Road. Bruce was offered a new contract and revealed the reason for turning it down was not financial, fuelling opinion he was one of a number of players who did not see eye-to-eye with Magilton. Town limped to a 0-2 defeat in front of the Sky cameras, leaving fans calling for Magilton's sacking after the woeful display, but he responded with the ironic comment: 'Unlike Roy Keane I am not going to walk away. I am here long term and have no intention of leaving.'

The national press reported that Magilton had lost the dressing room and, with Town 12th in the Championship at the halfway stage, the story of a 'secret meeting' broke. This incident was the beginning of the end for Magilton. Although results suggested his time was going to be up sooner rather than later, it revealed the breakdown of communication between management, playing staff and the local press, as Town sunk to their lowest ebb since Magilton took over. The pressure was telling, with the transfer funds spent and performances worsening. It was a question of when Evans would pull the plug, not if, although the lack of comment on Town's decline from the owner made many wonder if he would retain Magilton and save on the cost of paying up the remainder of his contract. The impact of the recession on Evans's finances was unknown, but like other wealthy businessmen, he was believed to have taken a hit from the global meltdown. His Ipswich Town holding was a drop in the ocean in terms of his empire, but like any astute businessman, which he clearly was based on his dealings outside of football, he would not spend money unless it made sense.

Whatever the truth regarding the secret meeting, it did nothing to help Magilton's cause. Claims of the meeting were doing the rounds at Carrow Road before, during and after the dismal defeat and wild speculation was filling message boards. Then *The East Anglian Daily Times* ran the story, with eight players – skipper Gareth McAuley, Richard Wright, David Wright, David Norris, Veliche Shumulikoski, Owen Garvan, Jon Walters and Shane Supple – understood to be those invited. They were said to be the chosen ones on which the team of the future would be built around. A source from within the squad was said to have revealed that the playing staff were uncomfortable about the meeting taking place.

Magilton admitted that he spoke to a few players before the Norwich match, but said the meeting was nothing unusual and added that he often held meetings, and would continue to do so. 'The meeting was not a secret one and there are a lot of negative stories being written about us at the moment,' he said. 'I wanted to make some points about the desire and passion I would like to see at this club, something that can be lost when talking to a bigger group. The same discussions I have had with other players at other times. There is no way I have singled out any player or players and I believe in the team ethos with the only way to success being as a team. I am adamant we will be successful and do that as a team.' Despite Magilton's protests, the performance at Norwich smacked of disharmony and discontent.

A day later, he was storming out of a press conference with the print media at Portman Road. Angered by more questions about secret meetings, the Northern Irishman's temper gave in. It was a clear indication of the increasing pressure he was coming under. Crowds at Portman Road were dwindling, drawn matches were met with boos, and whenever Town went behind it was greeted with chants of 'you don't know what you're doing', and not merely from the vocal North Stand.

'There is no question Jim had the potential to fall out with people,' said journalist Matt Plummer, who had covered Ipswich Town for more than a decade and wrote *Full English* – former Town defender Fabian

Wilnis's autobiography. 'He could be wonderfully friendly but he had this temper on him as well. Falling out with the local media didn't help and there was a really dark period during his last few months. He really clammed up and became extremely frosty to the point where for many weeks he didn't do the pre-match press conferences. He seemed to be feeling the strain and seemed to feel a deep-seated resentment towards the press coverage he was getting at the time.

'Jim was very cross with me at Barnsley [that season], literally one word answers and then the Chelsea cup game as well when he was terse with everyone and we sensed that it was the beginning of the end. Then there was the day he stormed out in front of five or six of us reporters. I felt it was going to happen because it was one of those days when he came in and tried to fulfil his obligation but there was an atmosphere and he became cross when pressed on certain subjects and walked out. I felt sorry for him that day and especially when the recording went online. He could always be a bit short and when speaking to him as a player after a defeat he wouldn't want to talk, but equally when he did want to he was great, really friendly, and I had plenty of nice chats with him and liked him. He was jovial, full of charisma and I was pleased when he got the job. You could see the excitement in his eyes on his first day as manager and I remember at his first pre-season friendly at Burton Albion you could see the excitement in him.'

Luciano Civelli was the last roll of the dice for Magilton. The Argentine was exactly what Town had been searching for for two years – a left-winger who could deliver dangerous balls into the box, as well as deal with the physical nature of the English game. Roberts found the Championship too much and fell back into League One with Huddersfield, while Ian Westlake was sold early in Magilton's reign as part of the deal to bring Dan Harding to the club. Essex-boy Westlake, an academy product, was not a player to whip the crowd into a frenzy, but he gave Joe Royle's side balance and a steady flow of goals from the left-hand side. Roberts's trademark was jinking runs with his peculiar, wiggling running-style, but after starting promisingly, his confidence fell apart. The onset of Town's long-ball habit did not help, as he stood either isolated on the wing, or tucked inside where he was out-muscled with little space to work in.

Civelli began his career as a full-back with Banfield before moving further forward. He cost £1.1 million and, after Town's previous experience of signing South Americans, Town fans hoped he would be more Mauricio Taricco, the popular full-back of the 1990s, than Adrian Paz, the expensive striker-cum-winger who left after a handful of games after the pair arrived in a joint deal. Town were unbeaten in Civelli's first three games but then a rot set in with an embarrassing 0-3 home defeat to Southampton on 3 March and a 1-3 home reverse against Doncaster on 4 April. The fans' patience was at an end and the play-offs were out of reach. Magilton took the blame for the Doncaster defeat and said some of the players performed as though the season was already over. A bright spot was the record-breaking debut of 16-year-old Connor Wickham, who broke Jason Dozzell's record of being Town's youngest ever player by 45 days.

Sandwiched in between the two shocking home results, Magilton produced the most glamorous signing of his time as Ipswich manager. It came completely out of the blue and could have altered the course of the season had it happened earlier. Giovani Dos Santos was out of the first team picture at Tottenham following his summer arrival from Barcelona, where he was dubbed the 'new Ronaldinho'. He was only at Town until the end of the season and, even though the chop was imminent for Magilton, the arrival of Dos Santos appeared a ploy by Evans to give the fans some entertainment before the season ended so they renewed their season tickets. Magilton knew he was getting something special in Dos Santos. His skill was phenomenal, combining impeccable balance with trickery, awareness and a goal-threat from anywhere on the pitch. His quality was way above the Championship, as well as Ipswich Town. Not since Kieron Dyer had Town fans seen such a gifted footballer. Civelli ruptured knee ligaments on Dos Santos's home debut, when the Mexican scored the equaliser against Burnley. It was cruel on the Argentine, but the damage was already done for Magilton.

How far Town's football had fallen was emphasised by the way Dos Santos was treated on the pitch. He played eight times during his spell with Town, including six starts, and scored four goals. When he gained control of the ball he headed in one direction – the goal, weaving past three or four defenders. But far from the stereotypical playground hogger, he was willing to play-in team-mates and create as well as score. However, the infrequency with which he was actually passed to by a Town team-mate was remarkable. Given licence to roam around the pitch, the instructions would predictably be to find Dos Santos's feet at every opportunity to let him wreak havoc. Strangely, the ball was still pumped long, leaving Dos Santos to wait up to ten minutes for a touch and the crowd was at a loss. The message was finally across by the time Norwich came to Portman Road for what turned out to be Magilton's final match in charge. Nevertheless, it took an injury to Ben Thatcher to make Town realise they would prosper if they kept the ball on the floor, and the introduction of forgotten man Jaime Peters, in an unfamiliar left-back role, sprung Town into life. With Dos Santos a threat on one side, Peters marauding up the wing on the other and Counago finally receiving the ball to feet, Town ran out 3-2 winners.

Three days later Magilton was sacked and assistant John Gorman also left. New chief executive Simon Clegg had joined the club a day earlier and a new era was set to begin. The timing was a surprise – two matches left in the season – but the actual decision made by Evans was not.

'You could see things falling apart on and off the pitch, all the problems off the pitch were being mirrored on it in terms of the way they were playing,' said Plummer. 'There was always the suspicion from the day that Evans took over that he may prefer a bigger name than Magilton. I don't think it was any great surprise when his departure did finally happen, except for perhaps the timing of it, having just beaten Norwich. It must have been sad for him because he had such a great affinity with the club.'

Magilton showed during his three seasons in charge that he was a competent Championship-level manager. He was able to take a well-financed club to within a point of the play-offs, which was no disgrace, but the lack of progression in his third season cost him his job. The majority of Town fans had turned against him, not because they disliked him, but because they could not see him as the man to take the club up. Protests against his in-match tactical decisions, team-selections and substitutions were voiced from the stands but without the burning hatred reserved for managers who are just unwelcome from the moment they set foot through the club gates.

The memory of Magilton's hat-trick heroics was faint, yet still existed. The fans knew he had the club at heart and was doing his utmost to win promotion, but it was difficult accepting that his best simply was not good enough. Although the calling for his head felt like a big fuss at the time, the inevitability of it meant an outpouring of sympathy followed his exit. He was no longer Jim Magilton, enemy number one. The fans who wanted him out had it their way after Evans decided the club could drift no further.

It was more underachievement than downright failure because Magilton assembled a squad of far greater quality than the one he inherited in 2006. Its pinnacle was the home form of 2007-08 when Town were a side to be feared. It fizzled out though, as Magilton's selection became confused. For a man whose vision for the club was built around winning in style, and whose playing career was based on ball retention, Town's attractive winning method faded. The constant change of systems and personnel was to blame, plus the lack of improvement of the playing staff during the summer of 2008. Players such as Lisbie, Volz and Thatcher brought little in terms of extra quality, and moving Bruce to right-back, playing David Wright at left-back and Norris on the right of midfield upset the team balance, while the sale of target man Alan Lee went against the grain of Town's direct playing style. Despite being taller than Lee, Stead was like a twig in the wind when it came to dealing with high balls, although his goal return was reasonable, and would have been greater had Magilton stuck with him and Counago as his first-choice pairing, rather than constantly switching to one upfront or dragging Walters away from his most effective position on the right.

The exclusion of Peters for all but his final game in charge was a mystery when Town needed more pace out wide to give them an alternative to long, straight balls. Danny Haynes never progressed further than cameo king or headless chicken, as Magilton tried and failed to harness the attributes of the fastest player in the division. With the exception of a couple of late bursts from Connor Wickham and a sprinkling of appearances by Liam Trotter, Jordan Rhodes and Dean Bowditch, Town's once famed trust in youth had gone. Billy Clarke and Rhodes were both making headlines during loan spells in League One and League Two, suggesting they had a bright future in the game. But Magilton stuck with the experience of Miller, Richard Naylor, Thatcher, Quinn and Campo.

'Jim Magilton kept going down blind alleys in his final season, changing the team and tinkering and then became entrenched in the end when he refused to speak to the press,' said Phil Ham, editor of the fanzine and website *Those Were the Days*. 'He needed a senior figure alongside him and although he had Bryan Klug and brought in John Gorman during his final few months it was really too late by then. I think if you look at the last months of Magilton's reign and then the winless run at the start of Keane's first full season, the seeds had already been sown.

'It was all falling down for Magilton, with the walking out of press conferences. He needed a new club to start at again and his sacking probably came a little too late. Town had been languishing around mid-table for the best part of three years and did not look like becoming promotion candidates. The media drummed up these fan protests and when about 25 people turned up it showed he still had the respect of many people but they questioned his judgment. He found it difficult coping when the pressure was on.'

Magilton left behind a squad which needed tweaking and the writing was on the wall for many of the 13 players whose contracts were up in the summer, but the club was left in a far better position than the one he inherited from Joe Royle. Millions of pounds were spent on transfer fees and wages during the last three seasons, which reaped nothing more than a place outside the play-offs.

Yet Town possessed the base of a quality side. Richard Wright was outstanding in goal and went on to win player-of-the-year, while McAuley grew in stature after an error-laden start to his Town career. Walters and David Wright were available to reform their partnership on the right-hand side, and it was hoped that Norris would begin to live up to his transfer fee.

Magilton's mistakes cost him his job. Would Roy Keane succeed where Magilton had failed? Would he spend wisely in the transfer market and make the adjustments which were needed? And would he bring back the passing style the fans demanded, on which Ipswich Town's reputation was built?

Chapter Two

The Appointment

'THE DAY I WORRY ABOUT TONY CASCARINO WILL BE A VERY SAD DAY IN MY LIFE.'

It was one of the most dramatic weeks in the history of Ipswich Town Football Club. The chain of events started on Tuesday, 21 April 2009 when Simon Clegg was announced as the club's new chief executive. Clegg, 49, had been leader of Britain's record-breaking Olympic team in Beijing the previous summer. He was chief executive of the British Olympic Association for 12 years and *chef de mission* of Team GB, but left in December following a restructuring of the organisation, before the former army officer in the Paras was offered his first role in football by Town owner Marcus Evans.

Clegg, awarded an OBE in 2000 and a CBE for his work on London's successful bid for the 2012 Olympics, took over from Derek Bowden, who was the public face of the club for seven years but would leave in the summer. Bowden guided the club through administration, along with David Sheepshanks, and said he was leaving the job pleased with where the club was heading. He told the *Ipswich Evening Star*: 'I am happy with what I have achieved here. We have put the club back on a firm footing and I believe made the right decisions. The financial situation has been improved since the dark days of administration and we now find ourselves in a stronger position than most of our Championship rivals.'

The former Saatchi & Saatchi executive was in charge when the club was controversially sold to Evans, but he felt that by selling the club, Town avoided the chance of a slide similar to that of Southampton 'Yes, it was the right thing to do,' he added. 'If not we would have been in danger of going the same way as Southampton, who now find themselves [in League One]. I am not saying we would, but there was a chance that could have happened. Now we are as competitive as any Championship side to make progress.'

The departure of Bowden was anticipated as Evans was expected to bring in his own men to run the club on a day-to-day basis. Bowden oversaw the transition from the 'old regime' to the 'new', but Evans was ready to implement further changes as he moulded the club to his liking – a club for the future, rather than one living on past traditions and values.

Town's owner, via the medium of the club media department, said of Clegg's appointment: 'Simon has built up an extensive knowledge of the sporting world through his role with the British Olympic Association and I'm delighted that he has agreed to join the club. Not only does he have a wealth of experience in the world of sport, but he has proved to be a highly successful businessman and team leader and will have a key role in moving Ipswich Town forward.'

From the club's tradition of being run by the Cobbold family, it was strange to find it owned by a reclusive hospitality tycoon and run by a man with a background in athletics. Clegg's credentials outside of football were never in doubt. Town fans, however, were left wondering if he could transfer his sporting and business acumen into the running of a football club which was, at that moment in time, a mediocre Championship team with a Premier League infrastructure.

Clegg faced the media for the first time that morning and told the gathered crowd he planned to take Town back to the Premier League at the earliest opportunity, rather than stipulating a specific time frame. He explained that the club's community feel was one of the main reasons for accepting the job, as well as its potential and sporting heritage. An incident earlier in the season was highlighted, when Clegg was sat quietly in one of the stands at Portman Road and saw a lady give a steward a box of chocolates for his efforts. This impressed him and helped make up his mind. He said he would draw on his experience of being involved in the Olympic Games and wanted everything at the club to be 'gold star level'.

With Evans having already promised money to spend in the transfer market during the summer, Clegg confirmed he would take an active part in transfer dealings, despite having never played a part in such a deal previously. Clegg, who had known Evans for more than a year, was effervescent and refreshing in front of the media. He spoke intelligently and freely about his role and his hopes for the future for the club. His guard went up quickly when asked about the future of current manager Jim Magilton. Speculation was mounting and Clegg would only say it was 'inappropriate' for him to comment – a small clue of what was to come.

In fact, it was only one day into Clegg's reign as the club's new chief executive when the announcement of Magilton's sacking was made. Assistant John Gorman was also relieved of his duties and Evans released a concise statement explaining that the time had come for a change: 'Today is a sad day for me. I have enjoyed working with Jim over the past 15 months and no one has worked harder to bring success to Ipswich Town in that time. Jim has a passion for the club but unfortunately we have not made the progress both he and I expected this season. I would like to put on record my thanks for his commitment to this football club and wish him every success for the future.'

Evans was working ruthlessly. Rather than bringing in a stop-gap manager earlier in the season and then a new chief executive before appointing another manager, or simply appointing a manager who was not his number one, he bided his time. Installing Clegg as chief executive was the first part of the jigsaw, sacking Magilton the second. This meant the infrastructure was in place for the new manager to come in and get straight on with the job – should it be before the end of the season or at the start of the summer – so the whole of pre-season could be used to build the squad he wanted. There were two games left in the season and Clegg was in front of the media for the second time in his first two days in the job to reveal Town were close to announcing their new manager.

Clegg revealed that Magilton's replacement would be installed by the end of the week, having already spoken to a number of candidates, with only final arrangements to be sorted. He said the club was looking for a manager with a proven track record, who had achieved some success and taken a club in the direction Ipswich were aspiring to go. More than anything, Clegg said Town wanted a 'winner'.

The sacking of Magilton was down to results not meeting the aspirations of the club when considering the level of financial investment, according to Clegg. He was unable to speak to Magilton himself about the sacking because the Northern Irishman returned to his homeland to be with his sick mother, so Evans delivered the bad news over the phone. The timing of the new manager being brought in was a big part of Clegg's discussions with Evans. The end of the season was most likely, but Clegg said Town's league position meant it was possible to bring the new man in before then, and give him a chance to assess the 13 players out-of-contract in the summer.

The identity of Jim Magilton's successor was subject of lengthy debate, if not since the day he was appointed, then certainly from the moment Evans took control of the club. With a stronger financial backing under the new owner, Town were expected to seek a bigger managerial name than Magilton. Reports in the national press of who Evans was lining up were being printed as early as January 2009, when Magilton was gamely clinging on to his job. Glenn Hoddle's name was repeatedly mentioned, even more so when John Gorman – who joined Town from Hoddle's Academy in Spain – arrived at Portman Road as Magilton's assistant, stoking up the speculation even more. Hoddle emerged as the bookies' favourite in the aftermath of Magilton's exit, but with Gorman departing as well, it was less likely the former England manager would be jetting in from his Spanish project to take the reins at Ipswich. Had Hoddle been appointed, he would have been well-received by the Ipswich

fans as his brand of flowing football was highly thought-of on the international stage and he would have added to the club's collection of
England managers who had also taken charge at Portman Road.

Former West Ham and Reading boss Alan Pardew was understood to
have spoken with Evans in recent weeks and Alan Curbishley was another whose name was forever mentioned in the press and on message
boards as a suitable candidate. Pardew oversaw West Ham's promotion to
the top flight in 2004-05. Curbishley spent more than a decade in charge
at Charlton Athletic, a club with parallels to Ipswich Town. He oversaw
two promotions to the Premier League and consolidation in the top flight
and had a reputation for unearthing top quality players for low prices,
including former Town striker Darren Bent, who was sold for a massive
profit and went on to play for England. Having worked wonders at West
Ham, where he kept the Hammers up when relegation looked a certainty in the 2006-07 season, Curbishley's stock as a Premier League manager was on the rise. He was reported to have been interviewed for the
vacant England managerial position when Steve McClaren was appointed in 2006, but, since leaving West Ham in 2008, he was yet to return to
football and spent time fighting a financial dispute with the club.

Neil Warnock, the Crystal Palace manager, was another to be linked
with the Town vacancy before Magilton departed. His uncompromising
and outspoken style was never popular among opposing fans, but he was
an experienced Championship manager, who had won promotion to the
Premier League with Sheffield United in 2005-06.

Roy Keane's name was tentatively mentioned in the run up to the
sacking of Magilton, but come Wednesday evening he was suddenly the
front-runner. His odds were slashed to 2/7. The website of Town fanzine
Those Were The Days revealed a close source had been informed by a Town
player that Keane was set to be appointed. By Thursday morning, confirmation had arrived – Roy Keane was new manager of Ipswich Town.
The common theme among the candidates was promotion. All apart
from Hoddle had achieved the feat in recent times and Keane was no
exception, having done so with Sunderland in circumstances which made
football sit up and take notice – for the right reasons.

'I wanted someone who would play decent football with consistency
and passion – none of which we had from Magilton – and a big name
courtesy of Marcus Evans's money,' said Oliver Procter, a Town fan of
more than 20 years and season-ticket holder in the Sir Bobby Robson
Stand. 'Alan Curbishley would have been good, as would have been a Joe
Royle equivalent. I was concerned that Keane spent a lot of money buying all sorts of players, with only a small number of decent players as an

outcome. I was disappointed when the news broke. I was listening in the car on talkSPORT, and was expecting more, but to take Sunderland up the way he did was impressive, and, after a little thinking, I was happy overall with the appointment.'

Marcus Evans provided his soundbite on the breaking news, without making an appearance, as Town fans had become used to: 'He has extensive contacts in the game and is a proven winner who encourages his team to play the attractive football that Ipswich Town fans have come to expect. I believe he is the right man to take this club where we want to be – the Premier League.'

The idea of having a manager with experience of winning promotion, being an outstandingly successful player and extolling the virtues of playing the game the right way (on the ground) sounded perfect. But in Roy Keane's case there was more than his medal collection from his days at Manchester United, and more than his one promotion as Sunderland manager.

The appointments of Keane and Clegg were greeted positively by the Official Ipswich Town Supporters Club, whose chairperson, Elizabeth Edwards, said the sudden changes were 'the biggest since the club turned professional in 1936'. She added: 'Although many fans have told me that they regret these changes, the majority would take success over structure. Marcus Evans is a successful owner of many businesses and is now imposing his preferred structure on the club. This means a CEO who rose to a high rank in the British Army, before masterminding some of our country's greatest sporting successes at Olympic level. His legacy in Olympic terms has been sustained even since he moved on. Roy Keane is a manager in similar vein – a proven winner in his first big day-job, captaining the most successful Manchester United team in history, before proving himself capable of promoting a Championship side and keeping them in the Premier League. Both Simon Clegg and Roy Keane have shown a ruthless dedication to getting the job done, and an attention to detail and discipline that ensured success in their different professions. This will inevitably mean deep-seated changes in the way the club is run, throughout the business. It proves Marcus Evans is committed to delivering the success that we all want for our club.'

What the Supporters Club failed to mentioned was the club had just appointed a manager with a track record for walking out – as both a player and a manager. With every achievement in Roy Keane's trophy cabinet, there was a dark tale. What were Ipswich Town letting themselves in for in their quest for success? An easy ride now they possessed a manager with experience of promotion? Or one of the biggest rollercoasters the club had ever experienced, with the press ready to pounce on Keane's every cough, sneeze and walk with his dog? No doubt being paid handsomely, there was no telling what Ipswich Town were going to get for the considerable amount of money it took to get Keane to sign his contract and move to Suffolk.

Expect the unexpected, was the best manner in which to deal with the club's bombshell announcement, for there was never any clue to what Keane would do from one day to the next. What was a certainty, was that Ipswich Town were back on the footballing map – not by winning football matches, but by appointing a high-profile manager with one of the most colourful histories in the game. If appointing Magilton three years earlier was a brave new step, giving Roy Keane the job, which gave Sir Alf Ramsey and Sir Bobby Robson the platform to greatness, was like taking a leap over a bottom-less chasm.

Keane was a name, more so than a manager. And this was important in Evans's decision to appoint him. The businessman was giving his brand a face-lift and letting the world know about it. From the instant the press releases were dispatched, the spotlight was switched on. Ipswich Town were up in lights and the great Keane soap opera was ready to restart – not just a new episode but a new series, possibly even a Christmas Special too – provided he had not walked out by then. Why was Keane causing such a stir? Because, in contrast to Ipswich's family club, do-goody persona, Keane was one of the most controversial characters to have played football domestically in the past 20 years. A hero to Manchester United fans for his never-say-die attitude, to many neutrals he was a snarling figure who harassed referees, stamped on opposition players, elbowed them, threw punches and spent nights in police cells. And that did not include the Alf-Inge-Haaland saga.

A small, shy boy who grew up in a working class family in Mayfield, Cork, Keane was forced to deal with rejection as a young footballer when he saw team-mates and friends selected for Ireland schoolboys and subsequently earn professional contracts in England. His size was given as a reason for his exclusion and, as a career in football looked uncertain, he worked at a local knitwear company, Murphy's Irish Stout factory, and did manual labour during a time of economic hardship in Ireland.

He was spotted by Nottingham Forest scout Noel McCabe while playing semi-professionally for Cobh Ramblers. Training full-time through the inaugural FAI/FAS scheme in Dublin, Keane began to show he was big enough, and more importantly, good enough. After coming over to England for a trial, he was signed by Brian Clough for £47,000 and made his first-team debut in 1990-91 at Anfield against Liverpool. Most of the

Forest team did not know who Keane was and Clough referred to him as 'Irishman', but he quickly established himself in the centre of midfield and Forest reached the FA Cup final in 1991, with Keane in the side which was beaten by Tottenham Hotspur.

An incident took place following the third round tie against Crystal Palace – one which gave Keane a lesson about professional football managers. He misplaced a pass which resulted in a Palace goal and was greeted by Clough's fist on returning to the dressing room. In *Keane: The Autobiography* he wrote: 'When I walked into the dressing room after the game Clough punched me straight in the face. 'Don't pass the ball back to the goalkeeper,' he screamed as I lay on the floor, him standing over me. Knowing the pressure he was under, I didn't hold this incident against him.'

Clough's treatment of Keane during his spell at Forest was important when considering the shaping of Keane's character, especially as a manager. Keane held Clough in high regard and certain characteristics are shared because of what Keane learned from him. He found Clough clever and daring. Would Ipswich Town find Keane to be a clever and daring boss? 'I would later have my differences with Brian Clough – none of them very serious – and would hear all the stories of bungs and booze, but I've never forgotten what he did for me – and how he did it,' Keane added in his autobiography. 'He was his own man, prepared to be daring, at odds with the conventional wisdom of any given day . . . for all his success Clough could be touchingly human, which is not too frequently the case with living legends.'

Keane was again on the losing side in a cup final in 1992 when Forest were beaten 0-1 by Manchester United. His performances were attracting the attention of bigger clubs and Blackburn Rovers were ready to do a deal at the end of the season. Before the campaign was out, Keane negotiated a new contract with a relegation escape-clause inserted in case Forest failed to avoid the drop – a fate they were unable to stave off. Blackburn manager Kenny Dalglish offered £4 million for Keane and the deal was set to go through when Alex Ferguson called. Keane had shaken hands on the deal on the Friday and was set to sign the paperwork on Monday, but Ferguson's call changed everything. Keane reneged on his agreement with Dalglish, whose fury fuelled swear-laden phone calls to his 'new signing', and Keane instead signed for Manchester United for £3.75 million – a British transfer record at the time.

The small matter of Bryan Robson and Paul Ince stood in Keane's way of a starting role at Old Trafford. Robson was injured at the beginning of the 1992-93 season and, at 36-years-old, was nearing the end of his career. Keane took his chance and lived up to his price tag, as United won their first ever Double. For Keane, it was an end to his Wembley hoodoo when Chelsea were swept aside 4-0 in the FA Cup final. His second season as a Red Devil was less successful, as United finished second to Blackburn Rovers and lost to Everton in the FA Cup final. Keane collected his first red card in professional football in the semi-final and the trophy-less campaign marked a period of change for United, as Andrei Kanchelskis, Mark Hughes and Ince were all sold. This left Keane the senior midfielder as Ferguson went for youngsters David Beckham, Nicky Butt and Paul Scholes. Newcastle were 12 points ahead at the top of the league by Christmas, only for Keane and United to drag back the deficit and go on to win another Double when they beat Liverpool in the FA Cup final. United won the title again in 1996-97 but Keane was in and out of the team due to injuries and he missed the second leg of the Champions League semi-final against Borussia Dortmund because of suspension.

The honour of the Manchester United captaincy came Keane's way when Eric Cantona decided to retire at the end of the season. However, Keane missed most of the 1997-98 season because of a serious knee-ligament injury, suffered at Leeds when he tripped Alf Inge-Haaland. The pair were involved in a running battle throughout the game and Keane could only watch from the sidelines as Arsenal took the title. His absence was viewed as a major reason for United relinquishing the Premier League trophy. They lacked his leadership and bite, as Arsenal, featuring the dominant force of Patrick Vieira, became the top side in the country.

Keane was fit and ready for the new season and overcame self-doubts about his effectiveness following the rebuilding of his knee. United won a historic treble of the League title, FA Cup and Champions League and his performance in the Champions League semi-final at Juventus was, and still is, regarded as one of the finest ever seen in the competition. He picked up a yellow card, which ruled him out of the final against Bayern Munich at the Nou Camp in Barcelona, but his will to win against Juventus inspired United to recover from 0-2 down at the Stadio Delle Alpi to win 3-2 and book their place in the final.

A new contract was signed midway through the 1999-2000 season which committed Keane to the club for another four years. It also made him one of the highest paid players in the country, although there was interest from abroad, with Bayern Munich and Juventus both ready to make him an offer. Keane was happy at Old Trafford, though, and, with an improved contract offer on the table and new players arriving, had no reason to leave. The club, however, put the reason for increased season ticket prices down to Keane's new contract, for which he demanded an apology. United won their sixth title in eight years and Keane was voted PFA Players' Player of the Year as well as Football Writers Association Footballer of the Year. United were trophy-less in 2001-02, finishing third in the league and as losing Champions League semi-finalists to Bayer Leverkusen.

A red-card in August 2002 and subsequent suspension gave Keane the chance to undergo a hip operation. While he was out injured and reflecting on his increasing fitness problems, he decided there was a need to tone down his all-action style and recklessness which was resulting in injuries as well as suspensions. Suggestions he was not the same player afterwards were quashed when he lifted another title in May 2003 – the nine major honours he led United to made him the most successful captain in the club's history.

Keane left United in November 2005 during an absence from the team due to injury. His relationship with the club was on a downward spiral and he suggested he would leave at the end of the season, anyway, when his contract expired. He signed for Celtic and helped them win the Scottish Premier League title and Scottish League Cup before retiring on medical grounds.

His international career is remembered more for the fallings out than what he did on the pitch. Although he won 66 caps for the Republic of Ireland, he perceived his nation's footballing set-up as a joke. He played in the 1994 World Cup in America, but it was to be the only major international tournament finals he would appear in.

Keane was a player driven by a thirst for success. From the moment Nottingham Forest gave him an opportunity, his ability was never in doubt. While he was still playing, every manager in the world wanted a Roy Keane in their midfield – a battler who never gave up, a leader who inspired those around him, and a talented footballer who was able to score goals, tackle ferociously and dictate the tempo of a match.

Many great players have had a dark side. For George Best it was alcohol, for Maradona it was drugs. Zinedine Zidane committed acts on the pitch which might result in a prison sentence if carried out on the street, and Keane was also controlled by a dark force. In his case, it was controlling his volcanic temper which could erupt anywhere and at any time. Keane puts it down to his thirst for victory and expectation of performing to the highest level possible but his troubles were off the pitch as well as on it.

For Ipswich Town supporters, the biggest fear was not being on the wrong end of a studs-up challenge or a verbal rebuke, but his penchant for walking out on situations he was angered by. His first big walkout was the highly publicised World Cup 2002 incident. Ireland manager Mick McCarthy was never at the top of Keane's Christmas list and he never would be again after events in Saipan. Keane was unimpressed with preparations at the training camp and gave an interview to the Irish press in which he voiced his displeasure. Keane said he had already told McCarthy to do something about the poor facilities and uninspiring training, but McCarthy rounded on Keane at a team meeting. Keane's response of 'I didn't rate you as a player . . . I don't rate you as a manager . . . and I don't rate you as a person. You can stick your world Cup up your B*******' was the end of his stay with the Irish squad.

Verbal confrontations were already a heavy feature of Keane's career. Before a televised clash between Manchester United and Arsenal at Highbury in 2005, Vieira was seen confronting Gary Neville in the tunnel about his fouling of Jose Antonio Reyes in a previous encounter. Keane, eyes wide and veins pumping, was then seen going chest to chest with the Arsenal captain, with threats echoing through the tunnel before referee Graham Poll took the teams on to the pitch. United won 4-2.

His Manchester United team-mates themselves were not exempt from feeling the wrath of Keane's tongue. A dressing down on the pitch was part of the game, but Keane went a step further when he said the treble-winning side should be broken up and, after United won nothing in 2001-02, he rounded on them, saying they had lost their hunger and were caught up in the excesses of a modern footballer's life. His team-mates were the subject of another rant when United were beaten 1-4 at Middlesbrough in 2005. The humiliation was too much for Keane, who lambasted the performances of Alan Smith, John O'Shea, Kieran Richardson and Darren Fletcher. Keane then turned on Rio Ferdinand, stating 'Just because you are paid £120,000 a week and play well for 20 minutes against Tottenham, you think you are a superstar'. The interview was for MUTV and never made an airing when the club put a stop to it. The United fans would not escape either. In November 2000 United had beaten Dynamo Kiev in the Champions League and Keane was next on the rota to speak to the press. He gave an honest view on the club's silent fans: 'Away from home our fans are fantastic, but at home they've had a few drinks and probably their prawn sandwiches and don't realise what is going on out on the pitch.'

Keane's notoriety grew from the day he implanted his studs into the chest of Gareth Southgate in the semi-final of the 1995 FA Cup. It was the first of 13 red cards in Keane's career. The worst on-pitch 'crime' came in the 2001 Manchester derby at Old Trafford when revenge was gained for the incident years earlier when Keane injured himself trying to foul Alf-Inge Haaland – then at Leeds United. The Norwegian was now with Manchester City and Keane had not forgotten how he accused him of faking injury when, in fact, his knee was in tatters. With five minutes to go, Keane gained revenge by committing one of the worst tackles seen in English football. It was late, high, and crude, sending Haaland flying off his feet. Keane admitted intent in his autobiography – an admission which resulted in the FA charging him for bringing the game into disrepute. The initial £5,000 fine and three-game ban for the red card was joined by a further five-match ban and a £150,000 fine.

Alan Shearer versus Roy Keane became much more than football in September 2001 when United lost 3-4 at St James' Park. Shearer, for the most part, possessed an attribute Keane was lacking – self-control. The Newcastle United striker prevented Keane from taking a throw-in late in the match so Keane threw the ball at Shearer, who gave Keane some abuse. The result was Keane throwing a punch at Shearer, who stayed cool and avoided the swinging fist before watching Keane traipse off for another early bath.

Less likely to be a physical match for Keane was his Ireland team-mate Jason McAteer, who would become their country's skipper after Keane. United were at Sunderland in 2002 and the pair had been embroiled in a personal battle throughout the game. McAteer responded to a Keane foul by gesturing with writing motions. The incident came days after McAteer said he would rather buy his son a Bob The Builder CD than Keane's autobiography. Soon afterwards the two went chasing after a loose ball and Keane landed an elbow to McAteer's head and was sent off.

The flashpoints were not restricted to the pitch or behind a microphone. Despite being a promising boxer in his youth, when out on the town Keane was a target for troublemakers, spurred on by the chance of making money from a scuffle with a famous footballer. After winning the title with Manchester United in 1999, Keane was out celebrating with team-mates when two women ordered him and Ryan Giggs to buy them a drink. They declined and Keane says in his autobiography he was hit by a champagne glass and all hell broke loose as he lunged at the man accompanying them. The women were asked to leave and called *The Sun* newspaper and the police. Keane was arrested and spent a night in the cells.

Keane's arrival in football management had a touch of fairytale about it. Sunderland were in the bottom three of the Championship and had lost four games on the trot under temporary boss Niall Quinn, who was also chairman of the club. Quinn and Keane had been on opposing sides when it came to the Saipan walk-out in 2002. Keane was in the stands at the Stadium of Light on 28 August 2006 as Sunderland faced West Bromwich Albion and, galvanised by the sight of Keane in the stand, the Black Cats ran out 2-1 winners – the effect of their potential new manager there for all to see before the paperwork was even signed. Quinn said afterwards: 'He brought a buzz to the place. They showed they wanted to play for the manager, they were playing for their futures. When Roy met the players, you could see them standing an inch or two taller thinking 'we are going to be working with that man, that is incredible'. Possibly the players are a bit scared. I hope they are, not in the sense that they will under-perform, but that they will give their all when they go training. This is a very demanding place but standards are going to have to be lifted. You only have to spend a short amount of time in Roy's company to realise just how impressive he is.'

A three-year contract was agreed and the honeymoon began. Six players – Dwight Yorke, Ross Wallace, Liam Miller, Stanislav Varga, Graham Kavanagh and David Connelly – were signed before the end of the August transfer window. By the turn of the year, Sunderland were in the top half of the table and five more players arrived before the January transfer window closed. The meteoric rise continued, as Sunderland moved into the automatic promotion places and stayed there, being crowned champions. Keane was named Championship Manager of the Year, but the celebrations were cut short as he decided against an open top bus parade through the city.

The 2007-08 season saw Sunderland retain their Premier League status with two matches to play. The lowest point was suffering a 1-7 thrashing at Everton, but Keane was regarded as having done a decent job in helping the club to prosper.

The high turnover of players continued, with expensive signings such as Anton Ferdinand. Keane had been backed financially, but results did not improve in the first half of 2008-09 and majority shareholder Ellis Short made it clear he expected more from his investment. By the end of November, Sunderland were in the relegation zone and had lost five of their last six matches. Keane resigned on 4 December – four days after he said he might walk away after Sunderland lost 1-4 at home to Bolton Wanderers.

It was not a simple departure based on poor results. At least it did not look that way. Quinn flew to Portugal to clear his head after the Bolton defeat, while Keane stayed away from the training ground. He informed Quinn by text that he was not coming back. There was no way forward and Quinn dealt with it diplomatically. 'Roy Keane hasn't been sacked because we've a bad team, he's resigning because we've a good team he feels he can't bring on any further,' he said. 'You hear the term amicable, that's actually the way it is here.'

Keane's solicitor Michael Kennedy released a statement thanking the club and its fans and Keane disappeared off the radar. The rumours started to spread, though. The players were reported to be celebrating Keane's departure, so fed up were they with his 'ruling by fear' technique and constant tinkering with team selection, while the length of time he had gone without speaking to Quinn was also the subject of wild speculation.

The truth was revealed by Keane to *Irish Times* journalist Tom Humphries on 21 February. The rest of the media would have to wait – for his thoughts and feelings on the words uttered by Ellis Short which made Keane realise his position was untenable.

The largest press turnout seen at Portman Road for years was present for the 4pm press conference. Back pages for the following day were cleared, TV schedules were altered and columnists prepared themselves for the column they had been waiting months to write. For the national press, it was not so much Keane's appointment as Ipswich manager which was at the forefront of their agenda, it was his return to football and the circus which followed it. For six months he had been out of the game, and for six months the press had been left without the possibility of a Keane rant or a Keane walkout. For the wider audience, the story was Keane himself, not Ipswich Town. This was a middle of the road Championship club floating along, living off the glory of Sir Bobby Robson's success, a nice club to visit for an away day, with a carpet-like playing surface and a chance of three points for the visitors – if they came with a physical and uncompromising approach. The press craved an insight into Keane's recent activities, where he had been, how many hours he had spent walking his dogs and the real reason why he walked out on Sunderland. National editors were demanding sensationalism, not Keane's hopes and his outlook on life in Suffolk.

Physically, Keane looked smaller in the flesh than expected for those gaining their first glimpse. Lean and healthy looking, he reminded me of a pixie when he was clean shaven. There was no sign of the footballing warrior, whose sins made bigger headlines than his glory. Ushered into Portman Road's Media Centre by Simon Clegg and director of communications Terry Baxter, who stuck close by like heavy security in case one of the press decided to re-enact the tackle on Haaland, and gain the story of the century when Keane came biting back with his own two-footed lunge, the new Town manager greeted everyone in his softly spoken Irish tone.

'The day Keane was appointed was one of my greatest days of covering Ipswich Town and certainly the most exciting,' said Matt Plummer. 'As soon as I arrived in the car park the Sky vans were there and the other TV companies. The car park was packed, and you could tell from just being outside the ground that something very exciting was happening. As you made your way in, there were signs on all the doors saying 'Press Conference', which was a first, and then going up the corridor towards the press room there were people everywhere and cables running up the floor. Everything was set up for the live broadcast and then when you stepped into the press room it was just a terrific atmosphere. There were so many people, lighting equipment, cameras, famous faces – I was sat next to Garth Crooks from the BBC, and all the big name reporters were there from the national papers. It was just very, very special – like the Hollywood of football. I had never seen anything like it at Portman Road. 'We got the signal that Roy was coming down the corridor and everyone was frantically adjusting microphones and cameras. He came in and sat down and Simon Clegg spoke first and there was this flashing – the noise from the cameras was incredible, they were really close to him and I was thinking how off-putting that must be. Neither of them batted an eyelid as they were both used to it.

'Compared to the old days under Jim [Magilton], sitting with him in a circle, talking about a hamstring injury or something, it was extraordinary. All of a sudden the spotlight was now on the club and now at Portman Road. I was there on the day Joe Royle was unveiled and again when Magilton was appointed and, while plenty of people attended those occasions, there just wasn't the same level of interest nationally. There were a lot of Irish journalists who came over for Keane's big day, as they just followed his every move.'

For the local press contingent and those reading about Keane with great interest in the local papers the following day, the big question was why Ipswich Town? Why would he want to come out of his self-imposed footballing exile to come to Suffolk? He responded by saying it was down to a gut feeling, that the ambition of the club and the feeling around it and its history gave him good vibes. The time was right for him to come back into the game after five-and-a-half months spent relaxing with his wife and five children. There were other offers, but it was the opportunity to try and take Ipswich back to the Premier League which was the most appealing.

Keane confirmed the details were sorted out quickly between himself and the club. 'I've signed a two-year contract but I'd like to try and do it [get promoted] in one year,' he said. 'That may be a challenge, but that's what challenges are. If I wasn't up for challenges I'd be out walking my dogs today. I think my dogs need a break. When I took over at Sunderland that was the challenge. I knew that was a very good football club and I managed to turn things around there, and it's the same here. I think what I did at Sunderland will stand me in good stead. In my first year at Sunderland in particular, we had a very, very good spirit, a never-say-die attitude. We had that up to when I left, believe it or not, we scored a lot of late goals, showed great desire, as much as we were short in certain areas. My team, I felt, would always go to the very end. That doesn't always win you football matches, but I want to get that from the Ipswich players. I think we had good success at Sunderland and we had success quickly, perhaps too quickly. Hopefully I'll be a bit more patient with myself. This summer there are lots of players' contracts up and I'll make sure I bring in the right characters, the right people.'

The idea of adding extra desire and a 'never-say-die' attitude was music to Town fans' ears. In many of Town's promotion quests during the last decade, the team could be taken to task for having the ability, but lacking the necessary mettle to see games out, show fight when the going got tough and take matches by the scruff of the neck when luck went against them. In simple terms, they were accused of being a bit soft. If Keane could stoke the fires and have Town's players performing that extra ten per cent that was lacking during Magilton's reign, it would make all the difference. Keane was making it clear he expected the same ethic and desire he showed as a player. No nonsense, play to win – at all costs. Keane predicted a busy few months with 13 Town players out-of-contract in the summer. His first training session at the club's Playford Road training ground had already taken place in the morning and he was not prepared to speculate on the futures of any players based on one training session. He admitted players would be coming in – no surprise considering his transfer dealings at Sunderland, and the financial backing of Marcus Evans. He then outlined his expectations of his players.

Punctuality had always been important in Keane's eyes. He berated Mark Bosnich in *Keane: The Autobiography* after the goalkeeper swaggered in 30 minutes late on his first day after signing for Manchester United. At Sunderland he dropped three players who were minutes late for the team bus which was ready to leave for an away game. Anthony Stokes, Tobias Hysen and Marton Fulop were the guilty offenders and Keane made it clear after his side's 2-0 win at Barnsley that such a misdemeanour would never be acceptable. Keane himself was late for the team bus while on international duty in America early in his playing career. His response to manager Jack Charlton was 'you should not have f****** waited for me'.

Now the boot was on the other foot. He made his expectations clear to the press and it was clear Town's players already knew. He said: 'All I've ever asked from my players as a manager is that they're on time for training and that they give one hundred per cent, and that's what I've asked of the Ipswich players. If they're up for that then they'll enjoy working for me, if not then we'll have a very brief relationship. We'll see how it goes.'

The main point Keane tried to get across during the press conference, was that one goal existed for both him and the club – promotion. His sole purpose was not to join the club as manager, be manager during the ups and downs and raise his own profile as a manager. There was one mission in place – to take the club back to the Premier League. The two-year deal he signed suggested there was little intention to hang around should the objective become impossible, be it because of financial restrictions, boardroom interference or the team's inability to raise a promotion challenge. The length of managers' contracts in modern football were shortening because of the unstable nature of clubs' finances, trigger-happy chairmen and managers' refusal to take on a job unless it was of the exact nature they are looking for.

Expectation levels rose for Jim Magilton when Marcus Evans took over the club. For Keane, those expectation levels were to move a step higher. His experience of winning promotion meant it could be expected again, and with Evans's millions to spend, there was no excuse.

To help him achieve the golden aim, Keane brought in Tony Loughlan as first-team coach. Loughlan was one of the few people in Keane's football career who he admitted to have kept a long-lasting friendship with. The pair had met at Nottingham Forest, where Loughlan's career went in the opposite direction to Keane's, as he went on to make two first-team appearances before spiraling down the footballing ladder with Kettering, Lincoln, Dundalk, Hinckley and Corby. His coaching career began at Leicester in 2001 and he joined Keane at Sunderland when his former team-mate took over in 2006. Like Keane, his time with the Black Cats ended in December 2008.

The national press were not interested in Loughlan. Nor were they excited by the start of Keane's quest to make Ipswich great again. Their big moment came when Keane was asked what qualities the likes of Mark Hughes, Steve Bruce, Bryan Robson and Paul Ince – all team-mates of his at Manchester United – possessed to make them such successful managers. Keane's response showed he had mellowed little during his time away from the dugout. 'Who are the good managers you are talking about?' he said. 'Sparky and Brucey have not won a trophy, have they? They have potential, but anyone can have potential. Steve Bruce has had a good season but Steve Bruce has been manager how many years? Sparky did a brilliant job at Blackburn, but is facing different challenges at Manchester City. We are all facing different challenges. Until an ex-team-mate of mine from 1994 goes on and really achieves something, then I would not agree with what you are saying about being a successful manager. You need a bit more than some of those managers have achieved. I believe I can potentially be a good football manager. I have done nothing in the game yet. I did OK at Sunderland, but I want to do better than OK. I've set my bar high by coming to Ipswich and looking to win something, but do you want me to set a low one? That's part of me. Anyone I've ever respected wants to achieve something in their lives.'

As much as Ipswich were discussed, the re-emergence of Keane provided the opportunity to grill him over his controversial departure from Sunderland. Had a new Ipswich Town manager ever had to endure such a testing press conference on his arrival? Keane said the time had come for him to leave the Wearsiders and went on to explain exactly why he called time on his stint in the North East. For the national press, his words were like gold dust.

'One of the big conditions I had when I went to Sunderland was that there would be no interference with team affairs,' he said. 'But when someone tries to move the goalposts . . . it is nothing to do with contracts, it is about a promise with people at the club. I was disappointed because I had signed a three-year contract and the three-year plan was on target, despite two or three poor results. Believe it or not, the results at the end had nothing to do with it. You have got to be relaxed and have trust in the people you are working with. I must have said it when I met Niall [Quinn] and the owners of the club about 5,000 times, that I would do it my way, particularly in team affairs. You might be better asking Niall or Ellis Short [majority shareholder] the reasons why I left. You have to respect the people who run the football club, as I did at Sunderland. But when people are telling you what you should be doing with the team, where you should be living, what days you should be in, it's over.' Ipswich Town had been warned.

Keane served up a stinging attack on former Republic of Ireland team-mate Tony Cascarino, who wrote when Keane left Sunderland 'you have to wonder who'd want him now when he has walked again'. Cascarino added he would be 'amazed if he [Keane] got another job in football'. With Keane employed again, he felt it was time to air his own views on Cascarino. 'I would not give him the time of day,' said Keane. 'I am quite happy to comment on people's opinion in football I respect, but Tony Cascarino is a man I certainly do not respect for a lot of reasons, and if I told you, you would be shocked. So the day I worry about Tony Cascarino will be a very sad day in my life.'

Bruce and Hughes brushed off the criticism the following day. Bruce told *The Daily Mail* it was good to have Keane back in football. 'For me, football is better with him back in it, because we were all intrigued yesterday – with how he looked, what he was going to do, what he was going to say, and whether he was going to come out with something outrageous,' he said. 'I am glad he is back in the game, and I am sure he will be a success at Ipswich. He'll put himself under enormous pressure – but that's Roy. He seems to be excited by the challenge, which can only be good. I've known him since he was 20 years old, so if there is somebody who can understand him a little bit, I know where he is coming from. And he's right! We haven't won anything. Two promotions means nothing in his book. You have got to win the Premier League and the European Cup as a manager to be a success in Roy's eyes. That's the sort of standards he sets himself – but it is very difficult to do that.'

Hughes, meanwhile, felt Keane was just making a statement by choosing to voice his opinion on the likes of Bruce and himself. He added: 'The media are very glad he is back on the scene because he is good value.'

Despite the negative headlines which followed, Matt Plummer's first impression of Keane in action in front of the microphone was positive. 'Keane was very confident and bold in stating his ambitions and you couldn't help but be impressed by the things he said that day,' he said. 'They were the kind of things you wanted to hear as a fan – this determination to get things right and do the best job he possibly could. He had a wonderful use of language, very eloquent, you could listen to him for a long while. He seemed friendly and was clearly a smooth operator, answering questions coolly. He was asked lots of questions about Manchester United, Sunderland and Ireland, which didn't happen with previous Town managers. The majority of the questions were about Roy Keane rather than Ipswich Town. There was a second conference in the board room with the nationals [newspapers] and there was this scrum of reporters who followed him off down the corridor. There was then all the negative headlines the next day to do with what Keane had said about people like Steve Bruce and Mark Hughes and I felt for him a bit as it was a sign of things to come. I don't think he was making out that they were losers or flops like the headlines suggested, I think he was just concentrating on what they had achieved rather than being derogatory.

'I was intrigued to see what he was going to be like and to see how things were going to be at the club, having come from a cosy scenario with Jim [Magilton], although his relationship with the local media did not finish on great terms. When he started the job we'd known him as a player and felt comfortable with him and this was going to be completely different. All of us sensed and had been led to believe from the Sunderland press people we were never going to have a relationship as such with Roy Keane. He would do everything that he needed to do in terms of press conferences and would speak very well and give the answers but in terms of forging a relationship, it was unlikely to ever happen. Even if he stayed there ten years we didn't expect him to know people's names. That was the way he operated and, to put it bluntly, he wasn't interested, which is just the way he is, and was, and probably always will be.

'I had reservations on whether he would fit in at a club such as Ipswich, in terms of his reputation and his background. The story was always going to be Roy Keane – it was Roy Keane's Ipswich. I am not sure how comfortable I was with that and I think a lot of people felt the same. I think some people felt bringing in a big name and personality like Keane was a step in the right direction, with Ipswich being this homely club, and they liked stepping into new territory. All of a sudden they had this manager who was brutally honest and forthright in his opinions and a lot of people liked the idea of exposure on places like Sky Sports News. However, I would soon come to resent that it was all about him and not the team. The face of the club had changed, as before we had David Sheepshanks, who was a good speaker and many of today's fans had grown up with him as the spokesman for the club. But there was now a different feel to the club emerging, with Simon Clegg the man in control on behalf of Marcus Evans.'

The profile of the club was launched skywards. If that is what Evans wanted, it is exactly what he got. When lottery winners buy a Ferrari, they do so to enjoy the car, but also to say 'look at me'. With Evans's money, he was able to make everyone take not just a glance, but a second look at Ipswich Town. The Keane story would run and run, but Evans was taking a massive risk. At the time of the appointment, he was bringing in a man with a track record of winning promotion – a pre-requisite. But why not a different manager who had successfully guided a side to the Premier League? Aidy Boothroyd did it with Watford, albeit with a reputation for playing 'hoofball'. Steve Coppell's name was mentioned, while Darren Ferguson was making a big name for himself at Peterborough. Evans could have brought in a manager from the Continent – a man with a taste for attractive, attacking football, the type of which the Portman Road faithful were yearning for. A risk, yes, but English football had cherry picked a number of foreign bosses, who subsequently turned out to be more useful than some of the 'names' employed by English clubs.

Joe Royle had taken the club a long way with little resources, so one wonders what he would have been capable of if he was given the kind of funds Magilton was handed. But he was sacked by the club for not gaining promotion. And his return would not have made the back pages of the national papers, or the Six O'Clock News. In employing Roy Keane, Evans believed he was getting a man who knew how to win and knew what made footballers tick.

However, great footballers do not always make great managers, as proven by the host of players who starred for England in the 1990 World Cup, only to be embarrassed when it came to running a side themselves. John Barnes, David Platt and Bryan Robson were the biggest casualties. Keane's Manchester United connections would have been of great appeal to Evans. He had played under Brian Clough at Nottingham Forest and Sir Alex Ferguson at Manchester United – was there a better tutelege? But Barnes played under Sir Bobby Robson for England and many successful managers during his playing career. In his selection, Evans wanted someone who would spend his money wisely. In Keane, Evans had chosen a manager with a questionable track record when it came to spending a club's cash.

'I wasn't expecting a name as big as Roy Keane as we were used to the Magiltons, Burleys and Lyalls, but Marcus Evans had made it clear he wanted to get Town into the Premier League and quickly,' said Phil Ham. 'I think the fans looked at what Roy Keane did at Sunderland, in taking them from the bottom of the Championship up into the Premier League and keeping them there and imagined he could do the same at Town. As to whether they liked him or not, I think people's minds were already made up and if they were not when he was appointed, they probably were after reading his book, which most of Suffolk did during the summer of 2009.'

Chapter Three

Impress or You're Out

'I CAN'T AND WON'T FORGET THE TRADITIONS OF THE CLUB AND THE WAY THE PLAYERS HAVE BEEN BROUGHT UP HERE TO PLAY FOOTBALL.'

The comfort zone was gone. There was no denying Magilton wanted promotion as much as anyone, but his players' desire failed to match that of their manager. The desperation to score was rarely evident during the final months, as opposition teams came to Portman Road and enjoyed the pristine playing surface, the facilities and the space and time given to them by Town's midfield, which sat deeper and deeper as the rot set in. In previous eras, when Town went behind at Portman Road with 20 minutes to go, they would lay siege on their opponents' goal. It was not pretty, with balls launched forward, and the strikers joined by a centre-half or two, and the flow of play resembled a game of Subbuteo instead of professional football – eight attackers praying on the next delivery from a goalkeeper stationed on the halfway line. Instead, under Magilton matches ended without even the slightest whimper, where the last minute was not too dissimilar to the first, and fans left the stadium with heart rates barely above resting norm. Only derby day, or the ball at the feet of little magician Dos Santos could whip up a modicum of frenetic behavior in the stands.

The ticket office phone lines buzzed as the club extended its early bird season ticket offer until the end of the season. Almost 13,000 had already been sold, but the club was expecting numbers to be down on the previous campaign because of the lack of a promotion assault and the recession. Keane's appointment stirred up huge interest and the final number would swell as fans bought into the new wave of hope.

The 13 out-of-contract players did not have long to impress and the ink was barely dry on Keane's contract when speculation began spreading on who he would try and sign. Sunderland players were the obvious names linked and Ricky Sbragia – the man who replaced Keane – said he expected the Town manager to be on the phone to him making enquiries to bring players from the North East to Suffolk.

An injury-hit squad for the trip to Cardiff saw a number of players handed an opportunity which would not have come to them had the likes of Gareth McAuley, Luciano Civelli, David Wright, Moritz Volz, Jon Walters, Ben Thatcher, Shane Supple and Jordan Rhodes been fit. Matt Richards was selected for his first Town game since March 2007, while

Jaime Peters made his first start since May 2007, at right-back. It was a position which suited Peters' attributes. His pacy bursts down the wing were often ruined by poor delivery into the box and long spells were spent on the periphery of the game. With only two Town goals to his name, he did not contribute in the final third as efficiently as Walters when occupying the right flank. The Canadian's impressive spring from a standing jump gave him an advantage when defending the far post and his stamina up and down the wing gave Town an extra dimension, with David Wright having rarely been played in his best position on the right side. Magilton tried Peters at right-back in pre-season without taking the experiment any further. Keane saw enough in his substitute appearance in the previous week's derby to see that he could be a potent weapon if played as an attacking full-back.

Pablo Counago, Jon Stead and David Norris netted as Town breezed past Cardiff, displaying the hunger which was missing from the previous seven months. It was the perfect start and suggested Town could be a force with Keane at the helm. The performance and result gave evidence that the squad Keane had taken charge of, despite being shorn of a number of first-team players, was far better than its league placing suggested. It just needed molding into a winning machine.

Keane was rightly impressed with what he saw and highlighted the hunger of the players in a match which was, other than showing the new manager what they could do, meaningless. It might have been different had Richard Wright not saved an early penalty. Stead, however, cast aside doubts surrounding his suitability under Keane, having been sold by him during their time together at Sunderland, by stepping off the bench and having a part in all three goals. Keane confirmed there was to be no mass invasion during the summer, unlike the transfer-merry-go-round which took place at Sunderland. He also played down his history of selling Stead, saying he was unable to stand in the striker's way when the opportunity arose for him to return to the Premier League with Sheffield United.

Coventry visited Portman Road for the final game of the 2008-09 season and Keane wanted to end the campaign on a high. Season ticket sales were now approaching 14,000 and a rousing performance on the final day would help to add as many as another 1,000 to that number. 'I think the season has been frustrating for a lot of people at the football club and we want to leave on a high on Sunday by getting a win in front of our supporters,' said Keane. 'Then we have a very busy summer starting next week, first dealing with the players whose contracts are up. I'll be meeting with the owner and the chief executive in the next week or two and possibly look at some targets. As for the players out on loan, I'll have to rely on feedback from the staff who have seen them through the season. I have been pleasantly surprised with the group of players here. It's not all doom and gloom.'

Keane was spot on – it was not all doom and gloom. Promised summer funds by Evans, Keane was safe in the knowledge he could clear out a large section of his squad without having to find a buyer, while there was no pressure to sell any of Town's best players, although very few were likely to be attracting interest after another season of under-achievement. The canvas was blank and he could, in effect, paint whatever picture he liked, as long as his transfer targets were willing to play for him.

Marcus Evans was also in a buoyant frame of mind. Keane's impact was instant – the club was making the headlines, first impressions on the playing side were that his new manager possessed a magic wand and the supporters were ready to return to Portman Road for another season at least. He wrote in the matchday programme ahead of the game: 'I would like to personally thank all our fans for their support this season and especially to the thousands who have committed to season tickets for next year. If ever there is a season to support Town and provide that extra something that will take us to the Premier League, it's the year ahead. There is a commitment from everyone at the club to get Ipswich back to where we belong. I've been to many games in the time I have been here and I have seen the passion the fans have for this club. I was at Chelsea when 6,000 Town fans drowned out the home support. I have loved every minute of being involved with Ipswich Town – well virtually every minute – and I have every confidence that we can move forward together. Ipswich Town will be a Premier League club sooner rather than later.'

All may have been rosy in the garden of Ipswich, but elsewhere in football Keane was upsetting people. Sbragia, the Sunderland manager, launched an attack on Keane for comments made at the unveiling press conference the previous week. 'Why doesn't he talk about Ipswich? Why is he always talking about Sunderland? That's what I don't understand,' said Sbragia. 'Roy Keane has left Sunderland. He's not here, we don't talk about him, don't discuss him, but for some reason he keeps coming back. I don't know why. Maybe he still thinks he's the manager, I don't know. I know I wouldn't go and criticise Ipswich. Maybe he's just bored and has nothing to do, so he thinks, 'I know, I will have a go at Sunderland'. Why did he leave? Why do I think he left? He knows the exact reason he left and I wouldn't want to say what I know about what he said and what he did. I won't go into that. It's up to Roy what he wants to do, but I think he should just concentrate on Ipswich. He's back in football and he should enjoy it.'

The excitement was palpable when Keane emerged from the Portman Road dressing room for his first home match as Town manager on Sunday, 3 May. More than 27,000 fans turned out for what was originally a meaningless end of season encounter, but they did not attend to watch the football – they went to see Keane. They were forced to wait until a matter of seconds before kick-off when Keane emerged to a cacophony of noise. The stadium was throbbing in a manner so rarely witnessed during that entire season. Eyes darted from the pitch to the dugout, to the pitch and back to the dugout again as Keane's actions drew as much fascination as what was happening in the game. Town's only scare came with virtually the last kick of the match when a Coventry free-kick bounced off the under-side of the crossbar, struck the post and came out again. Otherwise, Town were good value for their 2-1 victory, displaying the kind of commitment usually reserved for must-win encounters. Dos Santos netted in what was the final appearance of his loan spell, with the fans, and Keane, pained to relinquish his obvious talents. As the game faded late on, the Mexican waves started. Norwich were in the final throes of relegation to League One, the sun was out and all hope was renewed. The right man had been found. The potent mix of endeavor and entertainment was being injected into the veins of every Town fan at Portman Road.

While the neutral would have been impressed with Town's start under Keane, the manager himself felt he had seen both the good and bad side to what he had inherited. He said Town looked capable of scoring goals in the first half but forgot to do the basics – such as keep the ball – in the second. It was the Town of Jim Magilton which slowly slipped into play – a side used to bailing out and pumping the ball long at every given opportunity and unused to keeping possession for long periods, even though Magilton preached until he was red in the face how the players were made to pass the ball again and again in training each day. Keane admitted he sounded as though Town had lost 0-4, not won 2-1, but it was a sign of his high demands and expectations. Town would plan ahead without Dos Santos, who Keane said would almost certainly be playing at a higher level when the new season started in earnest.

The first sign of conflict between Keane and his players came only days after the season ended. As part of the changes he was implementing around the club, he told the players they had to move close to the training ground to avoid the risk of being late – a problem he encountered at Sunderland. Ben Thatcher and Kevin Lisbie lived near London and Lisbie publicly expressed his unwillingness to move. 'The gaffer has an issue with players driving up and down the A12 from London or wherever, and I can understand that,' said the striker. 'But I have a big family and I will not be moving them up here. We are a very close family too, so I don't want to be living away from them. This is something we have to resolve and I'm sure it will be as I would like to be with Ipswich next season, but I can't be sure I will.' With Jordan Rhodes and 16-year-old Connor Wickham expected to play an increasing role when the new season came around, Lisbie was carrying out his own agent's work in alerting other clubs to his availability. The striker's popularity with Town fans never took off because of his lackadaisical approach and inability to find the net at Portman Road – a feat he managed twice, compared to five times away from home.

The release of seven players came within a week of the final ball being kicked. Keane had seen enough of the players in training and gauged the views of the coaching staff sufficiently to tell Ivan Campo, Tommy Miller, Billy Clarke, Dean Bowditch, and youngsters Chris Casement, Jai Reason and Kurt Robinson they were not going to be kept on. Miller and Campo were the highest profile casualties, though neither were surprise departures. Miller, who signed for Sheffield Wednesday, was a favourite of Magilton, but he slowly fell out of favour after too many invisible performances and could not earn a place in the team solely on his regular success from the penalty spot. Campo, meanwhile, was an expensive flop. Only glimpses of the talent which earned him a Champions League winner's medal were seen during his single season at the club. A lack of fitness when he first signed did not help and he often played as though little training had been done during the week, fuelling stories of a commute to Suffolk from Mallorca.

Billy Clarke's situation was more complicated. Having burst on to the scene as a teenager, his appearances and goals dried up quickly. Loan spells at Darlington, Northampton and Brentford produced 16 goals, however, and many Town fans were keen for him to be given one last chance under Keane's control, especially as the bubbly young Irishman was from Cork and looked up to Keane as a messiah. Proven in the lower leagues, Clarke was ready to show he had the quality to make the grade in the Championship and rekindle the form which suggested he was going to be a Town star for years to come. His left-footedness made him versatile and, had he not been out on loan throughout 2008-09, he would have provided Magilton another option on the left side of midfield – a position he did reasonably well in during the 2007-08 season before heading out on loan to Falkirk. Keane decided Clarke would not add enough to his squad to warrant keeping him on, though, and he signed a two-year deal with Championship side Blackpool.

On the flip side, Alex Bruce agreed a new two-year deal. The new regime was certainly to his liking and Shane Supple also put pen to paper on a one-year deal. This left just Matt Richards, Dan Harding and Liam Trotter as players out of contract. Harding was involved in Reading's Championship play-off semi-final, which they lost, while Trotter was on loan at Scunthorpe, who successfully won promotion to the Championship via the play-offs. Only Trotter, who was offered a longer deal by Scunthorpe would sign a new deal, with the other two released. Neither player was a significant loss to Town. Richards showed potential as a teenager when becoming Town's youngest ever player in Europe, but his versatility eventually worked against him and his development stagnated at a time when he was expected to improve dramatically.

As Keane's first month in charge at the club drew to a close, Town were linked with names all over the world in the transfer market. Keane said players he worked with before were very much in his mind, fuelling even more speculation he would be approaching Sunderland for a number of their players.

Marcus Evans took over from David Sheepshanks as chairman – a position he had held for 14 years. He would continue as a club director and had already switched to a non-executive chairman's role 12 months earlier. Now that the club was in a new era, the time had come for Sheepshanks to move aside after a stint which took in many highs – such as promotion to the Premier League and a return to European action – and lows such as relegation and administration.

Fan opinion on Sheepshanks's success at the club was split as far as it was for players such as Pablo Counago and Marcus Bent. On one side there was the group highlighting his successful five-year plan with George Burley which resulted in promotion back to the Premier League, while the other side will point to the relegation back to the Championship which came about when Sheepshanks allowed Burley to spend millions on foreign imports – a spree which was partly to blame for the club going into administration.

After standing down, Sheepshanks admitted the club should have been sold six years earlier, after they finished fifth in the Premier League. 'Looking back, we could have sold the club in 2001,' he said. 'We never had an offer or any suggestion, apart from a share issue, to recapitalise the club, but then we didn't see the need then. I wish we had been bold enough because then we would have been able to cope with anything that would befall us. We never had any fat on the bone to withstand the worst sort of rainy day you could imagine. It was not so much a rainy day as a tempest.'

The Playford Road training ground was the next alteration under the Evans/Keane relationship. Hundreds of thousands of pounds were spent on the complex, which made it resemble Fort Knox compared to the recreation grounds some Football League clubs were forced to train at because of a lack of funds. A finger-print entry system was built in, stopping people not involved in day-to-day training activity from stepping foot on the premises. It was clear Town's players were there to work rather than socialise.

With the make-up of the Championship for 2009-10 decided, Keane was quietly confident of success. Bookmakers made them fourth favourites for the title – a feat last tasted by Town in 1991-92. 'We will have to deal with the expectation levels but expectation should come from within anyway, not so much from outside sources,' said Keane. 'There were levels of expectation here last season when money was spent on the squad, but throwing money around doesn't guarantee success anyway. It's about having the right environment, the right mentality – and having a little bit of luck along the way as well, which the club didn't have at the end of last season with all the injuries. We have to look at improving on last year, that's why I have been brought in. I'm quietly confident we can have a good season, but it's going to be tough. It's a very competitive league, the Championship, and with clubs the size of Newcastle and Middlesbrough in there next year, and West Brom, who know how to win promotion, it's going to be a big challenge, but maybe we can surprise a few people.'

Year-on-year, managers of Championship clubs and pundits labelled the division 'harder than ever' before the season started. Any club coming down from the Premier League was instantly expected to be among the title challengers. However, the Championship had not become more difficult. Just because any team could beat any other did not make promotion more unlikely. A side able to gain a modicum of consistency was likely to be in the play-offs, while a side performing well throughout the season would find themseves in the top two. For up to 15 of the 24 clubs in the division it was, then, a level playing field. The three relegated sides were slightly below their level, but not by much. The promoted sides were slightly better than the middle-of-the-road teams. It was not like the gap between the top and bottom of the Premier League where the chances of Manchester United or Chelsea losing at home to Hull are far less than West Brom losing to Plymouth. And it was this which made promotion from the Championship a more straightforward task than perceived. A good side was rewarded because the rest were swathed in a cloud of mediocrity. That Town won only three away games in 2007-08 and finished ten points off automatic promotion speaks volumes. In 2002-03 Town also finished one place off the play-offs, but were 22 points behind second placed Leicester. The gap between seventh (Cardiff) and second (Birmingham) in 2008-09 was only nine points.

Keane, like most footballers and managers of the last five years, spoke of turning Portman Road into a fortress after home fans saw only eight league victories in 2008-09. He wanted it to be more intimidating for visiting teams – certainly that would have been the case had he been playing for Town instead of standing on the touchline. 'Teams can still look forward to coming here. We can have that in a nice way but we can still win games here,' he said. 'It's all about getting the balance right. I can't and won't forget the traditions of the club and the way the players have been brought up here to play football. I was brought up the same way. When we've got the ball, we will play, but a lot of football is down to when you haven't got the ball and that is when you have to dig in. If we get that balance right we will win football matches.'

To get that balance right, Keane needed to spend wisely. Town's soft core saw them ship 53 goals – a total which would have been far higher were it not for player-of-the-year Richard Wright. Keane's two games in charge proved Town still had the flair of old, but could he instill the winning mentality? To do so, the side required more leaders. Gareth McAuley had been made captain as soon as he was signed by Magilton in the summer of 2008. It was a strange decision, given McAuley displayed none of the on-pitch skills usually attributed to a football captain. His own form was poor and his body language suggested he was uncomfortable playing in front of big crowds, let alone captaining the team.

McAuley's awkwardness was carried over when it came to press duty. I interviewed him in the autumn of 2008 at a time when the crowd were giving him stick for mistakes which were costing Town points. For a man who stood 6ft 4ins, he looked terrified of being in front of the camera, and when it came to a one-on-one interview with members of the written press, he went even further into his shell, almost whispering his answers, while curled up on a seat, displaying none of the fighting talk usually associated with a physical centre-half. Each question was met by a long pause as he considered what to say. It was like interviewing a trainee for a job, not asking an international footballer about a football match on Saturday. He was apologetic about his form and uncomfortable talking about it. This was not the type of player Keane would have leading his team, although he said McAuley would keep the captaincy.

Four new players would be enough for Town's promotion quest, according to Keane, who asked the fans to be patient over the club's summer recruitment. Youngster Ed Upson signed a new one-year deal and was followed by Trotter and Supple at the end of June, while young defender Troy Brown was also added to the squad, which began pre-season training on 1 July. The first purchase of Keane's reign arrived on 2 July, when Damien Delaney joined from Queens Park Rangers for an undisclosed fee. Delaney had been linked with Town for some months and the deal was said to have been held up by Paulo Sousa's departure as QPR manager – an exit which led to Magilton taking over at Loftus Road. A left-sided defender with international caps for the Republic of Ireland and experience of playing in the Premier League with Leicester City, Delaney, 28, was at the peak of his career at the time of signing for Town. Doubters pointed at his less than impressive display for QPR when Town won 3-1 at Loftus Road in February.

Lee Martin then signed a four-year deal for an undisclosed fee understood to be in the region of £1.5 million from Manchester United. Wideman Martin failed to establish himself at Old Trafford and had been out on loan to Royal Antwerp, Rangers, Stoke, Plymouth, Sheffield United and Nottingham Forest, without excelling at any of them. Keane saw Martin's progress at Old Trafford at close quarters and spoke to reserve team manager and former team-mate Ole Gunnar Solskjaer. Martin was keen to find a permanent home and, with Luciano Civelli injured, the signing, at least on paper, made sense – a young, hungry player from a top Premier League club able to play on either wing. Reports from Martin's loan clubs suggested he could dribble, but was easily knocked off the ball, injury-prone and inconsistent. With millions of pounds now spent on two players – neither of whom came with glowing references, a few question marks were beginning to hang over Keane's judgment in the transfer market, following on from the dissenters at Sunderland.

Town were beaten 1-2 by Irish side Finn Harps in their first pre-season encounter. Keane deployed a 4-5-1 formation, with Stead the lone front man in the absence of the injured Pablo Counago and Lisbie. Wickham netted the Town goal in what was an uninspiring display against poor opposition. There was more interest after the match in the two players Town had agreed a fee for than in the result. Sunderland duo Carlos Edwards and Daryl Murphy were names mentioned in the press, along with Paul McShane. The deal took many twists as Murphy was reported to have come to Suffolk for a medical before deciding he wanted to discuss terms with Hull City, whose bid was also accepted. The other player was confirmed as being Dean Whitehead, by Sunderland manager

Steve Bruce. The £5 million double deal broke down completely and Keane decided to move on to other targets.

As Town returned from a training trip to Portugal, Danny Haynes was sold to Bristol City for £400,000. Another case of unfulfilled potential, like Clarke and Bowditch. A place in a Premier League side had beckoned for Haynes when he burst into Championship action with blistering pace and a thumping, albeit often wayward, shot. Saddled by a poor first touch and failure to dribble anywhere but in a straight line, Haynes was more of an impact substitute during his time with Town, where he had progressed through the Academy. Famed for his goalscoring exploits in the East Anglian derby, he was also known for trouble off the pitch with court appearances for driving offences making the local papers. Keane decided Haynes would not progress any further at Portman Road and needed a fresh start.

Keane was happier with Town's 3-1 victory at Brentford, which was followed by another trip to Ireland. Town won their opening match 3-0 against Waterford, as Owen Garvan netted twice and Keane admitted afterwards that the club had rejected two bids for their players. An unacceptable 0-2 defeat by Cork was next. Somewhat surprisingly, it was a Cork player who would be the next arrival at Portman Road. Former Republic of Ireland midfielder Colin Healy had spent the majority of his career on the treatment table, but at 29 years of age, Keane felt he still had something to offer and a £70,000 deal was struck, prising him away from under the nose of Hartlepool United. The deal was largely met with derision by Town fans, who wondered why they were signing a player who had spent the last few years playing in England's lower leagues and then in Ireland and failed a trial at Town in 2006.

Lisbie was a notable absentee when Town beat Southend United 2-0 at Roots Hall and Keane confirmed the club had accepted an offer for one of its strikers. Lisbie was expected to depart after his refusal to move closer to Ipswich, but Swansea had been linked with Counago, who was out injured. One journalist tried to catch Keane out by asking: 'So Lisbie will be speaking to Swansea in the morning then?' The question was met by a glare.

It became clearer that Lisbie was not the player involved in the deal, and it was in fact fan-favourite Counago. An Arsenal fan once said to me that the Spaniard was the 'Dennis Bergkamp of the Championship'. From the western region of Galicia, Counago started his career with Celta Vigo and won the Golden Shoe at the World Youth Cup in 1999 – an Under-20 competition at which Xavi and Iker Casillas also starred for Spain on their way to lifting the trophy. Counago was signed by George

Burley (on a free transfer), played under Joe Royle, left when he contract expired, and was brought back, from Malaga (again on a free transfer), by Jim Magilton. Although popular with most Town fans, the disparity of opinion between those who rated him and those who did not was vast. He was the closest to a cult figure at the club, but would never be considered a club great after too many seasons lost to long spells on the bench or completely out of favour.

Few clubs in the Championship had a player regarded as a 'fantasista' at their disposal – a player providing, flair, guile and a touch of the unexpected, although often at the expense of other attributes, such as work-rate or physical presence. What was different about Counago, was not only his penchant for the spontaneous, but his physicality. Standing 5ft 11ins with strong thighs and thick waist, he was of average proportion for a striker, and won little in the air. However, he would back into defenders, keeping a low centre of gravity, twisting, turning, wriggling and dummying in a rare blend of footballing artistry. His trademarks were receiving the ball to feet on the edge of the box, either backing into the defender and turning past him, or laying the ball off to on-rushing teammates. There was back-heels aplenty at Portman Road, used as a method of creation rather than showboating. The goals were often spectacular.

For his detractors, such qualities would not take the club back into the Premier League. They pointed to Counago's lack of sustained pace, low success rate at winning aerial challenges and the frequency at which he was on the floor seeking a free-kick. Sometimes emotionless and brooding, Counago's Latin temperament resulted in an early bath on more than one occasion. You could put money on an exaggerated shrug of, the shoulders and glare at the linesman and referee within the first ten minutes. Then there were the lacklustre away performances – particularly during his second spell at the club. Like Marmite, Counago was loved or loathed – or should that be undervalued? He was a match-winner, a player who produced the one piece of skill in an 89-minute stalemate. But that one piece of skill would sometimes only arrive once a month, and some were not prepared to wait.

'I always thought he was a player who wouldn't fit the Keane 'mold', even though Keane had played with enough flair players in his time,' said Town fan Matthew Mehen, who attended his first game in 1992 and was a season ticket holder along with brother Andrew and father John (who had watched Town since Sir Alf Ramsey was manager). 'Pablo had that typical Spanish look of laziness, and perhaps arrogance at times.

'He was popular with the fans because he would get on top of teams by winning fouls and getting the crowd going and occasionally produce moments of pure brilliance. Everyone knew what Pablo could do but you needed time and patience to see it. For a new manager to come in and accept that was going to be very difficult for Pablo. I still expected to see him shunted out despite the two goals in Keane's first two games, and the same went for Kevin Lisbie.

'Pablo was deserving of his cult status. You could not compare him to any other player the club had produced or signed in recent times. You very rarely heard him speak publically – he basically did his talking on the pitch – and what you made of Pablo, the man, was irrelevant. The way he raised the spirits of the crowd was unique and his skills were probably unmatched in the Championship but he just didn't score enough goals.

'There were so many memorable moments from his Town career – which you would expect from a player who had been at the club for seven years. The main one which stood out was the back-heel at Charlton Athletic in 2007 which was probably the most ingenious, spontaneous moment I had seen in more than 15 years of watching Town.'

I interviewed Counago on a few occasions after Magilton had brought him back from Spain and I found him to be friendly, but guarded. His English was sufficiently advanced to hold a worthwhile conversation but he was wise enough to avoid talking about any kind of controversy. He knew how to play the media game, how to reverse a question in the same way he would reverse a pass on the pitch and how to play down subjects such as the disappointing end to his first spell at the club when Joe Royle was manager. 'I don't think about the past, only the future,' he would say in his deep voice.

Without this motivation to open up, it was difficult to find out what made Counago tick. He came across as the same brooding, distant Spaniard off the pitch as he was on it, but it caused no awkwardness on my part. His body language displayed a willingness to be there, just an unwillingness to give his forthright views. The politeness and handshake felt genuine and I would be forced to try again a few months later.

Sito Castro, the Spanish full-back, was also at the club at the time. His English was worse than Counago's, but his infectious personality brought no inhibitions in front of those portrayed as the devil – the press. He would readily laugh and joke, talk tactics after his interview duties were completed, and even ask everyone's opinion on why Magilton was leaving him out of the team. In return, he would offer his own off-the-record judgment on team selection and formations and talk animatedly about other clubs, especially those back home in Spain.

I saw this humbleness in Counago as well after a man-of-the-match display against Coventry at Portman Road in 2007. He scored twice as

Town won 4-1 and was summoned up to the Media Centre. Sitting in the centre of a cluster of reporters all leaning in to record his words, sweat was dripping off his forehead and down on to his suit as he explained that his goal celebration (a baby rocking motion made famous by Brazil in the 1994 World Cup) was due to the confirmation he was to become a father. He was asked if he would call the child 'Jim', after the manager, and on explaining that Magilton's forename would not be adorning his son's birth certificate he wrote down the correct spelling of the chosen Spanish name in the reporters' notebooks. It was a nice touch from a man who had been accused by fans, managers and the press of lacking heart for the game and for the club.

The fee offered by Swansea was reported as £500,000 – well below Counago's value to the team in the eyes of the majority. He was given permission to speak to Swansea boss Paulo Sousa and decided against the move. Keane then challenged the Spaniard to come out and fight for his place when he recovered from a groin injury that had kept him out of pre-season action. Keane said: 'I've no problem with Pablo staying and fighting for his place here, absolutely no problem at all. If the club receive an offer for a player that they think is acceptable, then you put it to the player, but if the player doesn't want to leave, then no problem. I spoke to Pablo and told him that if he wanted a new challenge at a new club then fair enough, but if wants to stay he has to come out fighting for his place. He knows I'm looking to bring in one or two new strikers, so he will have to battle for his place in the team and hopefully we will see him up for the challenge. It's the same with all my players. I expect them to have to fight for their place. It's part of football. It could be that Pablo goes on to make a big contribution for us this season. That's the way the game is.'

Jordan Rhodes staked his claim for an active role in the forthcoming season when he stepped off the bench to score in the Fabian Wilnis testimonial, which saw Town beat Colchester United 2-0. Keane revealed he turned down a bid for Rhodes earlier in the summer and fielded plenty of phone calls about the striker, who had proved his knack in front of goal while out on loan at Brentford. The Town boss wanted to see his players give a professional display and treat the match as a genuine pre-season game, not just a celebration for the former Town defender. There was little to set the pulse racing, as Town stuttered into gear and showed none of the fluency evident at the back end of the previous season.

While Dos Santos was playing fantasy football and scoring for Mexico in a 5-0 beating of USA, Town were struggling to shake themselves into life. Counago and Lisbie's absence saw Keane persevere with his 4-3-3 formation – a system which did not fit well with Town fans when Magilton was in charge. A static midfield and lack of a target man were a big hindrance, but with other sides in the Championship using the system, and Town finding it hard to win away, more often than not, Magilton would opt to deploy the in-vogue formation. However, Town's limitations meant it was more of a 4-5-1, and Keane's use of it did not look any more favourable, as Town were only beating sides well below Championship standard.

The next new face to join the Keane revolution was 19-year-old former Liverpool Academy scholar Shane O'Connor. Another Irishman, O'Connor impressed Keane during pre-season training and played in a few of the pre-season games. But everyone wondered when Town would add to their strike-force, which at that point consisted of Jon Stead, Jon Walters – better served in midfield – and youngsters Rhodes and Wickham. Counago was still some way from full fitness and Lisbie's future looked to be anywhere but Portman Road. A strong Town side was beaten 1-2 at Charlton Athletic, fuelling doubts about Town's progress since the back end of the season. Keane said he was finding shopping for new talent difficult, but was still hopeful of adding to his squad before the first game of the season at the Ricoh Arena, on 9 August.

Footballs were swapped for live ammunition as Town's shooting and endurance was put to the test during two days at Colchester Garrison with the 7th Parachute Regiment Royal Horse Artillery. The idea, according to Keane, was to take the players out of their comfort zone, and judging by the pictures the club released, they had never known physical tests like it. Some were snapped trying to fend off the nausea brought about by extreme exertion, while others looked like they had run from Ipswich in Suffolk to Ipswich, Australia. Keane was adamant the time spent with the army would help his players on the football pitch.

Another shock was in store for Town fans before the last of the pre-season friendlies. A bid was accepted from League One club Huddersfield for Rhodes and, after initial reports that he had discussed terms and had a medical before returning to Portman Road to fight for his place, his departure was confirmed. The fee was reported as £850,000, with possible add-ons. For Town fans it was an alarming sale. Rhodes had made only ten first-team appearances for Town, scoring one goal, but was expected to make a substantial impact in the new campaign. Recognised as the most natural goalscorer at the club, it was a question of when he became a regular part of Keane's plans, not if. As Keane had been insinuating all summer, if an offer came in for one of his players and it was acceptable, the player could leave. For a player yet to make his mark in the Championship, the price was high. But Rhodes's priceless knack of hitting the back of net, as shown by his loan spells and form in the reserves, led Town fans to scratch their heads. Why were they selling a young striker with a bright future when there was no apparent need to sell? Did Keane have an incoming transfer up his sleeve which would silence the growing doubts surrounding his transfer dealings?

Town were now down to two fit out-and-out strikers, and one of those was 16 years old. Keane was gambling, and, absurdly, his squad was getting thinner in the most important area – up front. The explanation given was that Town were not wealthy enough to simply keep buying players and not have any income from sales in return. Keane said: 'The offer that came in was acceptable. I'm under no illusion that, unfortunately, I have to let one or two players go to bring in one or two of my own players. I have already paid out to bring in Lee Martin and Damien Delaney and the club spent decent money last year, so you can't hold on to everybody. As much as I think Jordan has a good chance, that will be reflected in the fee and what will come in for him over the next few years. It was certainly a difficult decision without a shadow of a doubt, but that is part of my job.'

The sale of Rhodes paled in significance, though, when the death of Sir Bobby Robson was announced on the day that Real Valladolid of Spain came to Portman Road. Robson had managed Town from 1969 to 1982 and had been battling cancer for the fifth time. Tributes poured in from around the world and fans paid their respects at Portman Road long before the evening kick-off, laying flowers, shirts and scarves around his statue behind the Cobbold Stand. Keane thought his side's 3-1 victory was a fine tribute to one of the greatest managers the country had ever produced. A goal down early on, Town produced a brighter performance, particularly in the second half, when Wickham stepped off the bench, replacing the hapless Stead who could have scored at least four, to score one and have a leading part in an own-goal. Martin also shone, displaying his dribbling skills and ghosting into the penalty area to provide a goal threat.

The lack of strikers in Town's ranks saw them linked with Watford's Tamas Priskin, and Keane was spotted at Vicarage Road on 1 August, where he saw the Hornets beat Parma 3-2 in a friendly. A TV report stated a bid was already made, but Watford manager Malky Mackay denied it. Keane confirmed he was happy with his defence and midfield and was on the hunt for not one striker but two. The need for two was hightened when Lisbie joined Colchester United on a season-long loan with five days left until the new season. Also departing was Veliche Shumulikoski, who was holding talks with Preston North End after the two clubs agreed a £400,000 fee. Known as 'Shumi', the Macedonian failed to match his international form while in a blue shirt. Another player whose best position was never found, he was mostly used as a holding midfielder under Magilton, but videos on the internet and his early Town appearances gave weight to a feeling he was more effective as a box-to-box player – the type which gave him the tag 'the Steven Gerrard of the Balkans' when he came to England. It was clear he was not in Keane's long-term plans during pre-season. His time on the pitch was limited to half-an-hour here and there and he was known to be frustrated by the club's refusal to let him move on loan at the back end of the previous season, even though he was out of favour.

The belief that Keane did have a striker in his sights before the sale of Rhodes and the loaning out of Lisbie was proven when a bid for Priskin was announced by his agent József Vörösbaranyi. A fee reported to be between £1 million and £1.2 million was turned down, though, by Watford, who were keen to receive as high a price as possible for a player whose contract had only 12 months to run. Before any progress was made on that deal, Town signed 19-year-old Sunderland midfielder Jack Colback on loan until January. The player had yet to make a competitive appearance for the Black Cats, yet manager Steve Bruce wanted Colback to gain experience and Keane snapped up the chance to replace Shumulikoski. Again, replacing an experienced international with a bargain bucket buy from Ireland and a youngster with only reserve-team experience was a risk and one which sat uneasily with many Town fans.

With the season only days away, was the squad stronger than when Magilton departed? The answer was a categorical 'no'. Keane's striking options were down, an experienced centre-back to partner McAuley had not come in, and question marks hung over the effectiveness of big-money signings Martin and Delaney (who was expected to play at left-back) – both brought in to solve the club's dearth of left-sided players. It was difficult to see how the group of players assembled by Keane over the summer was going to ignite the club into promotion challengers, unless their manager's desire and will to win as a player would be transferred into what was a mediocre squad containing few stand-out players by Championship standards. Maybe Stead would defy his barren pre-season form by netting 20 goals? Or David Norris would justify his £2 million price tag by running the Town midfield and reaching double figures in the goals tally, with Delaney and Martin dovetailing beautifully down the left side? On the evidence of pre-season, this was all wishful thinking. At this point, the best Town could hope for was the return to fitness of Counago, the emergence of Wickham, and a stout defence holding on to 1-0 leads.

The Keane effect had worn off and Town fans had sobered up. A big-name manager did not mean big-name signings. Those who made the trip to Ireland witnessed at first hand how Town were some distance from bringing the good times back, unless they could start the season with a bang.

Chapter Four

The New Season Begins – August 2009

'THERE ARE GENUINE REASONS WHY WE HAVEN'T HIT THE GROUND RUN-
NING AND IT WOULD BE VERY TEMPTING TO MAKE EXCUSES.'

Football fans need not have left the comfort of their armchair to
watch Town's opening match at Coventry, as Sky TV was quick to latch
onto the Keane circus. Fears of a huge anti-climax were eased slightly
when Town sealed the signing of Tamas Priskin for £1.7 million in time
for the Hungarian to make his debut at the Ricoh Arena. Priskin's career
in England was slowly coming to the boil, having scored 14 times for
Watford in 2008-09. After joining the Hornets in 2006 from Hungarian
club Győri ETO, the languid frontman's appearances were infrequent as
Watford were relegated from the Premier League, but he did score twice
in the top flight and was scoring goals at international level – no mean
feat for a then 19-year-old.

A goalscoring record of 16 in 58 starts and 24 substitute appearances
gave Town fans more ammunition to question Keane's thinking, though.
Based on his performances the previous season, Priskin was coming
good and beginning to blossom in the English game and many of his
goals came from smart finishes inside the penalty area – the type of goals
Town lacked. Eight goals in 19 international games was impressive as
well. But time would tell whether he was significantly better than Jon
Stead, Jon Walters, Pablo Counago or Kevin Lisbie, and worth paying a
six-figure fee for. At his press conference, Priskin said he preferred
receiving the ball to feet from short passes. Would Town try and find his
feet or would they ignore his plea, like Counago, instead firing long balls
at his head?

In the build up to the game, Keane outlined once again Town's aim to
win promotion at the first time of asking under his management. 'If we
don't do it this year, certainly, if by the end of my contract in two years'
time we're not promoted, I would class that as failure. None of this mid-
table business, I think any half-decent manager can get teams to mid-
table in the Championship.

'I want to be one of the best managers around. That will come from
experience and, hopefully, my Sunderland experience will stand me in
good stead because, despite one or two bad decisions I made, I think I
did some decent stuff up there.' He said the team he built over the summer would have more pace and energy about it, but he refrained from

saying they would come out with all guns blazing and bulldoze their way to the top of the table. 'I think we're short, maybe, three players, but we'll be working hard over the next few days to put that right,' he said. 'We've got to focus on Sunday with the group of players that we have and I'm very pleased with them. When I took the job at the end of last season, I spoke to the players as a group and said we'd be pushing them, we'd be testing them and I said at the time that some players would fall by the wayside and a few already have. I think in your first few games you never know what you're going to get because it takes five or six games for the players to get up to speed. You can do all the training you want, it's the match sharpness you need, but I hope that like every time you come to see Ipswich, you're going to see a good, entertaining team. What I've tried to focus on is a lot more energy and a bit more pace in our team than last year. I think we were very predictable last year, we need to be like Ipswich have been over the years, we need to be nice on the eye, but winning.'

Keane was talking a good game, even if his side had failed to give the impression during pre-season of being a team to fear. He was saying what Town fans wanted to hear – the creation of an exciting, entertaining team with pace. But where was that pace going to come from? Danny Haynes had been sold, leaving Jaime Peters as the only player in the squad who was genuinely quick, and he had barely figured in the past two years. Midfielders David Norris, Owen Garvan, Colin Healy and Liam Trotter were at the slower end of the scale, while Counago, Stead and Walters were not renowned for leaving defenders in their wake.

The name 'Dos Santos' cropped up in Keane's interview with the press, when he admitted to having spoken with Tottenham manager Harry Redknapp. Speculation rumbled on all summer about the possible return of the Mexican and Keane was always realistic about Town's chances of re-signing the crowd-pleaser. He was certainly a more exciting prospect than Sunderland's Daryl Murphy, another player linked with Town and said to be the other half of the failed double deal involving Dean Whitehead.

Had Dos Santos been back at Town, expectations for the season would have been far different. As it was, a flatness surrounded the opening to the new campaign, simply because Town, on paper, did not have a side to get excited about. The bedlam which followed Keane's appointment had waned. Was he no longer the saviour of Ipswich Town Football Club? He stood on the same footing as Jim Magilton two years earlier – a manager given money to spend by the chairman, and whose every selection, signing and substitution would be analysed and torn apart by the fickle football fan. He would be judged on results, not on his glittering playing career, lack of public charm or the number of times he took his dogs for a walk. The Keane effect had impinged little on the players in pre-season. The rest of the world would now find out if it gave them that extra ten per cent with the season ready to begin.

Debates were raging among Town fans ahead of the season's opener. Lisbie had scored twice on his second Colchester United debut, and Jordan Rhodes and Dean Bowditch also found the net in League One. Many fans had renewed their season tickets after learning Keane would be in charge. They were prepared to ditch their club after becoming dis-illusioned with the poor value-for-money under Magilton and the corpo-rate direction the club was taking. They expected Town to be lining up on the first day of the season with a starting line-up to be proud of – sign-ings which signalled the club's intent.

'It was a surprise that more big-name players were not signed during pre-season after Keane outlined his and the club's ambition to win pro-motion within two years,' said Matt Plummer. 'But there was still this tidal wave of optimism and expectation and because of Keane's stature it was as though the club belonged in the Premier League.'

In typical bright August sunshine, a minute's silence was held before the match in memory of Sir Bobby Robson, and his name was still float-ing through the air when Coventry took a 10th minute lead. It was a moment to forget for keeper Richard Wright, who charged out to the edge of his box, only for Clinton Morrison to latch on to a long goal-kick and chip the ball into an empty net. Fifteen minutes later Morrison was celebrating again when his diving header flew past Wright. Keane sim-mered on the sidelines and expectations on the terraces were lowered by the minute. Walters pulled a goal back before half-time and Town were the better side in the second half, enjoying plenty of possession. Priskin was given his debut from the bench and Pim Balkestein's header was cleared off the line. It was the end of Keane's 100 per cent record as Town boss, and fears the side was not as strong as it should have been were proven. A draw may have been a fair result, but Town had lost 1-2. Their defending was not up to scratch and a lack of intent in and around the box left viewers exasperated.

Keane had sprung a surprise in his selection – picking Peters as a cen-tral midfielder – at the expense of Garvan (Healy was suspended), along-side Trotter and Norris. The triumvirate was short on quality going for-wards. Norris was chosen as the holding midfielder and went off injured shortly after half-time. Peters's vibrancy made his inclusion a success, although none of the three were likely to produce, or had produced in their Town careers, the kind of swashbuckling midfield showing which would haul Town to all three points away from home. As promised by Keane, energy levels were up as Town fought to get back into the game, whereas they could easily have gone 0-2 behind and remained that way. Neither Delaney or Martin were directly at fault for the defeat, although neither did their unflattering reputation a lot of good.

It was as much of an acceptable defeat as you are likely to find. First game of the season, 45 still to go, new players needing time to settle and gel, plenty of possession, and no need to worry. For the press, it was Roy Keane off to a bad start to the season, not Ipswich Town. Snide remarks, about giving the defence coaching on dealing with crosses and long-balls rather than lessons in how to fire a gun and live like a commando, were rife among supporters on their way home. Keane's frustration at his players' failure to carry out the simple tasks, such as keep possession or track runners, was clear to see on his face. It was masked, though, by a yearning to stay calm and let the players suffer during the week, not while plotting a way back into the match. Had he mellowed?

It was his family who would feel the force of his disappointment. His 38th birthday fell on the day after the match and cake was not high on his list of cravings. 'My whole family suffers when we lose,' he said. 'I can't sleep and my appetite goes. If I went home whistling and smiling after a defeat that would mean I don't care about my job which clearly isn't the case. Football is my vice. And I certainly need it more than the game needs me. And my wife and kids should certainly be more concerned about Ipswich's results than the most passionate supporter. I'm sure I'll end up eating tonight, but it won't be until much later.' Keane, like Town's 2,000 travelling support, was none too pleased with the defending on display. 'Someone should have taken Clinton's head off,' he said, referring to Morrison's diving header.

Coventry manager Chris Coleman was fully aware he and his team were like extras in a blockbuster movie. He did not mind playing second fiddle, however . 'It was all about Ipswich and Roy Keane,' he said. 'It was all about where they are going to finish. It wasn't about us at all. And that suited me. Roy will probably go home and kick the cat.' It was rare for Keane to talk about his home life. As far as he was concerned, his private life was his life, no one elses. He was once famously quoted as saying he had none of his Manchester United team-mates' phone numbers. It was hard to imagine what he was like at home, how he greeted his family after a defeat and whether he did, in fact, kick the cat. His autobiography is one of the best ever written of its genre. Yet it concentrates almost solely on football. The importance of his family is felt. But readers are given no more information about them than Keane felt necessary. No marital arguments, no toddler tales, and certainly none of the debauchery graphically portrayed by the likes of Stan Collymore and Dwight Yorke in their publications. To the outside world, Roy Keane meant football. And defeat at Coventry meant birthday joviality was kept to a minimum.

A few more candles were removed from the birthday cake when Keane learned of the extent of Norris's injury. The club's most senior midfielder had collided with team-mate Stead, damaging knee ligaments in the process. Five months on the sidelines and surgery was the initial prognosis and Keane said: 'It will be a big loss. He is a battler and he breaks up the play well and gets things going from there.'

Only two days separated Town's first and second fixtures of the season, as they headed to Shrewsbury for the first round of the Carling Cup. Keane chose to make wholesale changes, with Alex Bruce the sole survivor from the defeat at Coventry. Gareth McAuley and Priskin were on international duty, while Jack Ainsley, Reggie Lambe, Jack Colback and Colin Healy were all given Town debuts and Connor Wickham was handed his first senior start. The selection made it clear that the competition was at the bottom end of Keane's priorities, although he would argue it was a chance for the younger players to develop and stake a claim for a regular place.

Indeed, it was one of the club's great young hopes who made the headlines and had fans drooling on the long trip home. Of course, the cynics saw it as Town scraping through to the second round against League Two opposition. For Wickham, it was a statement that he was ready for first-team action. His two goals – his first at senior level – were taken superbly and left everyone at the ground purring. The last prodigal, fearless 16-year-old striker in a man's body had gone on to captain England and win every club title going for Manchester United. Alan Quinn netted a free-kick from the edge of the box to make it 2-2 going into half-time. As an entertaining and open encounter meandered its way to extra-time and then penalties – Town claimed their first spot-kick triumph for 18 years, and only the second in their history.

Wickham kept himself in the thick of the action by putting away one of the penalties and Keane, predictably, was quick to play down the impact of the new superstar in the ranks. 'He worked hard, showed a good attitude and put in a mature performance for a 16-year-old,' he said. 'We have to remember he's only 16 and we have to manage him properly. It might sound silly but the boy is still growing and we have to be mindful of that and not put too much workload on him. I don't know how far this boy can go. It's up to him but he has great potential. He works hard, but we will look after him. It's not good for him or the club to play him every week. For a 16-year-old boy to play against Shrewsbury, whose centre-halves were outstanding, it was very mature. We have to manage him carefully. It is a big ask, which is why I have brought in another striker.'

Shrewsbury manager Paul Simpson was left questioning Wickham's age, joking that he would like to see his passport. So there was now another reason for the world to take notice of Ipswich Town. They were now the club who Roy Keane managed, and the club with the 16-year-old man-boy striking sensation.

For one man, though, the pull of Roy Keane and Ipswich Town was not strong enough. Peterborough director of football Barry Fry labelled his club's second round tie with Town as a 'rubbish draw'. He had hoped to pull Manchester City or Tottenham Hotspur out of the hat and took consolation in Posh at least having a decent chance of progress in the competition.

Another Irishman was flying into Portman Road for a medical ahead of Town's first home match of the season. Fanzine website Those Were The Days (www.twtd.co.uk) revealed Bohemians keeper Brian Murphy was set to sign a pre-contract agreement with Town and subsequently join when the Irish season ended in November. Capped by Ireland at Under-21 level and winner of the FAI League of Ireland player-of-the-year for 2008, Murphy was tipped for further international honours and his arrival suggested number two Shane Supple was poised for a loan move away to gain more first-team experience after a couple of seasons of inactivity at Portman Road. Keane, however, remained tight-lipped and simply said Town had two keepers and would like a third. What he did confirm was that he was in the market for a replacement for the injured Norris and he invited clubs to make offers for his own players, saying: 'I still think there might be movement on one or two over the next week. I know there are clubs in the background, shall we say, making tentative enquiries. They can make all the enquiries they want, clubs need to put bids on the table if they're interested in my boys and not speak to every Tom, Dick and Harry about it, that's what I do. If I'm interested in a player, I make an offer.'

The sense of joy and excitement which usually greeted clear blue skies and a pitch worthy of royalty on the first home fixture of the season was downtrodden by the lingering grief of Sir Bobby Robson's passing. The roar which greeted Keane from the tunnel was a few decibels lower than the one which hailed his emergence four months earlier. The crowd was also nearly 5,000 down. Groups of fans who had not seen each other since the last day of the previous season chose to discuss the inevitable end to the great man's life, rather than the selection posers Keane had mulled over during the week.

A minute's applause in Robson's memory was the most memorable moment by the time the interval arrived. Keane chose to stick with the same 4-3-3 he had started with at Coventry, with Healy replacing the injured Norris in midfield. Wickham was deemed too tired to start after his 120-minute masterclass at Shrewsbury, so Stead was the lone front man, flanked by Walters and Martin. It was a system defended by Keane before the start. 'I've tried a few different things and I want my team to have variation and to be adaptable to 4-4-2, 4-3-3 or whatever it might be,' he explained. 'I think the players I have at the club at the moment, that [4-3-3] seems to suit us best. I would definitely see it as 4-3-3. I suppose if we get beaten people will say it's a 4-5-1 and that it's boring and defensive, but I see it as 4-3-3.'

By the time the players emerged after the break, lucky to still be level with Leicester, the system had been ditched. Healy's debut was cut short as he was axed along with an isolated and ineffective Stead, though sympathy was felt for his lack of service and support, as he was often the only Town player in and around the penalty area, swarmed by Leicester defenders. Priskin and Wickham emerged to form a twin strike-force.

The centre of midfield – arguably the most important area on the pitch – was now occupied by Trotter and Peters – two players who were not in Magilton's plans. Both had potential – Trotter was proven as a goal-getting midfielder in the reserves and had the physique to look after himself. Peters was a more rounded version of Danny Haynes, without the randomly directed fireworks at the end of a lightning quick run. Neither was experienced, comfortable dictating the play, used to tracking opposition runners through the middle of the pitch or likely to break down the Leicester defence with an inch-perfect pass. If any Town follower had been told 12 months earlier that Peters and Trotter were to be the central midfield pairing during the opening home fixture of the 2009-10 season, they would not only have dismissed it as poppycock, they would have laughed. Injury crisis? Player exodus after relegation to League One? It was all the more strange given that Owen Garvan, the best passer and midfield dictator at the club, was sitting on the bench, not required until midway through the second half. What had he done to upset Keane?

The players grew frustrated with the referee, Phil Crossley, while the fans grew frustrated at the disjointed mess on the pitch. And this was only the second match of the season. It was too much to expect a 16-year-old to win the match for the second time in a week and the match

finished 0-0. It could not have been a more underwhelming opening to
Town's home campaign. Excuses could again be made – early season,
players not yet settled, the league will sort itself out in time etc. But the
nagging doubts were now nagging that bit harder. Keane's signings failed
to impress. Delaney's distribution was an accident waiting to happen.
Martin was taken off after 63 minutes, Healy at half-time, and Priskin
offered no threat in his 45 minutes on the pitch.

Keane refused to give excuses, saying his side was 'sluggish'. There
was little positive spin he could put on what was a massive anti-climax.
The clean sheet was highlighted and the players' character in 'hanging in
there when they weren't at the races', but any football fan would have
been surprised to see how poor a side Town looked. To rub further salt
into Town's wounds, Jordan Rhodes took his Huddersfield tally to five
goals in three games.

Town were hoping to get their season up and running three days later
when Crystal Palace came to Portman Road. All eyes were on Keane's
attacking selections, as Town tried to find the sparkle in front of goal.
Would Keane be bold enough to start with 16-year-old Wickham? Or
would he keep the three-man attack of Stead, Walters and Martin, which
had so far mustered the only league goal of the season? 'If Jon Stead or
any of my other strikers had scored six or seven goals in pre-season and
wasn't starting, he'd probably come and see me,' said Keane at his pre-
match press-conference. 'If he'd scored a couple in the League Cup and
I'd left him out, then I'd be getting a knock at the door, so I'm expecting
one from Connor. The boy's doing everything he possibly can. What your
players have to do is make a statement to you – can you leave me out of
the next game?'

Richard Wright was one of the only Town players to make the statement Keane was asking for. A change in formation to 4-4-2, with Priskin
and, as expected, Wickham the strikeforce, made no difference to the way
Town played, or the result. Palace ran out comfortable 3-1 winners and
Darren Ambrose proved that, despite his unflattering loan spell the previous season, he had not lost the ability which enticed Newcastle to sign
him from Town as a teenager. His two goals came immediately after half-
time, leading Keane to remove Healy and Priskin, replacing them with
Stead and Garvan. It was from Garvan's cross that Bruce gave Town a
lifeline but Palace extended their lead through Neil Danns. Boos rang out
again at the final whistle. Wright had saved Town from a more embarrassing scoreline and again there was no sense of Keane having formed
a team which worked well as a unit. It was another blow for the club,
which announced it would be renaming the North Stand after Sir Bobby

Robson. Hopes of celebrating his memory with performances he would have been proud of had so far been dashed. In fact, Robson would have been thoroughly disappointed with their start to the season, but he would have understood a manager's need for time, after his own tenure at Ipswich did not begin gloriously.

Keane chose to take responsibility for the result, rather than criticise his players for their uninspiring display. 'In defence of the players, I take full responsibility,' he said. 'There were new players out there, young players and a new partnership up front. I know as well as anyone that sometimes these things don't happen straight away in football. It takes time to click. There are genuine reasons why we haven't hit the ground running and it would be very tempting to make excuses. In glimpses we looked dangerous, but we expect better and the players demand better of each other. There has been a lot of expectation around the place, particularly in the summer, and it's been a reality check for us all.'

Reality-check indeed. Town were expected to be firing straight from the off, not dallying with formations and who would play up front. Why had they not hit the ground running? Keane spent the whole summer preparing for the new season, shipping out the players he preferred to move on, and spending substantial money on those he did. New partnerships should have gelled during pre-season. In most areas of the pitch, Town's players were like strangers to one another.

'I think people think we are going to be the Chelsea of the Championship but I'm going to have to wheel and deal a bit more,' said Keane. Town's spending was way short of Chelsea's, even by Championship standards. For the outlay, though, progress was not unreasonably expected. Summer was the time for wheeling and dealing, and Keane was busy throughout. The east coast of England was hardly a big attraction for footballers, unless Newcastle come knocking – and the Magpies' appeal is not what it was. Although only three games were gone, the evidence so far indicated Town were a long, long way from being even a mid-table team.

What Town did not need now was for something else to go wrong. The press were warming to their poor start to the season and were watching and waiting for Keane to erupt. When second-choice goalkeeper Shane Supple announced he was retiring from the game, at 22-years-old, it helped to fuel theories that all was not well in the Town camp.

Supple's reasoning was that he had fallen out of the love with the game. His Town career had been in limbo since Richard Wright returned to the club. Easily good enough to be a number one at Championship level, the Irishman looked set to leave in the summer to seek regular action, but decided to stay for one more year. Unknown at the time, Supple was ready to quit football completely.

'It is something I have been thinking about for a long while,' he said in a statement released by the club. 'It's obviously a big decision but I feel that playing professional football is not something I want to continue doing as a career. There is no one reason why I have made my decision, there are a number of factors, but deep down my heart is not in the game any more and I'm not going to go into work every day trying to convince myself that it is, so it's the right time for me to walk away. I suppose that you could say I have fallen out of love with the game and when then happens I've always said to myself that I wouldn't hang around. All I wanted to do when I was younger was play in the Premier League, but as you grow up you realise that there are other things in life and, to be honest, the game is not what I thought it was. I want to thank the manager for the support he has given me. He was a bit shocked when I told him and I expected that but he understood my reasons. He's been first class. People probably think I'm crazy but I'm not going to stay in the game for anyone else, I'm making this decision for myself.'

Supple, a member of the FA Youth Cup winning side of 2005, said he was heading back to Ireland to spend time with his family and would consider his options – none of which would be in football. A month later, Supple expanded on his reasons for quitting football. In an interview with *The Daily Mail* he revealed how the lifestyle of a modern day footballer was not for him and how seeing his team-mates not caring whether they won or lost helped to make up his mind. He said: 'Even if I could afford to drive a Bentley, that was not what I was in it for. Some seem to think it is about flashiness, the big house, big money, cars. That wouldn't be my take on things. I remember Joe Royle saying some of them think they're stars and they're not even players. The decision was brewing over a number of years. The first time I thought this might not be the thing for me was the Christmas of 2005. That was my first Christmas away. My Dad came over for the Boxing Day game and I remember saying to him then 'I don't think this is the thing for me. I don't like what I'm seeing'.

'When you're a young lad your one aim is to get into the first team. You're in digs, you're training, you're resting, all you're looking at is the first team. Being away from home can be difficult on top of that, but at first it wasn't a problem for me. Then I got into the first team and I saw that some of the lads didn't really care whether we won or lost. I didn't really like that, that was disillusioning.' Supple denied any falling out with Keane and confirmed the new manager was the reason he decided to sign a new deal in the summer. He was not put off by the killing and eating of a pig at the pre-season army training and believed he would have been more suited to football 30 years ago, describing himself as a bit 'old-fashioned'. He started playing Gaelic football on his return to Ireland and liked that the players washed their own kit – a humbleness he enjoyed while on loan at Falkirk, where the players also brought their own packed lunch.

It is hard to imagine falling out of love with football to the extent that Supple did. No more last-minute glory, penalty saves like in the Carling Cup at Shrewsbury, or opening a pay slip to see the numbers run into thousands and thousands. Supple did not need Roy Keane, and nor did he need Ipswich Town. The appeal of Keane's new venture was too weak and, for that, Keane could not be blamed. It was football Supple was at odds with, not Keane. First the club lost the life of Sir Bobby Robson, now they had lost their young goalkeeper, a potential number one for years to come, to a yearning for a new life.

Keane said Supple was brave for making a decision most people thought he was crazy to make. Millions of youngsters around the world wanted to be in Supple's position – a professional footballer at a respected English club. But Keane said Supple was an intelligent man who would do well at whatever he choose to do and, although surprised, he understood the reasoning.

A replacement in Ipswich-born Arran Lee-Barrett was quickly signed. The 25-year-old was an Academy schoolboy at the club and had been released by Hartlepool in the summer. Not coming to Town, however, was Giovani Dos Santos. Keane, who received a letter from the FA asking him to explain his comments regarding referee Keith Hill prior to the game with Crystal Palace, but did not face any charge, was asked about the chances of the Mexican returning before Town's trip to West Brom and his response was 'very, very, very slim, I would have thought. Very slim'.

Town's showing at the Hawthorns was to be an accurate gauge of how they might fare in the Championship. The Baggies were one of the favourites to go up and were formidable opponents on home turf. 'Going nowhere fast,' was Keane's verdict of his own side, after Town were beaten 0-2 – again a scoreline which could have been far worse but for a string of saves by Wright, who also denied Luke Moore from the penalty spot.

'I always knew that the job would be difficult, but there is no getting away from the fact that it is a massive, massive challenge over the next few months,' said Keane. 'It is sink or swim for the players. We need to do better and I don't want to keep saying it. We don't look much of a goal threat and we are giving bad goals away. That is a recipe for trouble, so it is going to be very, very hard. But it can be done. You have to believe that we can turn it around.' It was only a few weeks previously when Keane was talking about promotion. The goalposts had been moved and it was a 'massive challenge' just to get Town's season up and running.

Four changes had been made from the side beaten by Crystal Palace, as captain Gareth McAuley, Damien Delaney, Healy and Priskin all dropped out. McAuley's absence was because of a midweek bust-up with Keane, according to reports. Garvan was given a recall in midfield, young defender Tommy Smith was included at the back, along with David Wright, and Stead was recalled up front alongside Wickham. Garvan and Stead only made it to half-time, as Keane plumped for a midfield of Trotter and Colback to try and gain a grip on the game. Barely 10 Championship appearances between them, only so much could be expected. Hauling back a two-goal deficit against one of the best teams in the division certainly could not be anticipated. Was Keane giving up at half-time? Where were the warriors in his side, players who personified their manager's own fearless desire as a player? The day was summed up by Lee Martin tripping over a corner-flag when attempting to take a corner-kick and the West Brom fans sung 'Keane's getting sacked in the morning'. The result left Town second bottom of the table. While still early in the season, it was clear Keane had no idea what his team best was.

The Town manager denied any bust-up with McAuley after the game, but he kept himself in the headlines for the wrong reasons when he announced that certain players who featured in the match were unlikely to ever play for the club again. 'There are certainly one or two players from the weekend who are unlikely to play for me again,' he told the gathered press. 'I've told them that. I'm still learning about these players, but eventually you have to make a decision about one or two and say "I don't like what I'm seeing". That's not just on Saturday's game, but the end of last season and pre-season as well. You can't keep waiting on people, you have to say that enough's enough. I'm not saying they're not good players, they're just not doing the business for me.' Keane's outburst led to deliberation over who he was referring to. The obvious two were Garvan and Stead as they were both taken off at half-time. But *The East Anglian Daily Times*'s Derek Davis named Alan Quinn as well in a story which would upset Keane, who felt hearsay was being presented as fact.

The team-sheet for Town's trip to Peterborough in the second round of the Carling Cup would give a strong indication of whom Keane was referring to in his outburst. Was it just in the heat of the moment? Or was Keane about to wield the axe? It was still early in the season for the Town manager to be making his mind up on players, or suddenly deciding that a chosen few would never play for the club again, despite featuring throughout pre-season and then in the opening matches of the new campaign.

Keane's craving for new personnel was growing stronger. The old guard was not up to it, he thought. A recent study by football writer Simon Kuper proved new managers who spent millions of pounds after joining a club did not enjoy any more success than those who kept the purse strings pulled tight. The correlation between transfer fees paid and success was a misnomer. It was high wages which were equal to success, according to Kuper. New managers were always keen to bring in new players when they began a new job. It was one of the first points they made when speaking publicly – the need to bring in fresh blood – whether prompted by the press or not. If a club was near the bottom of the table, there was an obvious need for new players. But what if it was a side just a couple of quality players in important positions short of being a top six side? It would make financial sense to spend larger fees on fewer players, so to bring in higher quality, and let the existing players try to thrive under the new manager – a change which would likely see their motivation and commitment increase as they would be playing for their future.

At this point in the season, had Keane brought in just Delaney, to fill the need of a left-sided defender, he would possibly have had the funds to buy either a top-rate striker or winger – not a Priskin or Lee Martin, based on the evidence of their early performances. Was there a need for Colin Healy and Jack Colback? Their wages could have been put towards a new, star-acquisition. Instead, Keane wanted an overhaul. He felt the existing squad was not good enough to win promotion and he would change it until it was. There was nothing wrong with such a strategy, as long as progression took place on the pitch. Each new signing had to add something extra to the team or the squad. Otherwise, six months down the line, the club would have a new team at great expense with nothing to show for it – a worthless exercise. Marcus Evans was backing his new manager, though. If Keane wanted to make more changes to the squad, he had the owner's blessing.

All managers have said they want a player who adds something to his squad. The problem Keane was facing was that so far his signings had added little, if anything, to the squad he inherited from Magilton. He needed his next signings to be the right players. It was clear before the Peterborough game, from his pre-game comments and his anger after the

West Brom defeat, that he did not rate a number of his players, although he did try and cover over the distrust in his players' ability. 'Saturday, I think, can be a watershed in terms of the club,' he said. 'You draw the line somewhere and say 'We need reinforcements'. But they've got to be good reinforcements. As much as I've said I've been wheeling and dealing, we need two or three to come in and say "This is how you do it". I wouldn't say the current players have let me down or that they aren't good enough, but it a takes a certain amount of time when you have new players coming into your club for the team to gel. I wouldn't say that people have let me down. I'm the manager, I'll take responsibility. It's just not quite clicked into gear. It's not a criticism of any individual players, but as a group we're just a bit short at this moment in time and we'll try and address that over the next few days.'

With a week to go before the transfer deadline, the Carling Cup-tie gave Keane a chance to see who was going to sink and who would swim. Counago was fit again to make his first start of the season after his groin problem. Keane said he looked 'half-decent' in training and would add a much-needed goal threat. It was ironic Keane was now having to turn to, and heavily rely on, the striker he tried to sell on the cheap during the summer.

Both Stead and Garvan were absent from the starting line-up. From Keane's comments, they appeared to have played their last games for the club. Stead, Town's top-scorer in 2008-09, had been unable to hold down a regular starting role even though his goal ratio was reasonable. The rest of his game left Town fans and players frustrated. Poor in the air, and on the ground, his saving grace was a knack for scoring a variety of goals – some spectacular, and for having a high work-rate.

Garvan, meanwhile, was expected to be the one player who would flourish most under Keane's leadership. They had plenty in common, being from Ireland and playing in midfield. Both liked to get on the ball and dictate play, but the difference was the lack of fire and bite in Garvan as a footballer. Whereas Keane would scythe through anything which moved and put his body on the brink, the spindly built Garvan was, by his own admission, an average tackler, whose ability on the ball covered up a weak defensive game. He was still Town's most effective midfielder, though, and had been since he made his debut as a 17-year-old. He always wanted the ball, and gave Town the chance to pass out of defence. Keane, however, had decided he could do without the Under-21 international, who was earmarked for full international caps and had been linked with a number of Premier League clubs since breaking into Town's first team.

Contrary to *The East Anglian Daily Times*'s assertion that Quinn was one of the chosen ones never to play for Town again, he was selected in the starting 11 at Peterborough. There was a glimmer of hope for Town's season when Priskin put them in front – from a Counago cross. On the evidence of the first half, Keane had found his regular strike-partnership. Priskin should have made it 2-0 when he earned a penalty before seeing his effort saved. Peterborough equalised before half-time and struck the winner midway through the second half when George Boyd capitalised on a Colback mistake. The game ebbed away from Town after Keane replaced Counago and Priskin shortly after the break.

Reports in Scotland stated that Town were about to sign Celtic captain Stephen McManus on loan with a view to a £2.5 million permanent deal, while Sunderland trio Daryl Murphy (yet again), Carlos Edwards and Nyron Nosworthy were also linked. Keane said after the Peterborough defeat he was not close to bringing anyone in. He then backtracked on his comments regarding players not playing for the club again. He said it was wrong to suggest Garvan and Stead's future lay elsewhere on the premise they were not in the 18-man squad for the Peterborough tie. 'Colin Healy and Damien Delaney were not in my squad for the Hawthorns [West Brom] but they were back last night,' he said. 'You cannot write off the Ipswich careers of Owen and Jon on the back of them not being at Peterborough. I read that Alan Quinn was also on his way out. But he was in my team last night and he will back up that he has not been told I am thinking about letting him go.' Did somebody have a word in Keane's ear about his dealings with the press? It was a bizarre backtrack from the Town manager, who only days earlier was adamant a number of players had played their last game.

McManus was not on his way to Portman Road, but Keane finally succeeded in bringing in a couple more players he knew well. It was reported that Town were keen on four Sunderland players – Nosworthy, Murphy, Edwards and Grant Leadbitter. It was Edwards and Leadbitter who made it down to Suffolk for talks in a joint deal worth £4 million. While Town were trying to persuade the duo to drop down from the Premier League, and in Leadbitter's case leave the club he began his career at, Stead was being linked with Crystal Palace and Doncaster following his omission from the Carling Cup squad, withdrawal at half-time at West Brom, and Keane's comments. Garvan was also being linked with a move away – to Premier League side Burnley.

The Leadbitter and Edwards deals had some way to go when Preston visited Portman Road on 29 August. Keane said he wanted to find out if they wanted to come and play for Ipswich and leave the Premier League before any deal was concluded, while he also confirmed Town had reject-ed an offer for one of their players – believed to be Stead. There was no bid from Burnley for Garvan. Keane saw the game as a chance to put right the wrongs which had marred Town's opening to the season. 'We're looking forward to it and it's an opportunity for our players to put a few things right that we've not really done so far this season,' he said. 'Same with the cup game the other night. We started the game well but we just don't seem to be able to finish the job off at this moment in time. I wouldn't say I'm angry, it just makes me more aware of how big the job is. I could make a few excuses for you, a few things haven't gone our way, but we'll keep battling on, trying to get it right.'

Alex Bruce skippered Town, having taken the armband from the pre-viously out-of-favour McAuley, who was brought back into the side to partner Balkestein. Bruce moved across to right-back, while Colback partnered Trotter in a central midfield substantially weaker than at any time in the previous five years. There was no place in the 18-man squad for David Wright – so often Town's best defender during the previous campaign. Priskin and Counago continued their partnership upfront after impressing at Peterborough, but Town were level for only 12 minutes as Ross Wallace – a player Keane managed at Sunderland – gave the visitors the lead. Town equalised on the stroke of half-time when Trotter's goal-bound shot was handled on the line by Callum Davidson, who was sent off, and Walters's spot-kick was saved by Andy Lonergan, only for him to put away the rebound. Town failed to make the most of their numerical advantage in the second half. Keane made a triple substitution 13 minutes after the break – taking off Counago, who looked the most likely player to open Preston up, Priskin, who had a header cleared off the line, and Martin. Town huffed and puffed against the ten men, but they were rely-ing on the goal-starved Stead and 16-year-old Wickham. Walters, a goal-threat from set-pieces and at the back post, was a likely source, but Quinn, Trotter and Colback were not proven match-winners. It finished 1-1, as Town's winless run was extended to five league games, seven including cup-ties, although they had beaten Shrewsbury on penalties.

The result was by no means a disaster. Keane had no complaints about it, although he and the 19,000 Town fans present were concerned by Preston looking more dangerous on the counter-attack than Town generally did with all their second-half possession. 'When Preston went down to 10 men, it should have been easier in terms of moving the ball a bit quicker and more penetration, but we huffed and puffed and never really opened them up,' said Keane. 'We had no player today with the quality that could go and get a goal for us, so I can have no complaints over the result. The effort was there, I can't fault the players for that, but we lacked the quality in the final third and that is what football is all about. I suppose this game shows why we're desperately trying to add to our squad. At the moment we're nowhere near but I'm expecting a busy couple of days. I certainly won't be putting my feet up and hopefully I can bring three, maybe four, players in before Tuesday. I have a very good idea of the areas I want to strengthen and there's a lot of hard work ahead.'

August had been an anti-climax. Keane's management was under fire and Town fans were left wondering why they had ever called for Magilton's head. But the new man would be given time. Ipswich Town fans were patient people. Knee-jerk reactions were not common in Suffolk, and Keane would be given the benefit of the doubt – for how long, only results would dictate.

Chapter Five

September 2009

'YOU SAID BEFORE THAT IT WAS THE WORST RUN IN 40 YEARS. YOU CAN STAND BEHIND THAT CAMERA AND QUESTION ME ALL YOU WANT. I THINK I HAVE ALWAYS BROUGHT SOMETHING TO MY CLUBS BUT AS YET I HAVE NOT BROUGHT ANYTHING TO IPSWICH.'

September had started with Town winless but, on the bright side, the deal taking Leadbitter and Edwards to Portman Road was still alive. Town were linked with Celtic defender Darren O'Dea and Birmingham midfielder Lee Carsley as the transfer window crept towards its close, and the rumour mill went into overdrive. Sheffield Wednesday's Richard Wood was reported to be close to moving to Portman Road, while McAuley was said to be a £1 million target for Middlesbrough. Derby County right-back Paul Connolly was also on Town's radar, according to the newspapers and internet. By Tuesday afternoon, the double Sunderland deal was confirmed. Edwards penned a two-year deal and Leadbitter three years for a combined fee of £4 million. Leadbitter was likened to Paul Scholes during Keane's time in charge at The Stadium of Light and was one of the first players Keane wanted to sign when he took over at Town in April. Sunderland's longest serving player until he left, Leadbitter was a feisty midfielder with an eye for goal. He was an England Under-21 international and a prominent part of Keane's side but was seen as surplus to requirements by new Sunderland manager Steve Bruce, who was spending big money to try and take the club to the next level.

Edwards, a Trinidad & Tobago international with 74 caps, had suffered an injury-hit spell in the North East. The right-midfielder or full-back started only 37 games in two-and-a-half years and spent a month on loan at Wolverhampton Wanderers. The need for a central midfielder was obvious, as Town could not carry on with a central pairing from Colback, Trotter, Peters and Healy and expect a top-six place. A weakness in such a vital area was foolhardy. Keane saw the problem and he did something about it, although the demotion of Garvan seemed odd, even though the young Irishman had not kicked on in his career as expected. With Norris injured, Town would rely heavily on Leadbitter and his credentials gave hope that he would be able to help arrest the slide and lead Town to their first victory of the season. The signing of Edwards was not as clear-cut as Leadbitter. In Walters, Town had the ideal right-sided midfielder, unless Keane planned on playing Edwards at right-back, or pushing

Walters upfront, where he was proven to be less effective. However, having played every minute of Trinidad & Tobago's 2006 World Cup final matches, Edwards was experienced and hardened to the demands of winning promotion from the Championship.

Keane felt the pair's willingness to drop down a division showed their hunger to succeed with Town, rather than stay in the Premier League and pick up their wages when it was increasingly unlikely they would figure under Steve Bruce. Their signing also dampened tales of players not wanting to sign for Keane because of his style of management, which had come under fire from more than one Sunderland player during his time in charge there.

The transfer window could not close without a final mention of Sunderland's Daryl Murphy. It was reported Town made a late bid for the front man but, thankfully for some Town fans who were none too impressed with his goalscoring record, nothing came of it. There was another addition, though, in full-back Liam Rosenior, who signed a loan deal from Reading until the end of the season. Like Leadbitter and Edwards, Rosenior had played in the Premier League – with Fulham – and was keen to get back there. His Reading contract was up at the end of the season and, if all went well, he was keen to stay on at Town, or at least put himself in the shop window at a club he expected to do better at than the Royals, who were not as strong as they were in previous years. It was also reported Town tried to swap Stead for Sheffield Wednesday defender Wood. Wednesday manager Brian Laws confirmed a swap deal was in place for Wood, but the identity of the Town player was not revealed.

September 5th was a blank date for Championship clubs as players were away on international duty. Carlos Edwards was one of them and, with a midweek international fixture as well, he was not due to meet up with the Town team until the night before their trip to Middlesbrough on 12 September. Speculation had been mounting all week that either Middlesbrough or Sheffield United were going to sign Gareth McAuley, who was also away on international duty, with Northern Ireland.

New-look side in place, Keane felt his team would now move up the table. 'We've had a couple of new players come in, who have had some decent hours on the training pitch, so there's been pluses,' he said. 'Obviously, we've not seen Carlos yet, but we've got some good training under our belts and we need to put that into action on match day. We've been working very hard, but there's no magic wand. We've got some good players, but it's taken a while to get going in terms of getting that first win under our belts, which I'm sure will give the players confidence and get that momentum going. But we've not managed to get that yet. With the two or three new faces coming in, I'm pretty confident that over the next few weeks and months we'll be going up the table.' The Town manager confirmed he had been in discussion with other clubs regarding two loan deals. If they were successful, he said it would probably see a couple of members of the Town squad move out on loan.

The most interesting part of Keane's pre-match press conference was his latest take on his 'players will never play for me again' outburst. He said: 'I'll admit I probably shouldn't have said that, it came across the wrong way. The point I was trying to make was that I think I have given players a certain amount of chances. One or two miss out and obviously one or two people jumped the gun, talking about Jon Stead and Quinner and a load of nonsense was written about that. I do believe that there does come a point when you have to say to a certain player that they're not part of your plans, but unfortunately the media go off on tangents and mention names and all this carry on, which I think is a bit out of order really. Having said that, every day you come to training players have a chance to impress their manager. We had a practice game last week and the reserves had a game during the week, so there's always an opportunity for players to stake their claim, but a lot of them don't seem to take it. That's what happens in football, that's why players move clubs.'

Whether it came across the wrong way or not, Keane was quite clear in what he was spelling out when he said it, and his players would have read what he said as well. Was he backtracking because results were not improving and he knew he was going to need some of the 'unwanted' players due to financial constraints? Three new players was a big enough change to the face of the team, but from what Keane had said, he wanted more than that. Evans was pouring money in fast to try and take Town forwards, but so far, he was getting little back in return. According to Keane, Town were improving and they would be OK. 'People need to relax and trust the manager, the players and the staff that we'll be fine come the end of the season,' he said before Town made the long trip north to Middlesbrough.

There was anything but relaxation on the minds of Town fans on the way home from the Riverside Stadium. If they thought Leadbitter, Edwards and Rosenior were going to turn Town into world beaters overnight, they could not have been more wrong. The defending was likened to a 'horror show' by Keane, as Town were beaten 1-3. Boro went into a 3-0 lead before Walters pulled one back in the dying minutes from the penalty-spot. Walters was moved back up front, at the expense of Priskin, to accommodate Edwards, while Peters, recovered from the injury suffered against Leicester, was preferred to the increasingly frustrating Lee Martin. Pim Balkestein, who started the season as first-choice centre-half, was not in the 18, nor was David Wright again as Rosenior took over at right-back. Town played like a team chock full of new signings and players with zero confidence. The first rumblings of discontent were coming from the away support, who called on Keane to 'sort it out'. For Middlesbrough manager Gareth Southgate, it was payback for Keane's conduct when the two came face-to-face as players at Villa Park in the FA Cup all those years earlier. Southgate's wounds from Keane's studs healed, but Keane's wounds from another humiliating result would run deep.

It was Keane's first footballing return to the North East since his controversial walkout on Sunderland and he was asked about the similarity between the two clubs at the point when he had just taken over at each. 'There are similarities,' he said. 'Sunderland had just come down so had that bit of strength. But we can't keep making excuses, we need to be better. It's up to the players, the staff and myself to sort it out. That's the beauty of the Championship. When you're down the bottom like us, sixth place is realistic. Even teams at the bottom in November can be up there challenging at the end of the season.'

Keane was less philosophical about Town's defending, which allowed Gary O'Neil to loop in a header after an embarrassing McAuley error when he missed his kick, and two goals from Jeremie Aliadiere. He was refusing to press the panic button, but it was becoming clearer by the week that there was a lot wrong with the team he had built so far. 'We have had decent possession and always looked a threat but as soon as we lose it we are in trouble and we've conceded a goal,' he said. 'We can't keep on giving the ball away. And up the other end too. We have put good balls into the area but not made them count. I wouldn't call it a crisis. Supporters may call it that, but I would call it a challenge. We are certainly not panicking. Are we disappointed? Yes. Are we frustrated? Yes. But we are not panicking. We have a decent squad here and between the boxes we are playing some good stuff. Maybe we are lacking a bit of confidence at the moment because of the lack of a win but it will come, it will gel. It is early days yet.'

The defensive nightmare led to Bolton Wanderers' centre-half Danny Shittu being linked with a move to Town. Keane refused to comment on Shittu and just said he would be making more calls ahead of Tuesday's home match against Nottingham Forest. Garvan spoke out in the Irish media ahead of the Forest clash, confirming he was not in Keane's plans. He admitted he needed to knuckle down, but his absence mystified most

Town followers, who felt he was a better player than Colback, Trotter, Peters and Healy in the middle of midfield. He wasn't the only one out in the cold. David Wright was cast adrift, with Rosenior, Bruce, Delaney and Smith now ahead of him in the full-back pecking order.

The points may not have been piling up, but it was not because of a lack of effort, according to Keane. And, if that was the case, it could only be because of one thing – a lack of quality, although Keane pointed at a shortage of luck. 'We need to keep working hard,' he said. 'You look at the first goal on Saturday, the boy was two yards offside as the cross came in, so we need a little bit of luck as well. We can't fault the players for their efforts, but nearly every league game we've played so far we've given teams a helping hand. Regardless of whether the boy was offside, we gave the ball away cheaply. We're making it hard for ourselves. And we're not scoring many goals, so the last thing we need to be doing is giving teams a helping hand.'

To the visible eye, Town were no less hard-working than any other team, but what stood out was the lack of support in the penalty area for the strikers and the absence of real tenacity – the kind Keane had no problem displaying during his playing career, even in training sessions. David Norris's absence did not help.

Town were lacking a player to put in a few beefy challenges to stoke up their team and put some fire into their performances. If they were to climb the table and get out of the mess they were becoming more and more tangled up in, it was going to take a physical and mental fight, and so far, even with the ultimate warrior as manager, they were falling well short. The lack of desperation to win games which plagued Magilton's final months was still there – basically because Town could not string together enough moves to reach the opposition's penalty area in the final ten minutes.

The lack of goals surprised Keane, but without Garvan providing the passes in midfield, Town were largely predictable. It was down to Leadbitter to get them flowing again. Matches at Portman Road could be scripted before the first whistle. Town would start brightly and then fade against a team with insufficient fire-power to pose enough threat to take all three points. It was not enjoyable viewing for the fans, many of whom feasted on the excitement of George Burley's football and the pride-filled displays of Mauricio Taricco, Matt Holland and Marcus Stewart. Fans knew such players would give their all and keep the ball on the ground. There was no telling what Keane's squad, Counago apart, would serve up, except 90 minutes littered with poor first-touches and misplaced passes. The Spaniard was different because Portman Road-goers could generally expect to see at least three moments of exciting skill per match – when he was selected.

Keane asked the crowd ahead of the visit of Nottingham Forest to stay with his side through the difficult times. 'I don't want to be patronising to supporters and say "give us a bit more time, a bit more patience", I think, hopefully, they're intelligent enough to understand what we're doing, where we're short and have a bit of faith in me,' he said. 'That doesn't mean to say they should be happy with results, of course not, it would be wrong for me to say that. Get behind the team, I think what the players need is the supporters behind them just now. We need the supporters, without a doubt.'

The Irishman was fortunate he was managing a club with fans whose allegiance was as strong as anywhere in the country, but bedded into their passion for the club was a willingness to give players and managers a chance before making strong judgments. Fans at other clubs would have reacted differently to the desperately disappointing start to the season and direction the club was taking – both on and off the field. A few boos at the final whistle brought no harm.

A string of poor results on the Continent could lead to death threats, fans storming the training ground, and sections of the stadium being ripped apart. In Suffolk, three years of underachievement at great expense had resulted in a few half-hearted chants from the North Stand (Sir Bobby Robson Stand) and an attempt to organise a protest – attended by a sparsely populated group of juveniles – against the previous manager before a home match. Times had to grow substantially worse for sleepy Suffolk to wake from its slumber and cause a real racket. Keane was also getting the benefit of the doubt because he was Roy Keane. And Roy Keane knew best, according to Roy Keane. He said it would take time for his team to gel, so time would have to be given. How would he react if Suffolk turned against him? If results continued to flunk, the world would be watching closely for the consequences, but not yet.

It was anyone's guess as to who would line up for Town against Forest. The days of knowing who was in the line-up before the team was announced were long gone. This time it was Lee Martin, Alan Quinn and Stead returning in place of Colback, Counago and Peters on a damp evening which McAuley would want to forget. It started so well for Town when Leadbitter scored in the first minute, latching on to Stead's flick-on from a long Edwards throw. It was one of Town's brightest halves of the season up to that point, with Quinn and Leadbitter dovetailing in the middle of midfield. The second half was a different story, as Town ran out of steam and former Norwich City striker Robert Earnshaw hit back at Town fans branding him as a species from outer space, by scoring within a minute of stepping off the bench. Town's strike duo of Stead and Walters were playing as individuals, not a partnership, and fed off long balls and scraps – neither of them comfortable receiving the ball to feet with their back to goal or running in behind the defence. A change up front was needed, but when the substitute board went up, it was Quinn and Carlos Edwards replaced by Colback and Peters, and then Liam Trotter coming on for Liam Rosenior. Keane revealed after the game that the three players taken off were all injured, and he agreed with the need to freshen up the strike-force.

The crowd was baffled by the substitutions. Counago and Priskin had both warmed up for a considerable amount of time, only for Keane to bring on three midfield players in a game they should have been going all out to win. Frowns turned to horror in the last minute when McAuley was caught in possession near the halfway line by Dele Adebola, leaving him clean through on goal. The Town defender chased back, tugged at the Forest striker and eventually sent him sprawling in the penalty area. Relief spread when the referee deemed the foul to be outside the box but McAuley was red-carded and, after his disastrous performance at Middlesbrough, was not given a peaceful walk back to the dressing room by the Town faithful. It was an awkward, ugly moment for McAuley, whose Town career was at crisis point. Already stripped of the captaincy by Keane and dropped, on current form he was a liability, although it was hard not to feel sorry for the softly spoken Irishman, whose slow plod off the pitch was like that of a jilted groom making his way from the altar after the bride told him she loved someone else. Keane said he would sleep well, despite heading home once again without all three points. The 1-1 draw meant the winless run extended to seven league games.

The Town players echoed their manager's thoughts on their poor start to the season – when a microphone was shoved under their nose anyway. When faced with the press they were talking a far better game than they were playing – speaking of going on a winning run which would send them flying up the table, saying it was still early in the season and everyone at the club was doing their utmost to turn it around. Little was said about Keane and his inglorious start as manager, as the players made sure they did not step out of line. The only comments relating to Keane were that he was calmer than the outside world believed and his signings would prove to be good business.

For all the talk, there was no sign, apart from the first half of the Forest match, that Town were going to win a game in the near future. Team selection was now a revolving door and McAuley verified that his agent had received a call from the club saying he could find himself a new employer. As error-ridden as he was at that moment, McAuley remained the best centre-half at the club. For three-quarters of the previous season he was outstanding. Keane's message to McAuley, and the other players who had vanished from the first-team picture, like Garvan and David Wright, was to keep grafting. He said: 'If an offer comes in for any our players that we think is acceptable, then we'll consider it. My advice to Gareth and any of the players is keep your head down and work hard. Every manager wheels and deals. Do you think Manchester United wanted to sell Ronaldo in the summer? Of course they didn't. Any player that comes into the club every single day, is on time and trains properly, has an opportunity to play.'

Keane, speaking ahead of Town's trip to Doncaster, then unleashed a verbal assault on football agents. 'Their [players'] agents run their lives. I speak to Gareth [McAuley], I spoke to him on Monday or Tuesday and he's fine, it's these agents. These agents are on the phone all the time, I spoke to an agent about one of my players yesterday. They don't like their players staying at clubs too long, they want them to move on. There's nothing wrong with doing well and staying at your own club. Good players do that, staying maybe 10, 11 years at a club.'

Keane's reputation for walking out, allied by his signing of only a two-year deal and Town's awful start to the season, led to talk of him leaving before the leaves fell off the trees, but he reiterated his commitment to the cause, saying he could have signed for three years but wanted the challenge of taking Town to the Premier League in two. 'I've had difficult periods before in my career, whether it's as a player or as a young manager, and I've always got through them,' he said. 'I'm fairly confident that come the end of the two-year contract that I've signed, we'll be in the Premiership. No one said it was going to be easy.'

Mention of Ipswich Town and the Premier League began to draw laughter from football fans around the country. The club had become a laughing stock – the club who risked all by appointing Roy Keane, paying him millions of pounds, handing him millions of pounds to spend, only to wind up in the relegation zone.

There was nothing Premier League about Town's defending at Doncaster's Keepmoat Stadium as they relinquished a lead to draw 3-3. Keane spoke before the game about his side's inability to keep the ball out of the net, as well as put the ball in it at the other end. He felt Town's play between the two penalty areas had not been all that bad. But games were won and lost in the final third and the first league win of the season remained elusive.

Changes to the side which drew with Forest were restricted to two, with Counago replacing Stead and Tommy Smith in for the suspended McAuley. Richard Wright dropped a cross for Doncaster's opening goal and Town waited until the 65th minute to get back into the game when substitute Colback drove in a low shot from the edge of the penalty area. A 35-yard strike by Martin Woods found its way past Richard Wright but Town hit back three minutes later when Priskin headed in Leadbitter's free-kick. Town thought they had won it with 12 minutes to go when Lee Martin bundled the ball home after a goalmouth scramble. He was mobbed by his team-mates as the players ran to celebrate in front of the visiting supporters, only for Doncaster to draw level five minutes later when Quinton Fortune – a former team-mate of Keane's – curled a brilliant 25-yard shot over Richard Wright. Keane said he never saw Fortune do anything like that when they were together at Old Trafford.

At least Town looked threatening and put themselves into a position where they should have won. Keane saw the season developing into a 'long, tough battle' where some of the players would have to be given the 'benefit of the doubt' as they settled into the club. 'We've got one or two injuries and we're lacking a bit of confidence, as you would expect, but no one is going to hand us a victory,' he said. 'We've got to keep battling away and do it for ourselves.' Keane was dealing with the pressure of managing a club without a victory in a manner far from his volcanic playing demeanour and reputation for erupting off the pitch as well. Apart from saying a few of the squad would not play for him again after the West Brom loss, he was taking regular defeat somewhat gracefully – in public anyway.

The occasion was all set up for Town to break their duck when the BBC cameras went to Portman Road on Saturday, 26 September for the visit of Newcastle. These were two of Sir Bobby Robson's former clubs and the two closest to his heart. The special day also saw the North Stand renamed in his honour. Both sides wore commemorative shirts and Robson's wife, Lady Elsie, was present, along with Town greats such as Mick Mills, Kevin Beattie and Frans Thijssen for an emotional day.

Town were expected, by the fans at least, to produce a stirring performance in Sir Bobby's memory. It was supposed to be the match which ignited their season, as they overcame one of English football's biggest clubs, who, like Town, were punching below their weight in terms of their position within the nation's footballing hierarchy. Unlike Town, Newcastle had made a decent start to the season and looked set for a quick return to the top flight, based on their early season form. Keane sounded a warning before the game. 'Good team, good players,' he said of Newcastle. 'Not many teams in the Championship have a couple of players who have won the Champions League. It's no surprise to me that they're doing well. They've had a good start, just like West Brom and Middlesbrough. Looking at the games we've played, we deservedly lost to West Brom and Middlesbrough, when you look at the teams who have come down, so we know it's going to be a tough game against Newcastle, but we're looking forward to it. The mood in our camp is pretty decent, pretty positive. The players have been pretty positive over the last few weeks, the new players have settled in well and the signs are certainly better from my point of view that we're making a little bit of progress.'

A little progress became no progress, as Town's worst start to a season in the club's 73-year history was confirmed. A huge gulf stood between Town and Newcastle in terms of quality, as the Geordies strolled to a 4-0 victory – made worse for Keane and Town by the full 90 minute screening live on terrestrial television, as families tucked into their evening meal before the X-Factor. Keane had made four changes from the team which drew at Doncaster, with Balkestein, Priskin, Colback and Trotter coming in for Smith, Counago, Quinn and Martin. Keane switched his formation to 4-5-1 and it was a strange decision, given Town's extra attacking zest at Doncaster, where Martin made his first meaningful contribution since joining Town, and Counago showed glimpses of finding top gear.

Sir Bobby would have shaken his head at the shambles displayed by Keane's team, and one wonders what he would have made of the choice to go with Colback and Trotter in midfield ahead of Garvan. And would he have trusted Delaney, who was playing like a goalkeeper being asked to play left-back, ahead of David Wright, or Ben Thatcher, who Keane confirmed was not in his plans – possibly because of his refusal to move closer to the town. There was effort, but no team pattern, no craft or cunning to create chances, no adventure from the midfield and, alarmingly, some pitiful defending.

Kevin Nolan helped himself to a hat-trick, Newcastle were three goals up inside 34 minutes and added a fourth after the break. There was little Richard Wright could do except pick the ball out of the net, although he was beaten from long range again – a common theme among recent goals conceded. Keane's signings showed up badly. Delaney was substituted after 59 minutes, as was Priskin, while Martin remained on the bench. The difference between Town and their opponents emphasised just how far backwards they had moved under Keane. The stadium was Premier League, the training facilities were fit for first-class footballers and more than 27,000 fans turned out to watch a side Keane said he planned on taking to the top flight. But the only thing on the pitch which was Premier League was Newcastle United.

'We gave some unbelievably bad goals away. I bet Nolan thought it was Christmas,' said Keane, whose patience almost snapped on the way to the dressing room after the final whistle. Unsurprisingly, the conclusion was met by boos and, as Keane made his way along the touchline, a number of Town fans voiced their displeasure at the club's plight under the big-name manager. Keane looked them in the eye and continued, but there was a hesitation when one fan in particular had something to say which Keane appeared to resent. It was all there to see on national television. Was his frustration at Town's winless run about to burst out? The moment passed and Keane stayed under control and continued to walk. It was a close call, though. It was clear he was ready to react as Town were now only kept off the bottom of the table by Plymouth Argyle.

'When I got us up at Sunderland, maybe I got a bit of luck,' said Keane. 'Maybe I was just very, very lucky and I'm being found out now.'

The first hint that all was not rosy behind the scenes came following the Newcastle debacle, when Keane was reported to have met with owner Marcus Evans, who attended the match. The Town manager, speaking ahead of his side's midweek trip to Sheffield United, told the gathered press he expected to be sacked if results did not improve soon. It was a speech of commendable honesty, and it cannot be said that he hid behind what he really thought, like so many in football. When asked a straight question, he gave a straight answer, and with Town having gained four points from nine winless matches, the ice underneath his feet was thinning by the week. He was riled by reminders of the club's position in the table and his achievement of managing the club to its worst ever start to a season, though. 'You have been telling me that for the last few weeks,' he snapped. 'You said before that it was the worst run in 40 years. You can stand behind that camera and question me all you want. I think I have always brought something to my clubs but as yet I have not brought anything to Ipswich. I'm doing my best – if that's not good enough, so be it. I'll be the one losing my job, not you. I don't think you'll be too worried about that, so that's fine.'

He could live with the booing from the crowd as well as the reminders of the dreadful start. 'That's life and we'll just have to deal with it,' he said. 'If I was a supporter, looking at our results, I would be booing me. It's part and parcel of our game. I've been booed before when I played for Ireland. We know there is frustration building up but I live in the real world.' The prawn sandwich eaters may have been picked out by Keane while at Manchester United for their unenthusiastic support, but at least there was entertaining football on the pitch that they should have been enjoying. Keane knew he could not round on Town's supporters because they had every right to be critical of what they had sat through so far.

Keane confirmed he was close to two loan signings – understood to have been sanctioned at the meeting with Evans, but as yet there was no official line from the club backing the beleaguered manager. He rejected claims he was chasing Sol Campbell, whose spell at Notts County in League Two was cut short by a Keane-esque walk-out.

If further evidence was needed for defensive reinforcements, it duly came at Bramall Lane. Four changes to the side – Colback, Balkestein, Delaney and Bruce replaced by Quinn, McAuley, Peters (at left-back) and Smith – failed to stop Town going behind from the first piece of goal-mouth action. Richard Wright looked as if he was fouled as he challenged for a high ball with United striker Darius Henderson, but nothing was given and Henderson tapped in from close range. Town levelled through a clever back-heel by Walters, and Leadbitter put them in front when his slow-motion long-ranger trickled into the bottom corner. Their lead was extended even further midway through the second half when McAuley gave Town fans a reason to get off his back by heading home a Leadbitter corner.

Surely Town could hold on to a two-goal advantage for the last 20 minutes? Seven minutes later Henderson beat Smith too easily and drove a shot past Wright to make it 3-2. Keane made substitutions and the game entered injury time when United won a corner. Richard Wright came off his line to catch the in-swinging delivery, the ball slipped through his grasp, and Chris Morgan slammed the loose ball into the net, via a deflection. As cruel as it was on Town, they only had themselves to blame. Their lead at Doncaster had been relinquished, and now they had done it again. How many goals did they need to score to win? Their performance for most of the match was fine, but ten goals had been conceded in the last three matches and the fundamentals of defending were lacking.

'Does it feel like a defeat? Probably not because we've scored three goals away from home but there was a spell in the second half where we were wanting one or two players to see the game through but nobody did tonight. It's very disappointing,' said a bemused Keane. It was hard to point the finger at him on this occasion. For 70 minutes his team selection and tactics worked. They could even have been 3-0 up had a foul on Richard Wright been given for the first goal. Instead, it was another long coach trip back to Suffolk without a victory. The players, management, fans and the rest of English football were still left wondering when Ipswich would actually win.

September ended with a vote of confidence for Keane from chief executive Simon Clegg. The club's fanbase and media were questioning when the club was going to comment on its worrying decline and it came with Town sitting bottom of the Championship table – the laughing stock of the land. There was no indication from Clegg that anything dramatic was about to happen behind the scenes when he addressed the press, but the severity of the situation was clear from his need to speak out. 'There's been absolutely no change in the situation,' he said. 'Roy and I continue to work very closely together. The three-way relationship between Marcus, Roy and myself is as strong today as it was in the close season. There's been no change to that. But I'm not in any way trying to shy away from the fact that it's been a hugely disappointing start. The fans deserve better, want better and I can assure you that it's not through lack of effort on Roy's part or the team's part that we're not delivering. The manager is under no additional pressure, he's a man who puts pressure on himself, he knows what he has to achieve.'

Clegg outlined Evans's commitment to Keane by saying there was money available for more signings. He would not be drawn on how much, or whom might be brought in, but he tried to make it clear the club was giving Keane all the backing it possibly could. On Keane's work with the team so far, Clegg described it as 'fine-tuning' and said he found the Town manager 'refreshing', having shared regular conversations during the season.

Receiving the backing of the board and club owner at the end of September is one thing, though. Not to sack the manager after reaching the end of October without a victory would be another. For all the positive spin being put on the situation by the media-savvy Clegg, Keane was testing the club's patience. Large sums of money spent meant expectations of promotion, not the worst start in the club's history. Two months of the season was considered a bedding-in period, but not three. Town had to improve in October, or else the club would have to admit they were in a position where the manager was held accountable for the debacle they found themselves in. And that would mean sacking Keane.

Chapter Six

October 2009

'WHEN I SAW DAVID IN THE BOX, I THOUGHT WHAT THE HELL IS HE DOING THERE?'

Those not up to speed on events in the Championship during the opening two months of the season may have thought Town were missing from the table when taking a glance at the standings at the beginning of October. Not in the promotion places or the top six after all the summer talk of this being *the* season, not in mid-table slowly moving towards the upper echelons, and not even in the top half. Sitting rock bottom, Town's season was yelling 'disaster'.

Another away game was not what Town needed in the first week of the month, but it was a return up to Yorkshire where they faced Barnsley on Saturday, 3 October. Keane was trying to deflect his players' thoughts from their league position, saying that if they just cut out the individual mistakes they would be fine. Easier said than done. It was a case of how many mistakes per game they would make and very few of the players were exempt. Richard Wright was to blame at Sheffield United, the whole defence against Newcastle, while Gareth McAuley had not endeared himself to his manager or the fans during September – likewise Delaney.

If the players wanted something to take their minds off their league position, they were given it by Keane's former Manchester United teammate Dwight Yorke, who played under the Town manager at Sunderland. Yorke's autobiography, *Born To Score*, was serialised in a national newspaper and Keane's management style came under close, and colourful, scrutiny from the Trinidad & Tobago international. The serialisation in the *News of the World* reported that Yorke had sent Keane a text message wishing him all the best after he dramatically quit as manager at Sunderland, only to receive an x-rated reply. Yorke said it shocked him, but at the same time it did not. It was not just his phone which received the wrath of Keane, according to Yorke. He told how Keane lost the plot during a Carling Cup-tie against Northampton. Sunderland came in 0-1 down at half-time and Keane asked for the kit manager to bring the tactics board out. Yorke wrote how Keane took a running jump at the board and smashed it with a flying kung-fu kick before telling the players he 'could not trust any of them'. The tactics board was again the target of Keane's foot following a goalless first half at Stoke. Yorke wrote that 'paranoia' was rampaging at the club and its players were fighting with one another. In his book, Yorke stated club management was not for Keane because of his temperament, although he did say he would be more suited to international football as an 'impact manager'.

The text message or the kung-fu kicks were not particularly pertinent to Keane's reign as Town manager, but instead it was Yorke's view that his former boss ruled by fear. He wrote: 'The intensity which drove the team [Sunderland] to those successes, however, never let up and, I think, ultimately, doomed Keano's managership. Even when we had secured promotion at the end of my first season, he wasn't satisfied. He wanted the title. He warned players he would not settle for anyone taking their foot off the pedal. It was leadership by inspiring fear. Keano had days when he would join in with the five-a-sides and any player on his team who misplaced a pass or miscontrolled the ball would be subjected to a stream of vicious lecturing or abuse. It reached the stage where nobody wanted to be on the same side as him.'

No Town player would readily admit they were scared of Keane, or that he ruled by fear. Any questions put to them about the manager were batted away with bland answers – they enjoyed playing for him, his team would gel eventually, and he deserved time. Judging by the performances on the pitch, there was an element of fear. Expression in the attacking third was a rarity, defenders hurried their clearances up the pitch providing the strikers with scraps to feed on, the midfield was choosing to pass sideways rather than forwards and nobody was committed to dribbling past an opponent. They were giving the ball away at their peril. Make a mistake and they were banished to train with the youth team – with Owen Garvan and David Wright.

Keane was less animated on the touchline than expected. The majority of matches were spent sat on the bench watching, jumping up to make a point when necessary, questioning his players' inability to make a short pass or demanding extra effort. His calmness during the second half against Newcastle annoyed some Town fans who felt he should have been bawling at his lame players from pitch-side, not sat watching like a spectator in the dugout. Compared to Jim Magilton, Keane was a picture of relaxation during a match. Sympathy poured in for anyone playing in a wide position when Magilton was only yards away in the technical area.

Keane said he had not read the serialisation in the newspaper but gave his frank view on Yorke, a footballer who had gone spiralling down in his estimations. 'I certainly wouldn't agree that I try to rule with fear,' he said. 'Players are entitled to their opinions and obviously they're selling books. I think that would be Yorkey's second or third book now, so he must be stuck for a few bob. I take on board comments from people who I have respect for in the game and Yorkey's not someone I've got respect for in the game. I had previously, but this was even at Sunderland. If he thought that, he was quick to sign a new contract and then didn't try a leg in his last season at Sunderland and went back to Trinidad for reasons that had nothing to do with football. Maybe he'll put that in his book. You'll have to ask the players. I don't think I rule with fear, I don't think that works, it might the odd weekend if you want a reaction from players. But I'm pretty sure if I want to be a manager over a long period it won't, be it at Ipswich or Sunderland. You'll maybe have to ask more than one player.'

Town had a history of conceding late goals at Barnsley – the home side's winner in November 2006 was the third time that month they had conceded in the final seconds on their travels, to be defeated each time. On this occasion, the away side's manager stood there in disbelief as the ball went past Richard Wright to leave Town still without a victory. There was a slight shake of the head as he leaned against the dugout and a troubled-looking walk to the tunnel when the final whistle blew almost instantly. The 1-2 defeat left Town's players in a state of shock which seemed to have engulfed Keane as well. That was until he faced the press. It is not known if he kung-fu kicked the tactics board, gave his defenders the 'hairdryer' or told the whole squad they could not be trusted. But he was certainly ready to blow a gasket when he was faced by middle-aged men with microphones and dictaphones. 'You've watched the game and nobody has asked me about the bloody penalty,' roared Keane, referring to Iain Hume's missed spot-kick. 'That about sums you up.' His ire wasn't spared on the BBC's Football League Show reporter who dared, no doubt prompted by senior officials, to ask if Keane intended to stick around? Keane's eyes answered the question before he replied 'I refuse to answer that'.

Journalist Matt Plummer saw the anger in Keane's eyes that day: 'Roy walked out at the press conference after the Barnsley game, although I felt sympathetic because it had been made out in some parts that he had been asked a question and just walked out but that was not the case – he had answered the last question and there was then a gap following which he'd stood up and left and then got into a bit of a spat with someone in the room. The atmosphere that day was just horrible, it was so tense. Very little was right on or off the pitch, team selections were erratic – somebody who was playing well would be dropped, and somebody who hadn't played for three weeks would come in.

'It was hard to see where a victory was coming from. There was so little to pin your hopes on – the style of football didn't entertain, nor did it inspire, with four centre-halves across the back and a midfield packed with industrious players. There was never enough width in the team, for example Jack Colback was on the left but you could tell he always wanted to be in the middle rather than bombing up and down the wing. In the home games he was playing 4-5-1 and it was sending out the wrong message. The crowd were used to seeing high scoring games and finishing in the play-offs and seeing great entertainment but this was absolutely chalk and cheese.'

It was a scrappy encounter in which Barnsley took the lead in the ninth minute through Hume – another long-range shot beating Richard Wright. Liam Rosenior equalised for Town with a diving header but they never showed enough to deserve all three points, though the 96th-minute Jon Macken strike was harsh. Keane insisted he was still as determined as ever and said it was the 'toughest time I have had in my career'. He felt the players deserved better than what they were getting and said they had to get out of the rut they were stuck in.

With an international break giving Town no opportunity to make instant amends, it also gave the club, Keane, and its fans a chance to take stock. The Sunday newspapers were reporting Steve McClaren, the former England manager as Keane's likely successor, with the tabloid press expecting the Town boss to either be pushed, or act as history suggested and walk.

The international break brought light relief to Owen Garvan. He was captaining the Republic of Ireland's Under-21 side, which along with the occasional run out for Town's reserves, whose fixtures came along as infrequently as Town clean sheets, was his only chance of playing in a competitve match. He turned down the chance of a loan move to League One side Colchester United, which would have been an almighty fall from grace for the 21-year-old. Keane had said Garvan's attitude was fine, adding further to the mystery of why he was not being used in a Town side desperately in need of a victory. A late equaliser for Ireland against Switzerland did his case no harm, but Keane expected more. A report in an Irish newspaper stated that Keane was not speaking to Garvan. His response: 'I was speaking to him on Thursday, I spoke to him two weeks ago. I take comments through the media, especially from Ireland, with a pinch of salt.'

The area Keane decided to strengthen during the break was in goal, with Portsmouth's Asmir Begovic signing on a three-month loan. A Bosnian international, Begovic had spent most of his time on the south coast on the bench and he said he was coming to Portman Road to play matches, not sit and watch Richard Wright play. Wright had been at fault for a number of goals and although he had also saved Town from a few hidings, he was not displaying the form which earned him player-of-the-year in 2008-09. He was beaten from shots outside the box and his handling at crosses was not as assured as normal. Keane's choice of goalkeeper was the big talking point ahead of Swansea's visit to Portman Road on 17 October. Would he stick with Wright, or drop him and risk shattering his confidence further?

At the other end of the pitch, Keane confirmed he would be recalling Kevin Lisbie from his loan spell at Colchester United where he was scoring regularly. Asked if Colchester manager Aidy Boothroyd knew about Keane's wish, he replied: 'He does now.' When Lisbie learned of the news he said it was a 'horrible' way to find out his loan spell was going to be cut short.

Only long-term absentees David Norris and Luciano Civelli were unavailable for selection as Keane decided to drop Richard Wright in favour of Begovic. Wright was dropped completely from the 18-man matchday squad, with Arran Lee-Barrett sitting on the bench.

The other expected changes to the side were in the shape of Pablo Counago returning up front in place of Tamas Priskin and David Wright made a surprise return at left-back – long overdue according to most Town fans. Jaime Peters, displaying bigger hair than usual, moved from full-back to right-wing where he took the place of Carlos Edwards, who was involved in Trinidad & Tobago's international fixtures. The international breaks were not helping either Edwards or Priskin, neither of whom had trained regularly with their new team-mates since joining Town. It was apparent in their performances as well, although Edwards was showing potential down the right side, with Rosenior playing behind him. Priskin was already coming in for abuse from the home support at Portman Road, unenthused by his body language and unwillingness to chase and harry defenders, as well as his poor goal return.

Begovic picked the ball out of the net after six minutes when Tommy Smith and Gareth McAuley were caught statuesque and Swansea's Craig Beattie raced onto a long ball and struck firmly through the new goalkeeper's legs. Eight minutes later, Town's best piece of football under Keane ended in an equaliser by Counago – the Spaniard's first goal of the season. A tippy-tappy exchange between the striker and Peters in the Swansea box ended with a cool, low finish. It was the simplicity of the goal which stood out. For months Town fans had begged for football to be played on the ground, and the move between Counago and Peters showed Keane's side was able to make a breakthrough without the need for brawn or luck. That Counago was involved in all Town's best work was no shock as he set about proving he was the best striker available to

Keane. Connor Wickham had a chance to win the match with only four minutes left as he ran onto a Trotter pass in behind the defence. The 16-year-old's low shot was saved, and, apart from displaying extraordinary distance on his throw-ins, the only other moment of note during the second half was the bizarre injury-time substitution of Colback for Trotter. It was as if Keane was wasting time and holding on for a draw. On the contrary, Town were never in serious danger of losing, although Swansea's ball retention was second-to-none. It ended 1-1.

Keane rejected claims that it was all doom and gloom at Portman Road after the winless run became one match longer. He thought Town looked like a side higher than their position and said they should have won, pointing at a probable offside for Swansea's goal. On Richard Wright's omission he said: 'I like to surprise people sometimes.' What would be the next surprise? More players coming in with Sunderland or Ireland connections? Or the sack?

Town's 13th league match of the season came three days later when Watford visited Portman Road. It was another golden opportunity for them to end the drought and move off the bottom of the table, especially with no new injury worries from the weekend. 'We're nearly there, but, as I've said many times before, we've never made it,' said Keane before the game. 'We've got to get over the finish line in terms of taking our chances and trying to stay as solid as we can at the back. Obviously, we conceded one on Saturday, but I thought we looked a lot more solid. It's frustrating for everyone at the football club, for the players, for the supporters, the staff and myself. But it's not really about me or what happens to me or how I feel, it's about the players going out and performing. If you're in the dressing room before the game or you come and watch us training, the players are very much focused, I don't feel I have to lift them.'

For a man who liked to surprise people, Keane himself was in for a surprise come the end of 90 minutes. It was not that Town had actually won – quite the opposite – and if the players required a lift prior to the game, they certainly did afterwards. That it all started so well just made it even crueler.

Unchanged line-ups were as likely as victories under Keane, who dropped Alan Quinn and Peters from the weekend, inserting Lee Martin and Edwards to the starting 11. Town were ahead after four minutes when Walters headed across goal and McAuley nodded past Watford keeper Scott Loach for his second goal in a matter of weeks. Walters hit the bar ten minutes later and Town were applauded off the pitch at half-time for the first time this season. They threatened with every attack, with Edwards enjoying his finest game in a Town shirt. The lack of a second goal was to prove crucial, though, as Watford equalised through Nathan Ellington in the 94th minute when he out-muscled Tommy Smith. It was the fourth occasion Town had been denied points late on, almost as if they were destined never to win another game. There was no anger or booing at the final whistle, just shock, and light applause rippled, letting the players know their efforts could not be criticised this time.

Keane laid the blame with poor finishing and said Town would not win a game until they started taking their chances. But as so often in their opening 13 matches, they were creating chances, but not clear-cut chances. Until Town set out to play attacking football, with penetration from wide areas and support from the midfield, there was to be no joy at the final whistle. The balance of the team was continually being altered, with right-footers on the left, different strike partnerships and changes seemingly being made for the sake of change. 'Maybe people outside the club say it's a crisis and results-wise it is, but the spirit and desire are there and the support from the fans is there for everyone to see, and that is much appreciated,' said Keane. 'We're bitterly disappointed not to have got the win and bitterly disappointed to be where we are. I've told the players that we have got to keep going, keep believing in what we're doing, but there is no doubt we face a massive test. It's a test that we have to stand up to.' Indeed this was a crisis, but at least Keane was not deflecting the blame elsewhere like some managers so often did. Yes, he questioned a few refereeing decisions, but overall, he was taking the criticism and gut-wrenching pain of failure on the chin.

So why were Town now 13 games without a win? Because six months after Keane took over as manager, his side still showed no signs of being a team. The only partnership to have developed was on the right side between Rosenior and Edwards and the latter had been affected by long-haul flights for international duty. The centre of defence was unsettled, a right-footer was now installed at left-back, no left-footed player was available to play on the left wing and Town's most creative midfielder was training and playing for the reserves.

Up front, Keane changed his personnel approximately on an hourly basis. No goals meant a stint on the bench. There was no attempt to find a partnership which could gel – a Kevin Phillips and Niall Quinn 'little and large' style like at Sunderland a few years ago, a crafty Peter Beardsley and livewire Andy Cole like at Newcastle in the 1990s or Alex Mathie and Ian Marshall at Town more than a decade ago. A decent strike-pairing was becoming a dying art, and it could not have rung more true at Portman Road. Stead and Counago performed reasonably well together before Keane took over, and in his first two matches in charge. But Keane was loath to play them together, preferring to use Walters up front and bring on the raw Wickham when Town needed a goal. Priskin was wandering about the pitch like a tortured soul, often completely ignoring his team-mates when they were placed for a pass, so it was difficult to say who he would be best paired with. His goal record at Watford gave weight to playing him on the shoulder of the defence and allowing Counago to drift deep and supply the passes. All Keane would say was that his strikers were not scoring.

The patience of the Town support and their reaction to the midweek heartache was not missed by Keane. He was quick to praise the fans at every opportunity and they were just about hanging in there for him. Their trust was fading by the day, but the discontent was being voiced behind closed doors. 'At any other club on this planet it probably wouldn't happen,' he said. 'After 13 games without a victory, it's strange that the players are getting applauded off the pitch but that's a credit to the supporters, they appreciate the players' efforts. I think from the other night they appreciated how well the players are playing. The signs have been a bit better the last few weeks but, of course, we need victories.'

Bottom against second bottom was unlikely to produce a pretty, free-flowing match and those who made the long trip to Plymouth were brave. Add in swirling, windy conditions and Town's persistent long balls forward and the outcome was expected to be grim. Keane may have forseen such a spectacle because he was happy with the point Town gained after going behind to a Carl Fletcher strike from outside the penalty area. The tinkering was kept to two changes – Colback for Trotter and Peters for Martin, though Keane was forced to replace the injured McAuley after 23 minutes. Rosenior was substituted at half-time and Counago shortly after as Town went in search of an equaliser, which they gained through Stead, when he cut out a short back-pass and rounded keeper Romain Larrieu. Plymouth were reduced to ten men for the last ten minutes when Darcy Blake was sent off for a two-footed lunge on Alan Quinn, but Town were too poor to take advantage and Plymouth could have snatched the winner. The 1-1 draw dented hopes following the Watford match, when Town appeared close to finding enough sustained quality to win.

'Everything was pointing towards us going down,' said Town season-ticket holder Andrew McGarry, a former professional cricketer with Essex, who also played for England at Under-19 level. 'The quality of football was terrible, the team had a habit of conceding in the last minute and they looked totally shot in terms of morale. Fifteen games is a bit too soon to push a manager out, though, especially when he had a lot of new players trying to gel and who were getting to know the club a bit better.

In terms of the way modern football works, however, I was surprised he did not get the sack at this point. Even though I had a season ticket, I actually found myself not being bothered whether I went or not as I was not enjoying it.'

The national press were reporting that Keane was seeking an experienced coach to help end the winless run. Keane had denied earlier in the season, when Brian Kidd was linked, that that was the case. Town's performances were begging questions of the effectiveness of their training. What were they doing all week to be playing so badly at the end of it? Fitness levels were not an obvious problem. Ability on the ball, confidence, awareness and finishing were. A worrying lack of shape was evident as well, with big holes opening up in midfield and in defence, where Town were fortunate their opposition's equal lack of quality meant they often went unpunished.

The coach link rumbled on into the latter days of October until former England caretaker manager Peter Taylor admitted he had held talks with Keane. Taylor was spotted at the Swansea and Watford home matches after leaving his job as manager of Wycombe Wanderers earlier in the month. By the time Town were ready to host Derby County on 31 October, they were embroiled in another mini-soap opera involving Keane. Taylor was reportedly taking Town's training sessions. Then the club announced he would not be joining the coaching staff. The statement read: 'Ipswich can confirm that Peter Taylor will not be joining the coaching staff at Portman Road. Senior management staff at the club and Mr Taylor held discussions over a possible role in support of the coaching team. However, there will be no further progression of those talks.' Taylor released his own short statement: 'We couldn't come to an agreement and it's best for all parties just to leave it at that. I don't want to add anything to the statement. The comments are fine by me. I don't think it would be in the interests of any of us to go any further into the reasons why.' *The Daily Mirror* reported Keane had changed his mind about Taylor coaching Town after 'he had thought about it'. The story stated Taylor had indeed been taking training sessions.

Keane was asked at his pre-match press conference about the Taylor saga and he denied the former Leicester City manager had been coaching his players. 'Peter Taylor hasn't taken any training sessions,' said Keane. 'I spoke with Peter during the week and we discussed a few things and we both decided we'd go our separate ways. It's very straightforward. Peter's a top coach and a good man, but we both decided we'd go our separate ways in terms of working together. It didn't work out and I wish Peter well.' Keane also denied he tried to sign Stoke defenders Danny

Higginbotham and Leon Cort on loan. So, according to him, the only player Town were close to bringing in to stop their free-fall towards relegation was unknown Senegalese trialist Ibrahima Faye.

The club was lurching from farce to farce. Confused fans were questioning what consisted of truth and what was media fabrication. Keane's version of events was difficult to accept after he had started to deal with his players' futures in the media instead of behind closed doors. The Lisbie situation impressed nobody, as Keane's mask slipped under the weight of holding on to his job.

Defeat against a Derby side shorn of 16 players through injury could have had drastic repercussions, but it never came to that as Town won at the 15th attempt and for the first time in the league in 181 days. It was not pretty, it was not entertaining and it was unsuccessful in taking Town off the foot of the table, with both Plymouth and Reading winning. Yet it granted Keane a lifeline and the players the crumb of comfort they were searching for. They could win, they could keep a clean sheet and now they could start moving on up the table.

'I still believed that Keane could take the club up,' said Town fan Oliver Procter, who made a round trip of 200 miles to get to home games. 'For the first time there was a work ethic at Portman Road! I thought he might do it in one season, but then we realised the quality just wasn't in the side. I was gutted when we could not find a win from anywhere. I think there was a serious fan problem though. The support was shocking and very quiet, and I think it has to work both ways. The side would have done better with stronger support.

'I didn't want him sacked, we had to give him time. If Sir Bobby was sacked early we would never have reaped the rewards of his time at the club. I think the two-year promise came more from Simon Clegg, not Roy, as he was trying to make a statement, so I think Clegg was also to blame. All clubs have bad runs and that was all it was. I think there was potential in the side. but a lot of the problem was too many individual errors, which cannot be managed. Then the crowd were on their backs, and it was an uphill struggle from there.'

The Derby win was a nail-biting affair, the end of which was greeted by celebrations more akin to a promotion party. It was fuelled by relief and the frustration of seeing such poor football for what had felt like an eternity. Town's lack of adventure and potency could be forgiven if Keane was building an impenetrable back line. For an hour Town threatened rarely, but the inclusion of Damien Delaney at centre-half alongside Alex Bruce was promising. Playing centrally, Delaney prospered, dealing with long, high balls and having cover either side of him. Trotter was back in for Colback and Stead for Counago, and neither made any headway before being replaced on the hour. Many wondered why Keane was persevering with Trotter. His distribution was wayward and his lack of mobility meant he was often either caught upfield or too deep. Touted as a future first-team regular, he was struggling to come to terms with the demands of the Championship. Physical strength was usually a bonus for a player who hoped to make it in the upper tiers of English football, but for Trotter it was proving a problem and Town fans were running out of patience with him, despite his being local born and bred. Town took the lead six minutes after he was substituted to sarcastic cheers. Liam Rosenior's cross from the right was met by fellow full-back David Wright at the far post and he powered home a header to spark delirious scenes. It was a nervy last 20 minutes, during which Priskin missed a gilt-edged one-on-one, but Town clung on.

The first win may have been in the bag, but there was no getting carried away. The best player on the pitch was Derby's 35-year-old Robbie Savage, and Town were defending against a one-man strikeforce of the soon-to-turn 37-year-old Paul Dickov. The significance of Wright's goal was not yet known, although for Wright himself it was the perfect way to tell Keane he should have been training with the first team, not the youth team. 'When I saw David in the box, I thought what the hell is he doing there?' said Keane. 'He's been out of the picture for a while but that's why you need good pros.' Wright was a rare commodity among professional footballers – a player whose complaints were not aired in public when inexplicably dropped – not just from the starting 11, but from the match-day squad. And Keane, like Sir Alex Ferguson was to Mark Robins back in 1990, would be thankful for the goal which could have saved his job.

Keane thought it was the worst his side had played for four or five weeks and they were set for another goalless performance until Counago and Priskin were brought on, allowing Walters to be pushed out wide, giving Town a semblance of team-work.

'Maybe the club should have dampened down the expectations when Keane was paraded, and then before his first full season – like Paul Jewell did when he would eventually take over and said it would take time for the club to build towards its goals,' said Phil Ham. 'Roy thought he could repeat what he did at Sunderland and everyone got carried away and I think he did too. He seemed to do his thinking in a "micro" sense. If Town were playing against a side with a quick winger, Keane would put Peters at full-back irrespective of how the other full-back was playing, be it on the right or left. He would pick teams for specific games which was to the detriment of a settled team.

'There were games such as Sheffield United away and Watford at home when Town really should have, and deserved to win and, overall, I do not think the side were playing that badly. The club had also spent a lot of money on Keane so I would have been surprised had they sacked him in October. I think the fans wanted him to succeed. It is part of the club's tradition to give managers time. It took Sir Bobby Robson a few years, as it did George Burley before his team gelled. I think the fans looked at what Keane had achieved in the game, and he could not achieve a lot more than he did, and they respected that.'

October had ended on the first high of the season and Town were unbeaten in their last four matches. Was it the start of a run? Or a smoke-screen hiding even darker times ahead? The heavy defeats had ceased, but for how long? And would Keane be around to find out, or had the vital three points against Derby bought him more time? With Town still bottom of the table, there was no reason to cheer or be satisfied, but as Keane and any Town player who had a microphone placed in front of them said, it was a massive monkey off their back.

Chapter Seven

November 2009

'Why don't you turn it off? That is the second time it has gone off. Why don't you put it on silent? Why don't you turn it off? . . . You're just going to let it ring?'

Five points from three matches, including a first away victory, sounded like a decent enough return from a team at the bottom of the table and scrapping for anything it can get before their highly paid manager was given the chop. We may never know how close Roy Keane was to being sacked – but he stated during November he believed he had six weeks to turn it around or he would be out. Having to wait until 29 November for that second win did not help his cause. A vast improvement was expected after the victory over Derby and it took nigh on a month for it to finally arrive.

While East Anglia waited to see if Marcus Evans would flex his business muscles and decide enough was enough, headlines and sub-plots were blowing up all around Keane and Ipswich Town. If Evans wanted his club to be in the news for the right reasons, it was not the case in November, but then what could he expect having appointed Roy Keane? The appointment had backfired and, as far as the media were concerned, the bullet was sitting in the gun with the trigger waiting to be pulled.

Relegation was fast becoming a reality, not a figment of the imagination, or a word associated with rivals Norwich City. For Evans and the Town board, there was very little in the way of encouragement and hope for the rest of the season. The win over Derby was papering over the cracks and the announcement of an operating loss of £10.32 million in the financial year (ending June) was a worry for the fans, if not Evans. The loss was expected in light of increased player wages and the number of players brought in, but it did not dampen concerns of what might happen should Evans walk away from the club, with his Premier League dream unfulfilled.

If Keane was going to keep his job he had to find a settled team, and one which excluded many of his summer signings. Lee Martin had made no impact at all during the opening third of the season. Too often he was either pushed off the ball, or flitted around like a moth stuck in a lampshade, contributing nothing except needless fouls.

'Keane had tried to start positively with a 4-3-3 and Martin was one of the three up front but he became a victim of the results and Keane felt he needed to go back to four or effectively five in midfield,' said Town fan Matthew Mehen. 'It was a narrow ploy, especially when Leadbitter and Colback joined. It knocked Martin's confidence and I think playing in a 4-3-3 was an ideal system for him rather than as a wide-man in a four. But who knows what went on behind the scenes? I think Martin did enough not to be dropped to the reserves. There were issues with his final ball but he was a winger who needed self-belief to take players on.'

Tamas Priskin was faring no better and the crowd were on his back for a perceived lack of effort. He could point at the poor service he was receiving, but when that is the case strikers earn their exorbitant wages by creating something out of nothing. Grant Leadbitter and Carlos Edwards were showing potential, but Damien Delaney had been a major disappointment and Colin Healy was looking like one of the biggest transfer mysteries in the club's history. Why did Keane sign him? If Town were going to get out of trouble they were going to have to score more goals. Keane, with approval from the terraces, canned the 4-3-3/4-5-1 system at Portman Road, and also away from home. But there was more than just a problematic system which was holding them back, according to *The News of The World*.

After drawing 1-1 at Reading and an enforced break due to internationals, Town had a long wait before Sheffield Wednesday came to Portman Road on 21 November, and the story everyone had been waiting for arrived – the inside track on what was going wrong. Rumours had already been spreading leading up to the newspaper article but this was the first time the so-called truth was revealed by 'dressing room snitches'. The story, under the headline 'It's the same old Keano', claimed he was making all the mistakes which soured his time at Sunderland. His communication skills came under fire, with no explanations presented to dropped players and a different 11 players selected each week – the exception being Jon Walters, Town's third captain of the season. The coaching came under fire, especially Keane's right-hand man, Tony Loughlan. The story claimed Keane was destroying the confidence of his players with 'hairdryer outbursts' and was undermining the club's strikers by not giving them a fair run in the side. There was no mention of Keane not working on his team's shape in training until well into October, but that was another unfounded story doing the rounds. Town had certainly been playing like a side who were unfamiliar with their roles.

On a lighter note, Keane's alleged behaviour during a behind closed-door friendly brought sniggers rather than widespread animosity. Fans were trying to watch the action at Portman Road via a window in the club shop. Keane spotted them and quickly ordered the curtains to be closed.

It was all water off a duck's back for Keane, but the perception was that he was becoming bigger than the club. The footballing world knew he did not care for the views of anyone but his employer and had no time for scurrilous stories in red-top newspapers.

An effort to improve the manager's public persona was made on 4 November when he made a surprise appearance at the Supporters' Club AGM at Portman Road. He admitted some of his signings were taking a while to bed in and his team had lacked experience at vital times. He also revealed he was refusing to take part in practice matches with the players because of his competitive streak. His appearance brought him back in touch with the fans who had felt his personal crusade at Ipswich Town was likely to cause long-lasting damage to the club, in terms of its image and reputation, as well as its playing power. He signed autographs and chatted away, leaving them with little doubt he was just another football manager.

The circus was back at Portman Road by the time Sheffield Wednesday arrived on 21 November. It was Keane in the headlines and not the club, though, after an explosive press conference in the Portman Road media suite. Gone was the smiley, happy man at ease with the fans. In his place was a manager with an agenda. Ireland's controversial failure to beat France in the World Cup qualifying play-off was the perfect ammunition for Keane. His views on the FAI had been lying dormant for a while, until Thierry Henry's hand came into contact with the ball and Ireland were not going to the World Cup.

Unshaven and with dark, tired eyes, Keane looked like he had been up walking his dogs all night when he took his seat in front of the press. Or had he been perfecting his speech? For he knew he was going to be asked about Ireland, with Sky Sports regular attendees at Portman Road now that there was a reason to be there. The press conference lasted 33 minutes, of which 21 minutes was spent on the subject of Ireland, who had requested for the match in Paris to be replayed. Keane made it clear he thought otherwise.

'I've been amazed by the commotion over the past few days. I think of course Henry handled it but I'd focus on why they didn't clear it,' said Keane, growing more and more animated as the minutes passed by without mention of Ipswich Town. 'I'd be more annoyed with my goalkeeper and defenders than Thierry Henry. How can you let a ball bounce in the six yard box? How can you let Henry get goal-side of you? If the ball bounces in the six-yard box I'd be saying where the hell is my goalkeeper?' Keane was asked if he had any sympathy for Ireland. 'No, not one bit,' he replied before starting off on another tirade. 'You look over the course of the campaign and Ireland had the chances over the two games. They never took them. They never performed in the first game. I heard a few interviews after the game where the manager said that none of the players got booked. Maybe that was the problem. They stood off France. The second leg we had opportunities to score but didn't take them. They weren't mentally strong enough. All these players can complain all they want. France are going to the World Cup – get over it!'

The subject of the FAI then arose. Keane could have brought the matter to an end, but continued. 'Usual FAI reaction: "we've been robbed, the honesty of the game . ." In one of the earlier group games, I think it was against Georgia, Ireland got a penalty. It was one of the worst decisions I have ever seen. It changed the course of the game. Robbie [Keane] scored a penalty and Ireland went on to win it. I don't remember the FAI after the game saying "I think we should give them a replay".'

FAI chief John Delaney was next on Keane's hit-list. Again, he had the chance to stop, but he was on a roll. It was exactly what the cameras wanted and the strength of Keane's disdain meant he was not bothered how he came across. 'John Delaney? He's on about honesty and integrity. I wouldn't take any notice of that man. People forget the last time I was at the World Cup in 2002. People seem to forget what was going on at that World Cup. I was one of the players, he didn't have the courtesy to ring me. He got interviewed and all he said was "I don't know where he is". I'd been with Ireland since I was 15 years of age and that man didn't even have the decency to ring me. He could have phoned me, tried the hotel room. And he's on about the honesty of the game. I think the Irish supporters probably deserve better, the manager, probably most of the players deserve it. But I don't think the FAI deserve better. What goes around comes around.'

The outspoken Irishman then defended Henry, who was receiving flak from all corners of the world for his mischievous act. Keane was right when he said there were far worse acts being carried out, but it was hard to accept the Town manager's views on bending the rules after the acts he committed during his playing career. While hardly Machiavellian in his style, Keane just broke the rules through acts of violence, causing physical pain rather than disappointment.

There was an interlude to Keane's tirade when a journalist's phone started to ring. Footage of what happened was released on the internet, but for those who were present, it was a moment of pure theatre. Keane's momentum was building at the time. He was on a roll and nothing would stop him from putting his point across. The room, containing television cameras, broadcast media and written press was silent apart from Keane's voice and the sound of him shifting on his seat as his contempt for the FAI came pouring out. Then a mobile phone started to ring. It belonged to national freelance writer and former Ipswich Town PR officer Mel Henderson, who worked for the club in the 1980s. From its first ring, Keane's focus was broken. His eyes darted about and it was obvious trouble was looming. He was pumped up enough without his speech being broken by a mobile phone, all of which were requested to be switched off at the beginning of the conference. The following was exchanged:

Roy Keane: 'Whose phone is that? It's the second time it has gone off.'

Mel Henderson: 'It's mine.'

Roy Keane: 'Why don't you turn it off? That is the second time it has gone off. Why don't you put it on silent? Why don't you turn it off? You're just going to let it ring?'

Mel Henderson: 'I thought I would let it ring out.'

Roy Keane: 'Oh right, that's good manners.'

Keane's reaction, the fury so visible in his eyes, exacerbated the stories of him ruling by fear. Mobile phones were checked and double-checked from that day. And Keane continued laying in to the FAI for another ten minutes.

His comments were not missed by FAI chief executive Delaney, whose message to Keane was to 'move on'. 'It's just a side-show. We've all moved on from Saipan – Niall Quinn, Mick McCarthy, the FAI and all the players – but it seems to me that he hasn't,' said Delaney. 'It's time for him now, in my opinion, to learn from the past – not live with it. I really thought the images shown around the world on Friday were very sad – it's sad to see a great former player reflected in the manner as he did. It's time to forget about Saipan and move on – because everyone else has.'

According to reports on the Monday after Town's goalless draw with Sheffield Wednesday, Keane had indeed moved on, because it was claimed he had been sacked. The tabloid newspapers were reporting that a number of Sunday crisis meetings had been held and Evans had called time on Keane's tenure. However, the club was quick to issue a statement, saying the stories were 'rubbish'.

The credibility of the stories was backed up by Town still waiting for their second victory of the season, with no alteration to their lifeless performances, despite being unbeaten in six matches going into the Sheffield Wednesday fixture. Town started the month by hanging on for a point at Reading – a side without a home victory in 15 games. Keane made only one change to the side which had beaten Derby – dropping Liam Trotter from the 18-man squad and starting Tamas Priskin alongside Jon Stead.

It was a kick in the teeth for Pablo Counago, whose industry in the second half was not enough to win favour over the misfiring Hungarian, who went on to miss a host of chances at the Madejski Stadium. Town made a flying start with Stead's volley from a long David Wright throw-in which had dropped invitingly in the penalty area. But Town lost their way, lost their lead and their heads in the second half when Alan Quinn was fortunate not to give away a blatant penalty for a clumsy challenge in the box. Reading hit the crossbar as Town rode their luck, although the visitors, spurred on by more than 2,000 travelling fans, could have nicked all three points in the final minutes when Priskin fluffed another excellent chance. The result left Town second bottom and there was a distinct lack of quality on display, with Town struggling to put a passing sequence of note together.

The draws had stacked up and Town had to wait two weeks before a chance to put right their season of woe. A host of players were linked with moves to Portman Road during the break, including Bolton's Gavin McCann, Sheffield Wednesday's Richard Wood, and Hearts pair Lee Wallace and Jose Goncalves. Many top Premier League sides were linked with Connor Wickham, a player Town's Alan Quinn said was the best he had ever seen at such a tender age.

Heading out of Town, according to the media, was Owen Garvan, who was linked with Nottingham Forest, Scunthorpe and Cardiff City. Keane left Town fans stunned on 21 November when Garvan was back in the starting 11, having finally impressed him in a midweek reserve outing. While his inclusion, at the expense of Quinn, was greeted by a huge cheer at Portman Road, the announcement of Martin in the line-up – as a striker – was met by a murmur of groans and disbelief. Where was Counago? Not on the pitch and not on the bench. Keane had chosen to rely on two of his worst signings to save his job. Martin lasted 57 minutes and the closest Priskin came was putting the ball in the back of the net when three yards offside as Town fired blanks. There was a new solidity about the side, with Delaney proving why Keane signed him, but the same could not be said about the players paid to perform at the opposite end of the pitch. Garvan brought more composure and possession to the midfield, but all too often attacks broke down because of a lack of pace and a holding player up front.

No explanation for the whereabouts of Counago was given by Keane after the match. There was talk of a training ground disagreement and the Spaniard's absence, despite his shortcomings, was Town's loss. If Keane believed the toothless Martin was more likely to fire Town out of trouble, then it seemed inconceivable he would make it to Christmas as manager. Keane, however, tried to spread the blame throughout the team, but said he would be seeking striking reinforcements. 'When you talk about the team scoring goals, you end up talking about the strikers, but it's not against the rules for defenders or midfielders to score either. And if you're going to achieve anything as a team, you need one or two of your strikers to put the ball in the back of the net on a regular basis. We'll keep trying different combinations and see if there's a striker outside our club that might be available.'

'I went to Portman Road during his [Keane's] reign, and on so few occasions did he set the team up with wingers,' said former Town striker Ted Phillips, who plundered 161 goals in 269 games for the club between 1953 and 1964 and was regarded as the finest kicker of a dead-ball of his era. 'When I played with Ray Crawford, Andy Nelson, Billy Baxter, Dougie Moran and Jimmy Leadbetter, Ray and I were always being supplied from the wing. Some of the players they have now, Sir Alf Ramsey would not have even looked at. Although Keane did manage to get his squad very fit, it just seemed to go wrong when they stepped on the pitch.'

The constant rejigging of Town's attack was benefiting no one. The midfield did not know who they were passing to or where they were passing it, and there was no sign of any of the strikers forging a partnership during their fleeting combinations. It was a tenth draw of the season and it kept the heat blazing on Keane. Draws were no good, despite the unbeaten record, as two difficult away matches loomed – matches which, it was believed, would decide Keane's fate, even though support was forthcoming from chief executive Simon Clegg. Concerns were intensifying as autumn turned to winter and the prospect of being in the bottom three at Christmas edged closer.

It was at the club's AGM where Keane made the admission to shareholders and supporters that he thought six weeks was an accurate timescale on how long he had to turn the club's fortunes around. The loyalty of Evans and the club's fans had been tested to the limit by a start to the season which had yielded just 13 points from the first 17 matches. Such form had made a mockery of Jim Magilton's sacking.

The addition of former Notts County manager Ian McParland to the coaching ranks indicated that Keane may have had closer to six weeks than two. Why bring in a new coach if the manager was going to be sacked? Also arriving before Town's trip to Cardiff City was striker Stern John on a month's loan from Crystal Palace. Keane tried to sign former Republic of Ireland defender Ian Harte earlier in the week from Carlisle in a loan deal with a view to making it permanent. The idea of bringing in a 32-year-old League One defender set few pulses racing among Town fans, and nor did the signing of John. A striker was needed – that was blatantly clear, unless Keane intended on bringing Counago back and handing him an opportunity to find top form next to a regular strike partner.

Trinidad & Tobago international John's goal record stood up to scrutiny. His 97 goals in English football had come in 250 starts and 105 substitute appearances, while 69 goals at international level was an impressive haul. He was a player Keane knew well as the pair had been together at Sunderland when John was also signed on loan. It was a move which worked, as John netted five times in ten starts. The pessimists at Town were pointing at the seven goalless appearances he had made so far at Palace after his season was disrupted early on by an elbow injury. At 33-years-old he was an unlikely revolutionary to Town's front line, yet he could do little worse than the previous incumbents.

'I think we get some good balls in the box and sometimes we've not had that person attacking it and I think Stern will do that,' said Keane on his new acquisition. 'As much as we've praised the players, particularly the strikers, for their work-rate and so on, we need someone who can put the ball in the back of the net, as that's what's been costing us.'

'I was far from pleased when they announced the signing of Stern John,' said Matthew Mehen. 'It was as if Keane was going back to his mates and I wondered who would be next? Graham Kavanagh? Dwight Yorke? [not after the release of Yorke's autobiography]. John was a baffling signing. How could he give more than Pablo, Lisbie, Stead?

'We always should have had Stead in the side – I think he gave us more than anyone else because of his energy and technique in front of goal. There was history between him and Keane, though, and I don't think he was the cheapest player in the squad. We should have built our strike partnerships around him, while Walters should have been used on the right where he had been so effective before Keane arrived.'

At the other end of the pitch, Keane was forced to make adjustments. Goalkeeper Asmir Begovic was recalled by Portsmouth after an injury to number one David James, leading to a recall for Richard Wright. The 90 minutes at Cardiff's new stadium finally offered Town and Keane some hope for the season. Although not particularly clear at the time, during November Town were starting to grow in strength and resilience – the silly, avoidable mistakes at the back had cleared up, the goalkeeping errors were a thing of the past, and the opposition were as frustrated as the Town fans begging to see a goal. They may not have been winning, but they had found a way in which to prevent defeat. However, until the draws turned to victories Keane's position would remain on a knife-edge.

An injury to Richard Wright and a stunning goal by Cardiff's Peter Whittingham in the first half could have marked the end of a short era, but Town responded, first through Jon Walters and then a deflected shot from Stead sneaked in with five minutes left on the clock – his third goal in three away games – to give Town victory against all odds. Arran Lee-Barrett, safeguarded by a defence including the regular trio of Liam Rosenior, Delaney and David Wright, hardly had anything to do, while Gareth McAuley, back in the side in place of the injured Alex Bruce, was back to his best. Town rode their luck at times, with Cardiff hitting the woodwork twice in the first half. It was an extension to the unbeaten run, though – and a first away victory of the season. Keane had discovered a way of making Town hard to beat, and at the same time winning. Garvan provided assists to both of the goals and, with both he and Leadbitter in midfield, Town were at least able to keep possession for more than five passes.

Keane said his side had come through a 'test of character' and reiterated his faith in the squad he had assembled. It was a contradiction from previous months when he said he would need fresh blood and some players would not play for the club again. He was happy with John's contribution – even though he missed when put through on goal – after handing his latest signing a starting role, and Town left Wales with a major shift in the atmosphere surrounding the club.

There was no let up for Richard Wright. His career had taken many twists and turns, from goalkeeping prodigy to England international, failed Premier League number one to bungling Championship custodian. The departure of Begovic was his way back in, until he collided with Cardiff striker Michael Chopra. The prognosis was four months on the sidelines due to a partial cruciate ligament tear in his knee, leaving Lee-Barrett as Town's only senior keeper. Brian Murphy was due to arrive in January and Town were unable to ask for special dispensation from the Football League to sign another keeper because young Ian McLoughlin, 18, was on a professional contract. In Lee-Barrett, Keane would have to trust.

The goalkeeping problem was an issue Keane could do nothing about. There was always a chance Begovic would be called back, and in Wright, he had an able, albeit out of form, deputy, and most people's money was on Town reaching January, when Murphy would be competing for a first-team place, without a goalkeeping hiccup.

The storm clouds over Portman Road were thinning as November ended. There was no predicting what would happen next, in a month when Keane had made headlines for entwining himself in national debate as much as he was for hanging onto his job at Ipswich by a whisker. With an away win in the bag, a tightening defence and plenty of talk of moving out of the relegation zone, Keane and Town had at least displayed strong hints of returning to a degree of normality – if that is ever possible for a football club with Roy Keane as manager. His target was to be out of the mire by Christmas – and in turn keep his job. Town had taken the first step, would the second prove too big?

Chapter Eight

December 2009

'THERE'S NOTHING EASIER THAN SHARING A DRINK AFTER A MATCH WITH THE OPPOSITION MANAGER, AFTER YOU'VE JUST WON. UNFORTUNATELY, THAT'S ONLY HAPPENED TO ME TWICE THIS SEASON!'

A strong hint towards a team's previous results lies in the mood of the club's manager at his pre-match press conference. Roy Keane's tetchiness and icy stare were typical of a man who was without a win for not weeks, but months. During Jim Magilton's better times, he would bound into the media centre, his Irish accent crackling down the corridor, then on entering the room and being greeted with familiar faces, a booming welcome would fill the air, followed by a few sarcastic jokes aimed at any one of the assembled press or club staff. It was only in the final months that the 'let's get this over with' atmosphere subdued what had previously been a jolly group of men talking about football, complete with profanities and toilet humour. Ipswich's unbeaten run under Keane brought about a changed man ahead of their trip to Bristol City on 5 December.

As usual, most of the 40-minute talk was centred on national issues – in this case the story of Arsene Wenger not shaking Mark Hughes's hand during a midweek Arsenal and Manchester City clash in the Carling Cup. Sky Sports wanted to know what Keane made of such an unsporting gesture and the Town manager gave his view. 'I don't know if it is just me – maybe I'm the oddball – but people should get over it,' he said, backing Wenger's quick exit down the tunnel. 'Arsene Wenger didn't kill anybody. People say he's a bad loser but we're all bad losers. I wouldn't think any less of him because of it. He deserves great credit because of what he has achieved. If it had been me I'd have been too busy celebrating the fact that my team had beaten Arsenal to worry too much about it. Sparky [Mark Hughes] wouldn't have lost any sleep over it. He's a big tough man and a good man. At least Wenger wasn't a hypocrite. I've had handshakes from managers who literally just grab the ends of your fingers. It's not about what you do in front of the cameras but what you do away from the cameras.'

Keane's body language was entertaining to watch. Rather than the deadpan, monosyllabic responses that many questions relating to football deserve, his movements were telling of his desire to emphasise what he was trying to say and his wish to answer each and every question. His hands cupped in front of him, he struggled to find the right words at times. His body was closed in making him look a lot smaller than he really was, and a photograph of the moment would have captured him looking like Oliver Twist asking for more – it was a far cry from the snarling Keane of earlier in the season. There was no shortage of his sharp wit, no doubt honed from spending two decades surrounded by wise-cracking footballers trying to out-humour one another. When asked if he had a points target in mind from the forthcoming festive period he responded by saying he was just glad to be in double figures and said current number two goalkeeper Ian McLoughlin would be playing for both teams in training matches, with number one Arran Lee-Barrett in need of a rest and a sanctuary to hide from risk of injury.

When the discussion went back to the handshake controversy he said: 'There's nothing easier than sharing a drink after a match with the opposition manager, after you've just won. Unfortunately, that's only happened to me twice this season!' The written press shuffled out of the room amused by Keane's final joke. The questioning appeared to be over when Mel Henderson jumped in with a final request. It was his first involvement in proceedings and Keane was quick to note it: 'I thought you were on your phone,' he quipped.

The change in persona laid to rest some of the tittle-tattle published about Keane in the tabloids. If he wanted the media onside, he was making headway, but if he was to have the fans completely on board as well, he needed to extend Town's unbeaten run.

The laughs and smiles for Keane did not last long. He could barely believe what he was seeing as Town came away from their trip to Bristol City with a point. There was only one reason why the game stayed goalless – atrocious finishing. Keane decided to change a winning side by selecting Alan Quinn ahead of Carlos Edwards, and Jon Stead ahead of Tamas Priskin, while Lee-Barrett made his first start for the club in goal. Stead could, and should have put Town two up in the first half when he ran clear of the Bristol defence, only to see the keeper save both efforts, neither of which were convincing. There were a couple of major scares early in the second half when former Town man Danny Haynes struck the post twice for City and he then cleared the ball off the line when Town were set to take the lead.

The biggest talking point of the match came with five minutes left on the clock. Grant Leadbitter's long-range half-volley beat City keeper Dean Gerken but rebounded off the post. Pablo Counago, on as a substitute for Stern John, having been reinstated to the matchday squad, pounced on the loose ball with the goal at his mercy. As he sprinted forward the ball took a slightly awkward bounce before he reached it and, instead of half-volleying into an empty net, he hesitated, controlled the ball on his thigh and waited for it to drop. By this time, Gerken was scrambling back across his goal and made a block with his foot, diverting the ball for a corner. Counago could not believe it, nor could the Town fans or anyone else in the ground. *The East Anglian Daily Times* asked on its website if it was the worst miss ever. It was bad, but there had been far worse. It was not on the same scale as Ronny Rosenthal's famous miss for Liverpool at Villa Park in 1992. The bounce off the post left Counago in two minds and he chose the wrong option. It cost Town three points and Keane was fuming with his striker. 'If you're telling me that Pablo Counago just had a good chance then good God! It was more than a good chance,' he said.

Keane was a little more forgiving ahead of the visit of Peterborough United three days later for what was a must-win game for Town. Peterborough were bottom of the table, four points behind Town and had recently changed manager, with Mark Cooper replacing Darren Ferguson. Town were 13 points behind the sixth-placed team and, if they could start scoring, Keane believed a march towards the top six was not the stuff of fantasy. 'The pluses are that for eight games now we've looked very, very solid,' he said. 'We look strong, the spirit is good, we stuck at it and if we keep playing like that and creating chances, no doubt the victories will come. Fitness levels are very, very good, the players looked very strong in the last 20 minutes. As an away team we looked like the home team. We'll always look at the strikers and say, 'You should be scoring', but credit to the opposition goalkeepers. The important thing is for our strikers to keep getting in there and eventually they'll score.'

A disallowed Stern John header was the closest they came against Posh, as the unbeaten run was extended to nine matches, but worryingly, Town had scored only twice in their last four games. The bulk of the possession was enjoyed once again and Town's defence and midfield were functioning in harmony. An inability to hit the back of the net was keeping Town in the relegation zone longer than they would have liked, and probably longer than they should have been. John, Stead, Priskin and Connor Wickham were all given a chance to score the elusive goal, but Counago was banished to the stands for his error at Ashton Gate. What message did that send to the strikers? Miss and you will be dropped?

To say the disallowed goal was harsh was an 'understatement' according to Keane, who pointed at the lack of reaction from the Peterborough players when the ball hit the net. He was unhappy with the number of long balls being played in the second half and felt it was a sign of edginess from a team low on confidence in the attacking third. The crowd did not help Priskin's confidence, and again Keane finished the match relying on an out-of-sorts recent loan signing and a 16-year-old.

It was a week when the behaviour of managers in England was in the news, and, for once, Keane's profile was low. There was an Ipswich Town connection, though, as Magilton followed Stoke City's Tony Pulis into the headlines. Pulis was involved in an altercation with Stoke striker James Beattie after their defeat to Arsenal. The argument was said to have been about the players' Christmas party. Meanwhile, Magilton's temper was well-known among Ipswich followers. His QPR team were on a bad run of results and, after a defeat at Watford which left them 12th in the Championship, Rangers midfielder Akos Buzsaky was spotted sitting in a stand at Vicarage Road in his kit and on his own. The club announced they had suspended Magilton pending an investigation and details emerged of an alleged head-butt on Buzsaky by Magilton, who denied any wrong-doing but left the club a week later by mutual consent.

The future of two of Town's players was under the spotlight. Full-back David Wright was seeking a new contract, with his current deal expiring in the summer, and Connor Wickham had been the talk of the tabloids for months. In and out of the first team, there was little doubt of Wickham's ability for his age and his potential. He could not sign a professional deal until March when he turned 17 and the opportunity was there to make a move to one of the biggest clubs in the country before that deadline, but Keane believed he would stay. 'Connor is playing in our first team at the moment, he's learning from myself and the good coaches we've got here,' said Keane. 'We're very confident, he's a level-headed type of guy and hopefully he believes his future is here. We've had some very positive talks [with Wickham and his father]. But obviously there are agents involved and we know the way they work, however, we're confident and I've not thought too much about it as there's only so much we can do. He's got a chance of being a top, top player, but that's just potential. We've all got the potential to be successful, but whether we can follow it through is another thing. You can go to one of these big clubs and get lost because they're signing everybody.'

Wickham was expected to be involved in the first-team picture when Keane took over. What was not expected was for Keane to be regularly turning to him when Town were desperately seeking a goal and also utilising him in preference to the likes of Stead, Counago and Priskin. It spoke volumes of where Town were at, in terms of being a team capable of challenging for promotion. Ideally, Wickham would have been coming on in the second half at Portman Road with the game all but over, not starting or having to come on and to save a sinking ship with the weight of the club's expectations on his broad shoulders. Keane's predilection towards Wickham was an example of his bizarre judgment when it came to selecting his team and employing his substitutes in the first half of the season.

The pressure was taken off the players by Keane, who claimed they were doing little wrong, ahead of Blackpool's visit to Portman Road on 12 December. Instead, Keane pointed the finger at himself. 'I have to say, I can't really fault them,' he said. 'That sounds crazy. I'll have to look at myself and say "Why aren't I winning them football matches?" I think I'm the one who needs to be doing better, not the players. I put the two subs on and we went too long. Maybe I should have gone with one off the front. I remember when we were 3-1 up at Sheffield United, we should have changed the shape then. When we were 3-2 up against Doncaster in the last few minutes we maybe should have changed it then too. You always have to look at yourself and your own performances.'

The teamsheet was met by puzzled expressions among Town fans, who wondered what Keane was doing in bringing Jack Colback and Jaime Peters into the starting 11 and pairing Stead and Walters up front. Was Keane about to face up to himself again? It took barely 30 seconds for him to find out as Stead set the ball rolling on what was to be their most enjoyable day of the season so far. The blond striker collected the ball outside the penalty area and curled a low, precise shot inside the post at the Sir Bobby Robson Stand end to settle the nerves. Town's domination, which saw Walters head against the bar, was rewarded before half-time when Stead sent Colback scampering clear of the Blackpool defence and the young loanee lifted his shot over goalkeeper Matt Gilks to provide a comfortable two-goal cushion.

There was a brief scare when towering centre-half Ian Evatt met a short-corner with a powerful header to bring Blackpool back into the game, but their interest did not last as Gareth McAuley headed in Grant Leadbitter's corner after 70 minutes. Town could, and should have been well ahead by then anyway. Walters miscued at the far post with the goal at his mercy after Leadbitter curled in a teasing low cross and an inventive move saw Peters screw a shot high and wide when steaming on to a pass which left the goal right in front of him.

The second period, with the exception of McAuley's header from a few yards out, provided some comical attacking from Town. Walters was played through on goal by Leadbitter, only for the midfielder-cum-striker to turn his back on the ball, thinking a defender had cut the pass out. The crowd hollered at him to wake up and realise the situation which had arisen, but it was too late. Blackpool's high defensive line left a yawning hole in behind as they pushed forward in the final quarter of the match – a hole Walters and Stead took advantage of, only to be found wanting when it came to the finishing touch. Walters ran through one-on-one, only to take too long and be dispossessed as he tried to round the keeper. Stead broke clear on the left, with Walters waiting for a cross with an open goal, only for the ball to be sent yards over his head. Stead produced the last act of appalling finishing when he was clean though, only to lob wide with the keeper stranded off his line. Blackpool's misery was compounded when David Vaughan was sent off for a second bookable offence in the 84th minute.

The 3-1 win did not reflect the one-sided nature of the match and the creativity displayed by a Town side which extended its unbeaten run to 10 matches. It was the first time their midfield and attack had finally clicked into gear, with the ball grounded and chances created through invention rather than defensive error. Although the Stead-Walters partnership had not worked previously, their movement off the ball was vastly improved and was aided by the performance of Garvan in midfield. From his position on the left, nearly every pass found a blue shirt, was played at the right angle, and he displayed bravery to take a risk rather than make the simple pass every time.

It was a complete contrast from the nervous, sideways passing rut Town had been stuck in during August and September. Garvan's lack of pace was of no cost, for his starting position for each attack was spot on. Tucked in when necessary, he was always available to collect a pass and did not shy away from staying wide when the play needed stretching. It was a lesson to be learned by a succession of Town players who tried and failed to nail down the left-wing spot during previous years, and also a message to Garvan's critics, who felt he was too slow to play out wide and too one-footed to be anything more than an average Championship footballer. He was the best player on the pitch, while Peters also produced his best display for months.

Town were out of the bottom three for the first time, moving up to fifth from bottom and within 11 points of the play-offs. Keane was deadpan afterwards, saying his side's shift out of the bottom three was nothing to be proud of. He was none too impressed with the finishing displayed by his strikers in the second half and said the scoreline should have been 6-1 or 7-1. 'They were unbelievable, thank God they didn't cost us, otherwise I'd be saying the same things I've been saying for the last few weeks,' said Keane. 'It would have been a nice boost for the players and sent a message out to everyone that we're not such a bad team. But let's not get too greedy or selfish. We'll take the three goals and move on.'

Another reason for Keane to grumble was the bookings picked up by Walters and Leadbitter – their fifth of the season, ruling them out of the next match. It would hardly leave Town depleted, though, such was their quantity of players, even with Pim Balkestein on loan at Brentford and Kevin Lisbie at Colchester United.

Expectation levels at Portman Road were on the rise. A side unbeaten in 10 matches and able to beat a team in the top ten 3-1, in what should have been a five or six-goal margin, should be able to beat all and sundry on home turf. Or should they? Languishing a few points above the relegation zone, Town were still, according to statistics, one of the worst sides in the division, but on this evidence it was a false position – a claim which could not be made weeks earlier when the football was dire, and the defending even worse.

There was more reason for cheer in the run up to Christmas, when Peters signed a new three-year contract. His current deal was set to expire at the end of the season and Keane was suitably impressed with the 22-year-old's versatility and attitude. At the club since 2005, his potential had only ever shown glimpses of blossoming. But Keane's decision to deploy him all over the pitch was paying off and a dependable defender as well as industrious midfielder was borne from the shell of a failing right-winger. David Norris was also closing in on a return from injury and chief executive Simon Clegg revealed Wickham had agreed to sign a pre-contract agreement which would see the young star sign a professional contract on his 17th birthday in March, although the agreement was not legally binding. Colback said he was keen to stay at Portman Road, with his loan spell from Sunderland up in the New Year, a period when Luciano Civelli was expected to be back in contention for a first-team place. Despite having a squad ready to burst, Town were linked with potential new signings in the run up to the January transfer window. Birmingham's Lee Carsley, linked earlier in the season, was said to be interesting Town again, and Derby striker Rob Hulse was also reported to be on Keane's wish-list.

At a time when Town were reportedly preparing to flex their financial muscle, the implications of not reaching the Premier League were spelled out by Clegg, who confirmed the club's debt would continue to grow. He said fans should not be worried by the £10.3 million loss, saying it was 'a matter of life in the Championship'. 'The most important thing here – and this is why we want to build a solid foundation for this football club – is that we don't become a yo-yo club,' he said. 'It's about going into the Premier League and staying in the Premier League and then we can mitigate those losses over the period of time that we're up there. To go up and come down, even with the parachute payments, does make it quite challenging. That's why we made the massive development at the training ground over the close season to try and bring the facilities up to the standard which you would expect of a Premier League club.'

A number of clubs up and down the country were being hit hard by the recession and the general struggle of being a football club in modern times. Premier League Portsmouth were facing administration, while Southend United were within a whisker of doing so. It was the clubs with a wealthy benefactor who were surviving and showing signs of progress. In the locality, Colchester United were in as strong a position as they had been in their history, because of the backing of owner Robbie Cowling, and Queens Park Rangers were running under the tag 'the richest club in the world' due to their ownership.

Town's league fixture at Scunthorpe on 19 December fell foul of the weather, as a great swath of snow blanketed a large area of the country. Ipswich itself was brought to a standstill, with motorists heading home after work ending up spending the night in their car, or having to find a way home away from the maelstrom on the roads. It was like the apocalypse had arrived early, as nature brought society to a grinding stop. It was no surprise the pitch was unplayable, with temperatures dipping to minus six. The cancellation forced Leadbitter and Walters to wait another week for their suspension to elapse and Town would also be without loanee John for the Boxing Day trip to Crystal Palace – his parent club.

It was a chance for Town to gain back-to-back victories for the first time in the season and, with the bad weather not affecting training at Playford Road, the only worry Keane had going into the game was the effect the absence of Leadbitter and Walters would have on the team. Leadbitter was now first choice in the middle of the pitch, having shown his Premier League pedigree. Walters, meanwhile, was still a shadow of the player linked with a Premier League move two seasons beforehand, but was the club's top scorer with five goals and was a favourite of Keane's because of his work ethic.

A recall for either Priskin or Counago was expected, but Keane instead recalled Colin Healy, the forgotten man of Ipswich Town, deploying him in an advanced midfield role behind lone sriker Stead. It was a bold decision by Keane, albeit a strange one, given how ineffective Healy had been at the start of the season and his lack of playing time since being dropped. A loan deal to Hartlepool was being lined up in January according to reports. It was not the happiest of returns, as Town's unbeaten run came to a controversial end. After a bright start, Peters, playing in the centre of midfield in place of Leadbitter, gave Town the lead when keeper Julian Speroni dropped a Delaney cross eight yards out. In the space of two minutes, disaster struck for Town. First, Palace equalised when Delaney's clearance inside the penalty area struck the back of Owen Garvan and Jose Fonte blasted the loose ball home. Then, only seconds after the re-start, Stead lunged into a tackle on Freddie Sears and was given a straight red card. It was a harsh decision, which left Town's players, and Keane, fuming, as Palace went on to score a second after half-time through Neil Danns and a late third through Victor Moses, which meant Town lost 1-3. Stead's tackle was late, but not high, nor two-footed and the reaction of the Palace players gave the referee, Paul Taylor, an extra incentive to reduce Town to ten men.

'I'm still amazed when people seem to enjoy seeing players get sent off,' said Keane. 'Some players get involved when they should have nothing to do with it. Other players, other managers, trying to get players sent off. It's ridiculous. That's the horrible side of football. It's up to the official but officials are put under pressure in different ways – but when players are sprinting up to the referee trying to get a fellow pro sent off? They're all supposed to be in a union together, they'll no doubt be at a dinner together at the end of the season. But I'll have nothing to do with it. I never want to see other players get sent off – even if there were a few tackles going in on our lads – unless there's something obviously over the top, the player's going to get a red card. But know your players, Jon Stead's not that type of player. It was a typical striker's tackle. But let's not talk all day about the tackle.'

Keane was unimpressed by the way his side floundered after being reduced to ten men, as possession was squandered and there was little chance of Town getting back in the game. Only Colback, who Keane said would become a top player because of his attitude, goalscorer Peters and Wickham came in for praise.

Stead's red card was appealed, at the risk of a three-game ban being turned into a four-game ban and the striker was insistent he should never have been sent off. He said he was shocked when he looked up and saw the red card. 'It wasn't two-footed, I didn't leave the ground,' he said. 'It was just a mistimed tackle and a yellow card would have been plenty. If anything I thought it was a foul on me [by Claude Davis] before the tackle but I didn't lunge at anyone or try and hurt the player. I tried to speak to the referee before he showed the card but their players made it difficult in the way they were surrounding him and that was disappointing. We're all fellow professionals playing the same game. But as soon as they saw the red card, some of the Palace players turned around and said to me 'It wasn't a red card, you are unlucky'. I'm hoping the appeal comes through because it kills me. I've just got back in the team and now I could be out for three games.'

Bank Holiday Monday gave Town the opportunity to put the disappointment of their unbeaten run coming to an end behind them, with Queens Park Rangers the visitors – albeit with Paul Hart in charge and not Jim Magilton following his acrimonious departure. Keane made four changes from the Crystal Palace match, bringing the previously suspended Leadbitter and Walters back in for Colback and Garvan, while John returned up front at the expense of Healy, who typically under Keane dropped completely out of the 18-man matchday squad. Norris made his first start since the opening day, playing in the centre of midfield, which saw Peters move to left-back in place of the injured David Wright.

Town made the perfect start when John sent Walters away down the left-hand side and he found enough space to angle home a deflected left-footed shot in only the third minute. More chances came in the opening 30 minutes and the match could have been over as a contest by half-time. However, Adel Taarabt was doing his best to avoid bringing the visitors level, missing two glorious chances.

The accustomed early second-half substitutions saw Norris replaced by Garvan, and Edwards, again failing to complete 90 minutes, taken off in place of Colback. Eight minutes later Town extended their lead. Garvan played a long ball into Stead's feet on the edge of the box and he turned and struck an inch-perfect, low shot past keeper Radek Cerny. Stead's second of the match and sixth goal of the season followed soon after when Walters was released down the right and his low cross was palmed by Cerny into the path of Stead, who had the easy task of slotting into the vacant goal. Stead then had two clear chances to seal his hat-trick. The first was blocked by Cerny and the second skidded wide of the far post with a clear sight of goal. It was typical Stead – scoring from an awkward position for his first and then missing two easier chances, a profligacy which had seen him drop out of the Premier League and at risk of becoming a Championship journeyman.

It was the halfway point in the season and Town were up to 19th in the table. Their search for back-to-back wins was stretching as far back as May, but one loss in 12 matches was promotion form, not that of a side near the foot of the table. Keane had been in this position before. His promoted Sunderland team started the season badly before gaining unstoppable momentum through the second half of the campaign and Town were showing signs of following suit.

They would have to make do without Stead, as the FA's Independent Regulatory Commission viewed the red card as the correct decision, and subsequently added the extra game to his initial three-match ban, meaning he would not be available for weeks. Keane held his tongue as tightly as he could but made it clear the decision was a joke. 'If that tackle deserves four games I'm glad I'm not playing any more,' he said. 'Steady is as honest as the day is long and I've seen the tackle over and over again and it's a yellow card at the most and he ends up being out for the best part of a month.'

It was the end of a tumultuous year for the club. From promotion hopefuls at the start of 2009, Town found themselves the talk of the country when the most controversial manager in their history was installed. They then found their promotion intent turn to fears of relegation when Keane's reign began in the worst possible manner and he scraped through to the end of the year. But slowly and surely the tide had turned and Town were able to look up and not down at the increasing number of teams below them in the table as the New Year and a new dawn broke.

Chapter Nine

January 2010

'THERE'S NO DOUBT IN MY MIND, JON WALTERS COULD EASILY BE PLAYING IN THE PREMIERSHIP, SO WE'RE VERY LUCKY TO HAVE HIM.'

On the pitch, the last 12 months had been some of the dullest in Ipswich Town's history. No end-of-season promotion push, no play-off drama and excitement, and totally unfulfilled suggestions of a title challenge when the new campaign dawned. Another year had passed, but with the exception of a new high-profile manager, Ipswich Town were still very much a Championship club dreaming of making it to the big time – just like every other club in the division, with the exception of Newcastle who, at the halfway point, were odds-on title winners and set for a quick return to the Premier League, where Chelsea and Manchester United were setting the pace.

In the space of a year, Town had gone backwards in terms of their on-pitch performances. Marcus Evans's masterplan was reaping no reward and the cost of not making the Premier League was set to sting him in the pocket to the tune of many millions of pounds. Attendances at Portman Road were steady, as fans slowly warmed to Roy Keane's view that the team needed rebuilding, even though it was a contradiction to the early season bleating from the club that they were targeting promotion – Keane in particular, saying he was there to complete the job inside his two-year contract. The money had been stumped up by Evans for new players, but Keane spectacularly mis-spent, resulting in many of his expensive flops not even making the bench. However, the initial expectation of Keane waving his money-laden magic wand and Town taking the fast-track to the Premier League had given way to the acceptance of a slow-burning transition on the pitch. Before becoming a ruthless winning machine, Town would have to be hard to beat and then begin the slow slog away from the relegation zone. Coming into the New Year, this part was well underway. But for how long would Town fans put up with their team battling their way to uninspiring away draws and the odd dominant home win? For all of Keane's endearment as a footballing winner, he was not winning enough matches as Ipswich Town manager.

The first stage of the recovery was complete. Now Town had to move up a gear and find a way to beat the teams below them convincingly, and take points off the top teams. The losing habit was gone thanks to an unpenetrable defence – potentially the best Town had found for many years. It was at the other end of the pitch where the question marks remained. If Keane was to be a success at Town, he would have to find a way of making his side score goals, because without them, Town were never going to surpass a mid-table position come May. His striking quota was fully stocked, but only Stead had stepped out from the pack to hit a flurry of goals.

The first action of the year came at Championship rivals Blackpool in the third round of the FA Cup. Keane secured an extension to Stern John's loan deal from Crystal Palace, making him available for the cup-tie. John was yet to open his Town account and his performances were receiving mixed reviews. The crowd was calling for Pablo Counago in the 3-0 win over QPR when John's lack of movement was leaving a bad taste in the mouth for some, but Keane felt he was performing an important role for the team in holding the ball up and providing an outlet. However, it was hard to see what John had done that Counago could not.

Keane admitted Town's winter form should have come in August, not when they found themselves bottom of the table and the laughing stock of the country. It was clear to him, and anyone who watched Town on a regular basis, that they were a far better team going into 2010 than they were in the opening weeks of the season. 'I think we're getting there,' he said. 'We've had to be patient the last few months, but I'm getting a lot more confident with the group I've got, and the staff. I should have been sussing everybody a bit quicker, but we're getting there, trust me.' On his wage, Keane should have been sussing his players out instantly, but he would be forgiven should Town rampage their way to a play-off place and go on a lengthy run in the FA Cup.

The latter became a possibility after Town beat Blackpool 2-1 in a game most notable for the two red cards handed to the home side's Ian Evatt and Rob Edwards – both for professional fouls. Keane moved Jaime Peters into a role just behind John, meaning Town's most advanced front pair had one goal between them all season. So it was surprising to see Town ahead in the opening minutes when Jack Colback drove a fierce shot high into the net from the edge of the penalty area. Colback's contribution was increasing with every game and he, along with other Keane signings such as Liam Rosenior and Damien Delaney, were producing displays containing far more consistency than when they first played for the club.

Town's lead disappeared in the 50th minute when Brett Ormerod headed past Arran Lee-Barrett and Keane instantly made changes, replacing the ineffective John and tiring David Norris with Owen Garvan and Connor Wickham. The game stayed even until the final 15 minutes, by which time Blackpool were down to nine men after Evatt flattened Colback on the edge of the box and Edwards pulled back Jon Walters when he was clean though. Garvan lined up the resultant free-kick and hit a low shot around the wall to put Town in the hat for the next round. They should have wrapped the game up more easily than they did, with Wickham and Colback squandering straightforward chances against the nine Blackpool men remaining.

It was all too much for Tangerines manager Ian Holloway, who was sent to the stands following the second red card, and threw his hat and coat on the ground before marching off. For Keane, it was a less emotional display, although he was none too impressed with the way Town performed once they had the numerical advantage. 'As far as our performance is concerned, we are turning in results now,' he said. 'We controlled the game well, although I was disappointed by the last 15 minutes. If you want to watch how not to play against nine men that was a display to watch. We had the chances to have killed the game off in the last 15 minutes but we're through to the next round and that is what I would have settled for at kick-off.'

A proven out-and-out front player would have helped Town kill the game off. Keane, happy to rely on the ageing John, willing Walters and raw Wickham, was showing no sign of going back to Tamas Priskin or Counago, neither of whom made the bench, even in the absence of the suspended Jon Stead. It was a risky tactic, should they have fallen behind and ended up chasing the game. Counago's instinct in and around the box had saved Town in the past, and in an age of seven substitutes, it was startling to not see him named among the replacements. Eager for Wickham to acclimatise to first-team football, Keane gave his brightest young star plenty of opportunity but, while the chances were falling to him, his finishing was not quite up to scratch.

The draw for the fourth round gave Town a trip to League One Southampton, who beat Luton 1-0 in the third round. With the January transfer window open, Derby striker Rob Hulse was again reported to be on Keane's wanted list, as was Giovani Dos Santos, who Keane said was most unlikely to be heading back to Portman Road because of the size of the other clubs interested in the Mexican. Priskin reiterated his desire to stay at Town, with reports in the press saying both he and Counago were likely to be on their way out of Portman Road as Keane attempted to trim his squad to free up money, and space, to bring in new players. Kevin Lisbie was called back from his loan spell at Colchester United, only for Keane to change his mind and allow him to stay at the League One club for the rest of the season, pending any cash bids from other clubs.

Town's lack of goals gave rise to suggestions Lisbie may come straight back into the Town team. However, his return to Colchester made it clear his future lay away from Town while Keane was in charge.

Liam Trotter joined Millwall on a month-long loan deal. His playing time had been severely cut since the reintroduction of Garvan and the emergence of Colback, whose loan had been extended until the end of the season, and return to fitness of Norris. Tommy Smith followed him out of Portman Road, ahead of the visit to Leicester's Walkers Stadium, joining Brentford for a month. The Bees were seeking a straight replacement for Pim Balkestein, who Keane recalled from his loan spell when Delaney and David Wright were injury doubts.

The country was experiencing its worst cold snap for decades and the football calender was taking a pounding as a result. The big freeze saw the majority of Premier League matches postponed on 9 January, even with undersoil heating and a variety of snow-clearing devices available. It was the roads which were causing most of the problems, as heavy snow had settled on top of a layer of ice and a national shortage of grit led the government to tell the nation only to drive if absolutely necessary.

Keane failed to make it to Portman Road for his usual Friday morning press conference, such was the snowfall and Arctic conditions in Suffolk. It was somewhat ironic that the Town manager could not attend, given his demands when he took over that his players live close to the Town to avoid poor punctuality and tiredness. While housebound, Keane was no doubt giving thought to ways of combating Leicester's direct style of play. The outcome, when the teams emerged in front of the Sky TV cameras on a biting cold Sunday afternoon (the scheduled West Ham versus Wolves match was postponed) was a line-up featuring four centre-halves. Keane appeared in the Walkers Stadium press room prior to the match. He fetched a cup of tea and stood watching the television, which was screening Sky Sports News. He spoke to no one, and no one spoke to him. Ten minutes later he was gone and re-emerged on the touchline at kick-off.

The pitch was slippery but perfectly playable as Alex Bruce started at right-back and Balkestein at left-back, with Gareth McAuley and Delaney the central pair. Rosenior had been suffering from a knock, but was fit enough for a place on the bench, which featured only one striker in John. New keeper Brian Murphy, in the squad for the first time after his signing was finalised, injured an ankle in the warm-up and would have played no part, even if required. Wickham started up front alongside Walters and Town were ahead inside the first minute when Colback's low cross was bundled in by Norris, with the aid of a deflection. The home crowd grew restless as Town defended strongly and looked a decent bet for a second goal. McAuley saw a header excellently tipped over by Leicester keeper Chris Weale, and Colback should have tapped home Leadbitter's driven cross. It was Leicester who scored the next goal, however, when Delaney's weak clearance was charged down by Steve Howard on the edge of the penalty area and he slid the loose ball past Lee-Barrett. It was an avoidable goal and one Delaney would not want to see again. Town were unable to gain control of the second half and were indebted to a brilliant one-handed save by Lee-Barrett who prevented Foxes top-scorer Matt Fryatt from scoring from point-blank range.

The contest became scrappy with little passing and plenty of aerial challenges. Town's back line, which was altered when Rosenior replaced Bruce with half an hour to go, were content in distributing the ball high and anywhere. Norris was energetic without producing anything other than the first-minute goal, as Town struggled to find a way of breaking down an uninspiring Leicester side. Keane withdrew Wickham for Garvan, leaving Walters as the lone striker, giving Town, in effect, six midfielders on the pitch. Walters headed wide when well-placed and Town's chances of winning were gone. It ended 1-1.

Two points dropped or a point gained? It was Town's 13th draw of the season, and despite it coming against a side in the top five, Leicester's lack of quality was obvious – it did not take a miracle, or a lot of money, to be in the upper ranks of the Championship. As a spectacle, the match was a drab affair. Like many Championship fixtures it was a physical battle between two teams, neither of whom was prepared to gamble to win. Keane's selection pointed towards a fear of defeat. Neither full-back went past the midfield, and the exclusion of Garvan, playing only a bit-part again despite his form in December, gave Town a predictability going forwards. With only John on the bench, there was no one Keane could turn to in order to change the flow of the game. He was intent on filling his side with battling players, those he could rely on to give their all and not shirk a challenge, like Norris, rather than those who might just win him a match occasionally.

Keane talked up Norris afterwards, saying how much he thought Town had missed him. 'He's been a massive loss to us,' he said. 'He's just getting up to speed with his match fitness. His passing will improve over the course of the next few months, but we've missed his tenacity and his energy. I've got a lot of time for David, he's my type of player, he gets stuck in and he's been a big plus for us over the last few weeks. I'm pretty sure that if he hadn't got injured at the beginning of the season we wouldn't be where we are in the league, which is a compliment to him.'

Keane was continually saying it was victories Town needed, so why go into the match with so few attacking options? 'Because we've had such a poor start to the season, it's victories we're after but Leicester are obviously having a good season and maybe it's a point gained,' he said. 'I think we probably had the better of the chances but our keeper probably pulled off the best save. Draws won't get you too far up the table but I still think we are capable of having a good season, and that would include getting into the play-offs.'

Keane's habit of contradicting himself was becoming more and more noticeable as the season wore on. He wanted his strikers to score more goals, but would not play them, or sign a proven one for that matter. There was nothing but praise for John's performances, yet he had not scored all season. Players were one minute cast adrift and the next would be back in the reckoning and replacing those who had been playing reasonably well – David Wright and Garvan the prime examples. It seemed like Keane was suffering from a similar ailment to Magilton – he could not work out his best team. Instead, he said his selected sides were those best to win the game in question. But how could Town come back and win if they went behind against Leicester with only one striker (with no goals to his name) out of seven players on the substitutes bench?

Keane said a deluge of new signings should not be expected in the transfer window. Transfers were another of Keane's contradictions. One week he would say he was likely to sign one, maybe two new players, and a few weeks later, after the signings failed to arrive, he would say he was happy with his squad. He said after the Leicester match: 'We won't be doing much business, I wouldn't have thought. We've made enquiries for one or two players, but that's as far as it's gone. We've got one or two lads coming back from injury and the balance isn't too bad. I've got a big squad, I've got a lot of good players who didn't even travel with us, so I want to be careful and if I do bring one or two players to the club, then they'll have to be of real quality, and trying to get a player of that quality in January is very difficult, and it's the same for every club.'

As a side near the bottom of the table and having under-performed during the first half of the season, Town fans were expecting new signings – and decent ones to boot – during January, to help Keane's side, lacking players capable of playing in the Premier League, climb into the top half of the table.

While signings were not forthcoming, a few surprises certainly were in a week of high drama at Portman Road. First, the club announced the sacking of coach Bryan Klug. The 49-year-old had taken on all manner of roles at the club, including youth-team player, academy director and assistant manager to Magilton. Well-regarded by all, Klug oversaw the development of top young talents such as Richard Wright, Kieron Dyer and Titus Bramble, all of whom were sold on in big-money transfers. Keane had said at the start of the season that there may be changes off the pitch as well as on it, and the introduction of Ian McParland to the coaching staff was another sign that some of the old guard may be moved on. Keane said: 'He's [Klug's] done very well at the club, he's been a very good servant, but I've been in the job now five or six months and I've decided to make a few changes. Charlie [Ian McParland] came in, Antonio Gomez and Tony Loughlan came in. I just decided to make that change. He's a very, very good coach, he's got vast experience, he's worked at different levels at the club – the first team, the academy, the reserves – and we wish him well.'

Also departing was Colin Healy in a loan move to Falkirk for the remainder of the season. Keane took the blame for Healy's non-existent impact since joining the club in the summer. 'It's not quite happened here for Colin so far but that happens in football and I take some of the blame for that,' said Keane. 'I look at the games I played him in, against Palace when he hadn't played for months, and then we went down to 10 men and I put him on the right. At home to Leicester, when he sat in midfield in a system I played that didn't work for us on the day. It's been difficult for him but it's not been his fault. It's been mine, if anything. Maybe I've not really given him a good run in the side. One or two things went against him, even at the start of the season when he suffered from blisters after the army training.'

One player who was staying, for now, was Priskin who turned down a loan move to League One club Charlton Athletic. Town were linked with Nottingham Forest's Dele Adebola, who had been mentioned in connection with the club under Magilton, but before Keane brought in a new striker he was understood to have to ship at least one out. Rumours of a return of Kieron Dyer to Portman Road were quickly scotched, but in the case of Luciano Civelli, he would not be turning out for Town at all during the 2009-10 season, after Keane allowed him to head back to Argentina. Written off until pre-season, Civelli had suffered setbacks in his return from the terrible knee injury and Keane agreed it would be better for him to go home and recuperate, with family and friends close by.

With the rain pouring down and mid-table Coventry City the visitors to Portman Road on 16 January, a damp squib of a game was to be expected. Keane abandoned his tall back-four policy in favour of Jaime Peters and Rosenior at full-back, while John came in up front in place of Wickham, who joined Counago on the bench. Peters had by now moved ahead of David Wright in the full-back pecking order, with his pace and stamina, together with a sound defensive mind and the ability to play anywhere on the pitch making him difficult to leave out of the starting 11.

Early goals had usually been of Town's making, but they found themselves behind after only three minutes when Clinton Morrison, the scourge of Town for many years, finished a sweet move with a 20-yard shot which went in off the inside of the post – most of the crowd was still wringing out umbrellas and overcoats when the water fell from the shuddering goal-frame.

Town fought back admirably, spending most of the first half in Coventry territory. Peters and Rosenior had acres of room and it was from a Rosenior cross that Town drew level, John heading in his first Town goal – and his first for any club in his previous 32 appearances. The momentum continued in the second half and Town were 2-1 ahead when the imperious Garvan, whose passing was inch-perfect despite the skiddy conditions, split the defence with a pass into the path of Walters. His low cross was helped on by Leadbitter and Colback came steaming in from the back post to side-foot past a succession of Coventry defenders sliding in to block his shot. Colback's knack for a goal was growing, as was his influence on matches. Playing on the left, with Garvan drifting in from an unusual right-hand role, he gave Town width when needed and tucked in, allowing Peters to charge on when space opened up. Having an attacking full-back like Peters had made a huge difference to Town's pattern of play.

Gone were the long aimless balls, replaced by passing through the midfield and a switch of play to the advanced Peters or Rosenior. Counago and Wickham replaced Norris and John after 63 minutes. There were a couple of scares for Town when Lee-Barrett was forced into a fantastic point-blank save and another from distance. Town should have extended their lead when Colback was put in the clear by Wickham but his attempted chip from 30-yards was fluffed. A typical piece of Counago skill then came even closer to sealing the match when he chased the rebound from a Wickham shot which was saved. The ball was rolling out to the side of the penalty area when the Spaniard won a challenge with a Coventry defender, rounded the advancing keeper and another defender before seeing his shot agonisingly stopped on the line by Martin Cranie's toe. The ball stood stationary, just in front of the goal-line, for what seemed an age, with Counago left on the floor near the penalty spot with his head in his hands.

Thousands of fans up and down the country leave matches early, despite paying up to £40 for a ticket, sometimes more, only to head for the exit before the referee had blown the final whistle. Where were they going? The season-ticket holder in the adjacent seat to mine left Portman Road seconds after the ball hit the Town net from the head of Coventry's Richard Wood, who had moved on from Sheffield Wednesday. Four minutes of injury-time were signalled by referee Michael Oliver, and the four minutes were up by the time Wood scored. Coventry celebrated for a couple of minutes, taking an age to return to their half, by which time spectators were pouring out of Portman Road. Those who stayed were rewarded to one of the most extraordinary passages of play seen for years, which gave Town an extraordinary 3-2 win.

Twelve seconds passed between the moment the game was restarted and when Counago netted the winner. It was deep into the seventh minute of time added on and the pandemonium which followed was as manic as at any time during the past decade. It was the contrasting emotion of thinking the game had been snatched away, only for it to be won, all during time which should never had been played and it sent the stadium into delirium. The goal itself was 'worthy of winning any game', according to Keane, who was remarkably calm on the touchline when Counago latched onto Wickham's pass and scooped the ball over the on-rushing Kieren Westwood. It was an ice-cool finish from the Spaniard, who was mobbed by the whole Town team – including keeper Lee-Barrett, who charged the length of the pitch to join in. Keane made do with a punch of the air and a big smile. The crowd was stoked up even more by the tannoy announcer singing 'Ole Ole Ole' which then rang out in the streets around the ground after the whistle was finally blown.

It was a moment for Town fans to cherish for ever – the kind which came around only once a decade. It was compared to Shefki Kuqi's late, late winner at Crystal Palace in October 2003 when Palace had equalised in the 88th minute, with Kuqi making it 4-3 to Town a minute later. But Counago's goal was in the seventh minute of time added on, making it even more unlikely, particularly as it was scored by a player who had been out of the first-team picture and seemingly on his way out of the club, despite his popularity with the fans.

The late drama overshadowed what had been a competent display by Town. The midfield clicked with Garvan, Norris, Leadbitter and Colback all playing in the same side, and any fears about a lack of width were dampened by the rampaging runs of Peters. Keane had no complaints about the time added on at the end of the match, saying the four minutes were a 'minimum of four minutes'. 'Ultimately, though, we got what we deserved,' Keane said. 'We played some decent stuff and Pablo's finish at the end was worthy of winning most games. It was a good pass by

Connor and a brilliant finish by Pablo and you can see what it meant to everyone, the players, the staff and obviously the fans. We've not had too many highs. We've won games but we've had setbacks and it was a hammer blow with them scoring right at the end. You think we have seen the end of those days of conceding goals right at the end, so to come back and win it has given everyone a big boost at the club.' Coventry boss Chris Coleman saw the mystery minutes situation somewhat differently, saying 'two wrongs don't make a right'.

It was the first real excitement felt at Portman Road all season and a further step in the right direction for the club, which was now sitting ten points off the play-offs and six clear of the relegation zone. In response to Keane's criticism of a lack of goals from the strikers, two of his quota were on the scoresheet, and Counago showed a flash of the quality which should have made him a more regular starter, and scorer. There was now a reason for football fans to go to Portman Road again. Instead of looking at the league table and hearing the negative vibes surrounding Keane during the first half of the season, the feelgood factor was returning and Town were winning more games than they were losing.

'I can't think of a finish as dramatic as the one in the Coventry match during the last couple of decades and it turned out to be the biggest high during Keane's time in charge,' said Matt Plummer. 'Everyone was so deflated when Coventry equalised, there was even despair in the press box. There were some people from Coventry sitting behind me and they celebrated with clenched fists when their goal went in. There weren't many times under Keane's regime when everyone left the ground feeling positive but on that day the fans were able to believe that just maybe everything would be alright in the end.'

The reshuffle behind the scenes continued, with Steve Foley taking over the running of Town's reserve side from the departed Klug. After weeks of waiting, keeper Lee-Barrett finally confirmed he had signed a new 18-month contract. The 25-year-old's jump from training with the club in an attempt to keep fit, to being number one was a fairytale story for the player who was with the club's Academy as a teenager. Other clubs were said to be interested until he signed the new deal which was expected to be a formality, given the opportunities presented to him and Richard Wright's injury which was likely to keep Lee-Barrett in the first-team picture for some time to come.

Any hopes of a long and exciting run in the FA Cup were dashed at Southampton. It was typical Town, in that they went into the tie on such a high after the drama at Portman Road, only to produce one of their worst performances since the debacle against Newcastle in September.

Keane talked up the magic of the FA Cup before the game, but the urgency to get their name in the hat for the next round was never there until Counago pulled a goal back in the last minute after Saints led 2-0 – the first a long-range rocket from full-back Wayne Thomas, the second after Lee-Barrett was unable to hold a 20-yard free-kick and Antonio reacted quickest to net from close range. Town were noticeably poorer after skipper Walters was forced off at half-time with a hamstring injury.

Walters's impact had not gone unnoticed by Keane, who raved about the Republic of Ireland 'B' international. 'There's no doubt in my mind, Jon Walters could easily be playing in the Premiership, so we're very lucky to have him,' said Keane. 'He's a very, very important player for us. The game he missed at Palace, we missed him. It's not just what we see on a Saturday but it's what happens the rest of the week, obviously the supporters and media don't see that. He's a big, big player for us.' Walters's form had been a mixed bag for the previous 12 months. Certainly, he had not been one of Town's worst players under Keane's management, but he had not set the Championship alight since the season started. Keane fancied him as a striker and his return of six goals from his opening 24 matches was average at best. However, once he went off at St Mary's, Town were punchless, as Keane even called on Priskin to try and shake them into life in the second half.

Town could have scored when Carlos Edwards's long throw appeared to have been brushed in by Counago, but the referee deemed the ball had not touched the Spaniard – a fact later confirmed by the striker – and disallowed the goal. It was the only major contribution Edwards made, having been brought in for the rested Norris. He was following the suit of Lee Martin and Priskin in drifting out of Keane's preferred starting line-ups, despite only being at the club a few months and arriving on the back of a considerable transfer fee. Keane felt Town did not deserve to lose, although he said they were not good enough to win the match either, – a worry considering they were facing League One opposition.

It was further confirmation that if Town were to be a side with play-off, and even promotion aspirations, they were going to have to improve considerably and were still more than capable of serving up a stinking performance. The January transfer window was entering its final week and Keane's only business had been to let players go out on loan and extend John's loan deal. Left-backs Kevin Kilbane, of Hull, and Lee Naylor, of Celtic, were linked and Keane refused to comment on any player contracted to another club.

There was a patent lack of interest in Town's players from clubs in the Premier League. The days of having to sell off the crown jewels to stay afloat financially were gone, but none of Keane's squad was producing the kind of form linking them with a move to a bigger club – Wickham the exception because of his contract situation and potential.

The players had the chance to show they were good enough to mix with, at the very least, the top teams in the Championship when West Bromwich Albion came to Portman Road on 26 January. Going into the match on the back of a 1-2 defeat by a League One side in the cup was not ideal. Town, though, could still point to one defeat in 14 league games as proof they were a match for most teams in the division. West Brom were challenging Newcastle for the title and had already given Town a lesson in how to move the ball around and play expansive football when the they ran out 2-0 winners at the Hawthorns earlier in the season.

It was a return to the scene of one of Portman Road's classic moments, with Counago's late winner against Coventry ingrained in fans' minds. So it was ironic when Town were given a spoonful of their own medicine. Keane made four changes to the line-up from the Southampton clash, bringing David Wright back in at left-back, moving Peters to right-wing and starting Counago and Stead up front.

From the beginning West Brom showed they were in a different class to many of the mediocre sides filling the Championship. McAuley cleared a Chris Brunt looping effort off the line and Town's defending was increasingly desperate and they were fortunate to make it to half-time goalless, although Peters could have put them in front. When played in behind the defence by Counago, his shot was blocked by keeper Scott Carson. Referee Stuart Attwell, renowned for making questionable decisions, gave Town a helping hand with 25 minutes to go with a penalty for the apparent man-handling of Delaney in the box. Leadbitter scored from the spot. West Brom laid siege to Town's goal and but Town could have gone two ahead when substitute Priskin was in the clear, only to see his shot saved by Carson. The bitter blow arrived near the end of the four minutes of injury-time when Brunt buried a rebound from close range to leave Portman Road in disbelief for the second game in a row.

As hard as it was to take for Town, there was no denying West Brom were a class act, who deserved at least a share of the points. Town's backline held on manfully, displaying the doggedness Keane demanded of his side. However, their failure to hold on during the final minutes of matches had now cost them nine points over the course of the season. Keane stayed on the pitch and shook the hand of each of his players and later exclaimed how they showed spirit and desire in going ahead against a 'cracking' side. He said: 'We had chances to have finished them off but that will come. It's the sign of the progress we are making that we can hold a team as good as West Brom, but it's a sign of how far we have to go, as well. When I was driving to the game I knew that we would have to defend well if we were going to have a chance and they did that. A blind man could see that West Brom have a very good chance of winning promotion. They play very good football and move the ball well and we knew that, but in terms of clear-cut chances we had the better ones. We are nearly a good team but we all know 'nearly never made it'. Are we short in certain areas? You bet we are. But we are improving all the time and they gave it their all tonight.'

For all of the talk of improvement, and the club spin on reaching the play-offs, Town found themselves back in the mire only four days later thanks to a dire display at Preston North End. Most of the other strugglers – Derby, Crystal Palace, Scunthorpe, Reading, Sheffield Wednesday – won, leaving Town, beaten 0-2 at Deepdale, only one place and three points above the drop zone. Two of their last three performances smacked of a side lacking every ingredient required to challenge for promotion, and worryingly, many of Town's problems from earlier in the season had reared their head again.

One of these was Keane's muddled team selection and tactics. After starting with two strikers – Counago and Stead against West Brom – he dropped the former to the bench and moved the latter to the right wing in a 4-5-1 formation. In his pre-match press conference he talked up flop signing Priskin, and duly gave him a place in the starting 11. 'Tamas is going nowhere,' said Keane. 'He's staying at the football club. I think the boy deserves a chance, I think the boy's a talented player. We're obviously hoping for a bit more from him but, like I said when we signed him, some players take longer than others to settle in. People are on about him being a goalscorer. Our top goalscorer has six goals and Tamás has got two and he's probably played the least minutes of all the strikers. I think the boy deserves more of an opportunity and he's going to get that over the next few months with the games we have and with Jon Walters being injured. We've had plenty of enquiries for him but I made the decision that he's going to stay with us. Tamas is staying, Tamas is going to be part of our squad, definitely.'

The decision to start Priskin backfired, as he missed Town's best chance early in the second half when he blazed over with only the keeper to beat. He then had a header disallowed and again failed to last 90 minutes. Neill Collins gave Preston the lead and on-loan Manchester United striker Danny Welbeck sealed the points six minutes from time, lobbing Lee-Barrett. Keane bemoaned Town's defending and his side's lack of cutting edge – a combination made for relegation.

With the closure of the transfer window only two days away, Keane was asked about the possible signing of Cardiff's Michael Chopra, who played for him at Sunderland and was scoring regularly for the Welsh side. Keane said the club would probably not be able to afford him. It begged the question, why would Chopra want to sign for Ipswich, now embroiled in a relegation scrap, and a team showing little creativity?

The constant switching had again failed to reap rewards for Keane. Counago had found himself back on the bench, alongside John who returned to Crystal Palace after the match, bringing an end to a largely forgettable loan spell. Stead had been spoken of as the club's number one striker before his suspension, but was played on the wing. How was Keane going to improve a team he was constantly changing? By bringing more players in before the transfer window closed? Or by biting the bullet and sticking with players such as Garvan and Counago, who had done it in the past but not quite done enough to suggest they were going to do the business regularly in the future?

Chapter Ten

February 2010

'DON'T THINK FOR ONE MINUTE IT WILL BE THE SAME TEAM ON TUESDAY NIGHT. I'M SURE YOU'LL HAVE A GOOD GUESS BUT I BET YOU GET IT WRONG. I USUALLY GET IT WRONG!'

If a player was Irish, played for Sunderland, or played with or against Roy Keane during his playing days, he was linked, if not signed by Keane himself on transfer deadline day. The window closed on 1 February and Ipswich Town's activity was somewhat predictable, with the exception of the mystery surrounding Tamas Priskin.

Alex Bruce was the first to depart, to Leicester City on loan for the remainder of the season. It looked an excellent move for Bruce, whose opportunities had been limited due to the centre-back partnership of Gareth McAuley and Damien Delaney. Leicester were eighth in the table and only two points off the play-off zone. The loan deals of Liam Trotter, at Millwall, and Tommy Smith, at Brentford, were extended, but the big news was Priskin.

After Keane's unprovoked outburst regarding Priskin's future at the club three days earlier, Town fans were astonished when the club announced the Hungarian had gone on loan to Queens Park Rangers. Why did Keane say Priskin was 'definitely staying' and would be a regular in the coming weeks, only to get rid of him? It was another of Keane's grand contradictions and made a mockery of all he had said. Such U-turns were making it even harder for Town fans to buy into the 'Keane dream' of the former Manchester United legend being the right man to mastermind the club back into the Premier League, and quickly. His muddled selections and hit-and-miss transfer dealings were a disease suffered by many a manager. But telling the world one thing and then immediately doing the total opposite was quite another. Why should anyone believe anything he or anyone else at the club had to say when its credibility was waning by the month?

Priskin's performance at Preston did not help his case for a permanent place in Town's starting 11 and, after ten starts, nine substitute appearances and two goals, he would play out the rest of the season at Loftus Road.

'Keane signed him to score goals and he didn't,' said Matthew Mehen. 'You could tell Priskin was affected by it as well. Like Pablo, he was another who the supporters did not hear from or about [other than observing him on the pitch on a Saturday afternoon], which added a certain amount of intrigue. He was very good with his feet – you could see he had a nice touch but the goals just didn't happen. He cost a lot of money and a lot was expected of him – perhaps too much. He was not too dissimilar to Pablo in the way he wanted the ball to feet – rather than a Shefki Kuqi-type who would chase sweet wrappers. However, I wondered why we had signed Priskin when Keane was hardly enamoured with Pablo. Maybe he did want a skilful striker and Priskin was younger than Pablo?'

In Priskin's place came two attacking players. Both Daryl Murphy and David Healy had been linked with Town in previous seasons and Murphy had been on trial at Portman Road in 2005 before signing for Sunderland. Keane signed Healy, a prolific scorer in international football for Northern Ireland, while at Sunderland, but not once had he started a league fixture for the Black Cats. The loan deals until the end of the season were completed before the 5pm deadline and concluded Town's business in the transfer market.

Two players with Premier League and international experience – Murphy possessed nine Republic of Ireland caps – gave Town greater quality on paper. But would it turn out to be a transfer masterstroke by Keane? He had already raided Sunderland for Grant Leadbitter, Carlos Edwards and Jack Colback, and, while Leadbitter and Colback had done well, Edwards had shown little to back up his transfer fee and Town were three points above the relegation zone. Murphy's playing time in 2009-10 had been sporadic – seven appearances, four from the start, the last of which was in Sunderland's 2-7 defeat at Chelsea in January. Healy's club career had been a disappointment compared to his international exploits. Awarded an MBE for services to football in 2008, the 30-year-old had started his career at Manchester United when Keane was also at the club, and while his international performances had made him a star in his homeland, he had made no impact in the Premier League and slumped into regular bench-warming duties. Seven appearances and no goals in 2009-10 for Sunderland was not a record he was happy with. Town's two new signings were not players in top form – they were players with reputations who were at a club on the big stage.

The two new Irishmen brought Town's first-team Irish quota up to 11, including the loaned out Colin Healy. There were two Murphys, two Healys and two Wrights (none related) adding to Keane's strange squad composition. The arrival of a striker or two had been on the cards after Keane's public disapproval of his side's goal output. That he brought in two loan players and said Cardiff's Michael Chopra was likely to be too expensive was evidence that the transfer kitty was running low. Murphy was a versatile player able to play on the left or up front. Keane said he preferred him to play in a more advanced role, although sceptics pointed at his record of 14 goals in 114 games, 55 of them as substitute, for Sunderland. His record suggested he was unlikely to be any more prolific than Jon Stead or Pablo Counago.

Town fans were afforded an instant sight of Murphy and Healy lining up as a strike pair, as Keane stuck them straight in for their debut against Gordon Strachan's Middlesbrough. It was harsh on Stead and Counago, whose goal output was only nine between them, but the service they had received, along with Wickham and Walters, when played up front, was hardly providing goals on a plate.

He may not have scored since February 2008, but Murphy showed he had not forgotten where the goal was, making a dream start to his spell with Town, putting them ahead after a mere 23 seconds – even quicker than Stead's strike against Blackpool. The Irishman slid in ahead of Middlesbrough keeper Danny Coyne after Healy's low cross was deflected across the edge of the six-yard box. That was as good as it got for Town, who slowly fell back into their bad habits of lumping long balls forward. The initial excitement of two new strikers soon wore off and Healy was replaced by Counago after an unflattering hour. Both debutants were short of game time, and were unable to prevent Town from relinquishing their lead when David Wheater headed in a corner just after the hour mark. It finished 1-1.

It had been far from a classic encounter and followed the pattern of so many of Town's matches in the campaign – go ahead, concede and then play out an unspectacular remainder of the match with no lack of effort, but no quality on the ball. The Portman Road pitch was cutting up and made slick passing tricky, but the supposed ball-players – Leadbitter and Colback – were bypassed for most of the 90 minutes and the line-up – lacking the benched Jaime Peters – contained no pace or width. Keane included Walters in the starting 11, despite telling the press the day before that he would not be fit in time. It was as though Keane would have Walters in the side even if he was missing a leg.

Keane himself summed up the display aptly afterwards: 'boring'. A point against a team that had been in the Premier League in recent years was no disaster. Town's position in the table – one point and one place above the relegation zone – was, and Middlebrough were forced into starting the match with three centre-halves and three full-backs because of injuries. Draw after draw was sending Town in the wrong direction and they were not just looking over their shoulder, they were every inch in the thick of a relegation dogfight. Little time had elapsed since all the talk had been about the play-offs and the table remained tight in the bottom half, with a couple of victories pushing teams up five or six places. Town, however, were stuck in what had become an endless rut of uninspiring displays, matched by uninspiring results.

The optimism from the festive period when the goals had started to return, and the excitement generated by the last-gasp winner against Coventry, was flushed away by the reality that Keane's side was changing, evolving, yet getting no better, and was all the while costing more and more money. They were unable to break away from the chains of Championship football, with its barrage of long balls, physical contests and reliance on set-pieces – the success of which kept more than half of the sides in the division each season. West Brom and Newcastle were playing football which belonged in the Premier League. Cardiff were scoring goals left, right and centre. Meanwhile, Town were still struggling to put three passes and a shot on goal together.

'But this was a typical Championship game,' said Keane. 'Both teams had chances, it finished 1-1 and we all go home. Boring. Scoring goals has been a problem for us all season. In the second half we got in some really good positions but we just needed the final ball. The final ball is the most important one in football.'

Keane was having no problem in pointing out what was going wrong. Fixing it was proving somewhat trickier. The final ball had been lacking all season, though no wingers had been purchased, apart from the failed signing of Lee Martin. Murphy showed decent touches which gave Town fans some hope for the future and Healy could be expected to get better. With four away matches on the trot to come, and only one away win in the bag all season, it was dawning once again that Town were in a mess. A new year was now into its second month and no method of play was apparent. Four changes to the starting line-up for the 1-1 draw provided fuel for the doubters, who stood by their claims that Keane was not tactically astute enough to get Town promoted, and for all his straight-talking persona off the pitch, what he was producing on it was falling way short of expectations.

Keane had three days to sort his side out and stop Town from finding themselves back in the bottom three, with Queens Park Rangers the first of the quartet of away fixtures. Having slept on the Middlesbrough match, he still insisted he generally liked what he saw, even if many others did not. The club was quiet on the play-off front and the word 'promotion' had all but been erased, except from the mouth of full-back Liam Rosenior, who appeared hell bent on gaining brownie points for his public relations work. His future was yet to be sorted out, with his contract running down at Reading, and Town had offered nothing beyond the loan deal to the end of the season. Rosenior, though, was prepared to put money on Town being promoted to the Premier League the following season.

Optimism was not a feeling shared elsewhere in football. Portsmouth, Cardiff City and Southend United were in the High Court on winding-up orders for unpaid tax bills, while Norwich City's financial troubles following their relegation to League One were filling the news in Norfolk. The plight of Town's biggest rivals, although they were set for a quick return to the Championship, was a stark warning. No team was too good to go down and Town had proved a prime example of a club spending money but not buying success. Norwich and Newcastle had shown in the previous 12 months how the impossible could happen, and if Town were to lose at Loftus Road, the club was going to have to start considering the implications of a step down.

Maybe Rosenior had a crystal ball, because Town answered their critics with an outstanding first-half performance against Queens Park Rangers, going 2-0 up with goals from Norris and Murphy, and it could have been more. Keane took a gamble by going for all-out attack in his line-up, with Rangers sliding down the table and low on confidence following more managerial upheaval. Colback and Peters were deployed at full-back, in place of Wright, dropped from the 18, and Rosenior, who took his place on the bench, after both failed to make any attacking impact against Middlesbrough. Garvan and Counago were brought in and Town instantly found the way to goal. It did not last, as QPR came back strongly in the second half, pulling a goal back through Jay Simpson, but Town could have put the game out of sight. 'It was an important night for us,' said Keane, out sharpish from his team debriefing. 'Obviously we should have done better in terms of killing the game off but I have to be pleased, in the end we got the win. It was a very important three points, especially with the run of away games we have coming up.'

The night was dampened by Reading beating Plymouth, leaving Town in an improved 20th place, but with only one point separating them and the relegation zone, with Scunthorpe sandwiched in between. The shape of the table changed little before Town were next in action, even though they had a weekend off due to Cardiff's involvement in the FA Cup.

They were kept in the public eye by owner Marcus Evans, who was reported by *The Daily Mail* to be offering hospitality packages for the London Olympic Games. Tables of ten, with the champagne trimmings, a transfer to the stadium and viewing of the best events, including the 100m final was quoted at the small matter of £98,500, plus a 24 per cent service charge and exclusive of VAT. The package made no mention of tickets, which was not surprising, seeing as they were not on sale to any-one until 2011, by which time West Ham had won the bid to use the Olympic Stadium in Stratford after the 2012 Games.

By the time Town were ready for the trip to Peterborough United on 16 February, they were a striker down. Coventry City had come in for Stead, offering an initial loan deal until the end of the season, with a chance to make the deal permanent in the summer. Stead took a couple of days to mull over the offer, as his pregnant wife was settled in Suffolk. Keane, in one of his darker moods at his press conference the day before the game at London Road, said the impending birth of a child would make no difference to his choice of football club. 'I don't know if that comes into a player's mindset, I know it wouldn't come into mine, but some players are different,' said Keane, of Stead's consideration of his wife.

Six-goal top-scorer Stead had never truly settled in Town's front line. His goal record of 18 in 49 league starts was better than any other Town striker during the same period, but Keane had lost patience with his lack of team-work and inconsistency. When in top form, Stead was as good as the top strikers in the Championship. He was badly let down by far too many poor games, though, and was often substituted either at half-time or by the hour mark. On first and second impressions, Town had gained a better striker in Daryl Murphy – a player of similar size, yet more effec-tive both in the air and on the ground. Stead's red card against Crystal Palace proved to be the end point of his Town career, even though Keane talked him up during his four-game suspension, given he was in fine scor-ing form at the time of his dismissal. His comeback was an anti-climax and Keane acted by bringing in Murphy and Healy.

'Stead was being talked about as the club's big, main striker and how it was going to be a great loss when he was suspended but then he found himself surplus to requirements which was strange,' said Matt Plummer. 'Given the problems scoring goals and the distrust in Pablo, I couldn't understand why they let Stead go. But then I had also winced when they sold Jordan Rhodes to Huddersfield – you just wondered what the think-ing was behind these odd decisions. The one which I couldn't get my head around the most was the treatment of David Wright and I still can't to this day. Keane did not have a right-back, as they were playing people like Alex Bruce or Jaime Peters there. Wright was a dependable full-back, but like so many of the others he just fell out of favour. We got to know him well because he was one of the few put forward to speak to the press under Magilton and he was always professional.'

A grizzly Keane was full of pessimism as he talked down Town's previous away victory and he even conceded that thoughts of the play-offs should be banished. The assembled press gang delved into Keane's selection policy, suggesting he may buck the trend by picking the same starting 11, only to be told gruffly that some of the players who did so well in gaining a 2-0 lead at Loftus Road were unlikely to be starting again. 'Don't think for one minute it will be the same team on Tuesday night,' said Keane. 'I'm sure you'll have a good guess but I bet you get it wrong. I usually get it wrong! Last week it was just my gut feeling, what we thought we could add by bringing Garvs [Owen Garvan] into the team and weighing up the way the players had been training. But, as I say, if people think that's going to be the starting line-up on Tuesday night, I'd be surprised. I'm not necessarily sure whether we played well or QPR were poor on the night. We certainly should have finished the game off a lot earlier than we did. Instead of enjoying the first half or the first hour, I focus on the disappointment of the last 20-25 minutes when the game should have been dead and buried.'

Rarely satisfied, Keane reminded all that his team was finding it hard to hit the back of the net, effectively blaming the club's strikers for the season of struggling. He said: 'We really can't be thinking of the play-offs at this moment in time. You say the gap's only 13 points, but 13 points is a lot when you've only won five or six games all season. It's not as if we're a free-scoring team where we can go on one of those runs. We showed that again last week, missing opportunities.'

Next in Keane's line of fire were reserve-team players Ed Upson and recent acquisition Devann Yao, who failed to impress in a 1-0 win over Norwich, in which Upson scored the only goal. 'Ed was poor,' said Keane. 'Just because you score a penalty doesn't mean you've played well. He needs to get a move on with his fitness because his contract's up in three or four months. He did a bleep test yesterday and his score wasn't the best. Devann didn't play well in the game. He was poor, but we'll give him the benefit of the doubt as it was his first game as he's still getting up to speed in terms of his fitness levels.'

Town's concerns were running deeper than under-performing reserve-team players and Keane's public show of tension marked a prelude to the major blow which came at London Road. He stuck to his prediction of making changes to a winning team – dropping Peters and Counago, in favour of Healy and Rosenior. There was nothing the dissenters could complain about in the opening half an hour as Town took an early lead through Murphy's header from a Leadbitter corner. Peterborough, like Queens Park Rangers, were unstable and in shocking form, having won one of their last ten matches, leaving them well adrift at the bottom of the table. More chances came and went to wrap the game up by half-time and the 3,000 Town fans had reason to expect a dominant second 45 minutes which would have moved Town up the table and away from the relegation zone.

Instead, they produced one of their worst 45 minutes under Keane and totally capitulated, conceding three goals. Peterborough manager Jim Gannon changed his side's system after just 35 minutes, replacing striker Craig Mackail-Smith with winger Reuban Reid, and switching to a five-man midfield. It left Town bamboozled and there was no tactical response from Keane, other than to replace Garvan with Peters and put the Canadian at left-back, where Colback was being given a torrid time by Reid. Healy lasted 72 minutes and was replaced by Counago, while Leadbitter, Town's most influential midfielder, was hauled off in place of Alan Quinn, whose appearances had all but dried up, and Town failed to improve.

The 1-3 defeat was a blow to the players, to Keane, and the Town fans who witnessed the manner in which their side had folded against a team in dire straits. They were left wondering how long they were going to be treated to such under-achievement, and whether there was any hope left under Keane's management. It was one step forward and two steps back. Progress was stalling fast and the previous victory over QPR was papering over the cracks. The final whistle was greeted by boos from the travelling fans and the after-match airwaves were filled with callers demanding the club act on its perilous position – one point above Reading, who were in the relegation zone with a game in hand.

Keane was in a brighter mood than the previous day when he exited the dressing room to face the press, and those expecting a tetchy question and answer, cut short by an angry exchange and a quick march out of the building, were left disappointed as he worked through the rights and wrongs of the performance.

'We live in the real world,' he said. 'We defend each other but when you have three thousand fans here to see you, you must be better. It is not good players that get you out of trouble, it is characters and in the last 25 minutes I never felt we were going to get back into it. I have defended the players this season as they have always given their all, but we died out in the second half and I need to put my finger on why tonight and we must do more. You can have 90 per cent of the possession but if you don't score and don't defend set-pieces you will lose games. There is no hiding place. In any walk of life you have got to show some character and we had none.'

Keane's assessment of needing character rather than quality to get out of their predicament was alarming, for there was no shortage of endeavour and effort from his side during the season. It was the quality they were lacking – quality from set-pieces, quality defending set-pieces and the quality to open the opposition up in open play and finish off the openings. Were they short of quality because of the players within the squad? Or was it the way the team had been moulded and its tactical instruction?

The squad had certainly cost enough to assemble and owner Marcus Evans had enough evidence to say enough was enough. With 16 matches remaining in the season there was time for a new manager to come in and bail the water out of the leaky and slowly sinking ship. Keane, however, could point to his record of four defeats in the last 21 matches. Progress was in short supply because when they did play well it was in patches and their lack of sustainability over 90 minutes was turning possible draws into defeats and, most importantly, victories into draws, allowing teams around them in the table to catch up and overtake with a single result. Six victories in 30 league games was a chronic situation and one that Keane had found himself in earlier in the season when Town were breaking the wrong kind of records. His straight-talking style was still accepted by a large quota of the fans, but, with the club back in the mire, it was wearing thin again for many.

In the days following the Peterborough defeat, there were few excuses for one of the poorest results in years. Full-back Liam Rosenior told the press the loss was 'embarrassing', while skipper Jon Walters issued an apology to the fans. Keane refused to shy away from the blame and continued to play the media game with a straight bat in the lead up to the third of Town's four away matches on the trot. He admitted the fans had every right to have lost patience with both him and his side, particularly after the final 20 minutes at London Road.

'The buck stops with the manager, absolutely. I pick the players, I pick the systems, make the substitutions and it's not been good enough so far this season,' he admitted. 'Whatever decisions I've been trying to make just haven't been falling into place, and that comes down to the manager. I've never shied away from that. We get all the stats of second-half performances and I think we're the second worst (in the division) and that's not good enough. Our fitness levels are very, very good, there's no doubt about that, but maybe the players get tentative or get a bit nervous because we had such a bad start to the season and start stepping back a bit rather than being on the front foot. Then you invite trouble on your-self.'

Defeat at Sheffield Wednesday could have had drastic consequences, especially if it was heavy. But again Keane and his side found strength, resolve and a result at a time when the pressure was at its most severe. They were helped by facing another side in need, with Wednesday also scrapping for their lives, just a point ahead of Town and going into the game on the back of a 0-2 home defeat by Doncaster. The match itself at Hillsborough, on a freezing Saturday in front of more than 21,000, was like 22 men trying to move through treacle. The pitch was rutted and a bane for anyone trying to keep the ball on the ground. In the end it suit-ed Town, for they were able to conjure up the one successful move of the match when Carlos Edwards, recalled for the first time in a month, unleashed an arrow of a shot from 20 yards which flew past keeper Lee Grant.

It wasn't pretty, but the 1-0 win meant Town were out of the relega-tion zone, and that was all that mattered for Keane and the club. There was certainly little quality on display, from either team, and having said character would be the key to keeping them up, it was that which sent Town on the journey home happy with three points in tow. Keane had made expected changes, with Brian Murphy making his long-awaited debut in goal in place of Lee-Barrett, who had performed reasonably but was never destined to be the club's regular number one, and 19-year-old Shane O'Connor made his League debut at left-back. Edwards took over from Owen Garvan, who was dropped from the squad, and David Wright was back in for Rosenior, who was ill.

Murphy was called into action after just 12 seconds, making the first of three excellent saves, but otherwise Town were able to deal with the long balls and aimless attacks posed by Wednesday, who provoked hos-tility from the home crowd throughout the game. Daryl Murphy hit the post from close range in the first half and Edwards should have made it two in the second when Town broke clear in a three-on-one situation. Walters's late header was disallowed for a mystery push but it failed to dampen the day for Town.

The result relaxed Keane and he was composed after the game when he faced the press. 'The game should have been dead and buried and we put ourselves under pressure by missing chances,' he said. 'What you've seen today has been the problem all season. We haven't been killing the game off with the second and third goals. We were hurt by the criticism from the defeat at Peterborough and I was pleased with the way the play-ers bounced back from that.'

I spoke to Carlos Edwards after his match-winning goal – his first strike for almost three years – and there was no sign of tension or pressure. The Trindad & Tobago international laughed and smiled as he told of his wife-to-be in the Caribbean, and how she would have to stay there now he had ended his goal-drought. Edwards spoke up for his manager, as all of the Town players had done since Keane took over, in the knowledge that anyone who stepped out of line would not play again while he was in charge. Edwards was open enough to say it was as much down to the manager to scratch the players' backs as it was the players to scratch the manager's. So far, the players had not been doing it for Keane. But nor was Keane being fair to the players, given his constant chopping and changing of systems and line-ups.

Keane appeared to have learned the error of his ways when he named an unchanged line-up for only the second time of the season when Town went to Scunthorpe United three days later. It was the final game of the testing run of four away matches on the trot and a 1-1 draw gave them an encouraging record of seven points from a possible 12.

They had opened the season unable to gain even a solitary victory, but were now able to go on an unbeaten away run – the drawn matches were hampering them, though, and the point gained at Glanford Park was their 16th draw of the season. It was far from a classic, as Scunthorpe's Cliff Byrne gave the home side the lead with a close-range header in the 69th minute, before substitute David Healy poached his first Town from inside the penalty area four minutes later.

Keane predicted it would be the first of many goals for Healy in a Town shirt, giving further credence to the belief that the Northern Irishman would be part of his first-choice strike partnership for the remainder of the season. 'It was a real poacher's goal from David and he is capable of that,' said Keane. 'All good goalscorers score a majority of their goals around the six-yard box. I think once a goalscorer, always a goalscorer, and I think he probably just needs a run of games. He's got a decent goal record. Obviously you look at what happened with him at Fulham and Sunderland and sometimes for a striker it doesn't work at a club. I've known David from my younger days at Manchester United and he's a goalscorer. You try and find the right level and he's just come a little bit short in the Premiership, but that's no insult to any goalscorer. He will probably say he's also not had a run of games. Listen, if you've scored that amount at international level it says a lot about you.'

The end of the away-day trawl had seen the pressure lift off Keane, whose team had claimed seven points from four away games. With a run of five home matches in the next eight fixtures, Town were expected to

make quick progress up the table. The final game of the month saw
Bristol City come to Portman Road on 27 February and it was a chance
to see if Keane's prediction of a goal-glut from Healy would come true.
However, it was a frustrating day for Healy, and for every Town player, as
they came up against an inspired goalkeeper in Dean Gerken.

Keane recalled Healy to the starting line-up and brought another loanee – Rosenior – back into the 11 at the expense of David Wright and
Shane O'Connor, which saw Colback move into the left-back role to
mark former Town man Danny Haynes. A dour first half failed to inspire
the home fans who had been starved of action for a couple of weeks. All
the optimism from the away-days points haul was seeping out of Town
as they made difficult work of breaking down a mid-table Robins side,
unable to put the ball in front of the jet-heeled Haynes.

City almost went in front when Chris Iwelumo headed against the
crossbar, aided by the fingertips of Brian Murphy. Luckily, for those doz-
ing off in their seats and already deciding not to renew season tickets
despite a price freeze, the second half was far livelier. Gerken denied
Gareth McAuley his fourth goal of the season with a wonderful finger-
tip save, while Colback saw his stabbed effort come back off the post
after Leadbitter had put him in the clear. Town slipped into some of their
best play for weeks but there was no way past Gerken, or so it seemed.
Substitute Wickham hurled a last-minute throw into the box, only for
Gerken to miss his attempted punch. The Portman Road crowd rose as
the ball bounced into the net, but referee Nigel Miller correctly deemed
the ball did not touch any player on its way in. It ended goalless.

Town's failure to beat the unbeatable keeper – who later claimed he
meant to miss his punch – was not down to poor finishing, according to
Keane, who was pleased with his side, despite having plenty to say at half-
time – as revealed afterwards by McAuley. Keane said: 'He [Gerken] was
brilliant and sometimes you have to praise the opposition. I couldn't wait
to get the team in at half-time because we couldn't have been any worse
in the first half. We waited for something to happen. You've got to make
it happen. We were completely different in the second half. The players
were outstanding but we just couldn't put the ball in the net. It's a clean
sheet, so that's another positive but it's another draw and that's incredibly
frustrating.'

It was frustrating for all, but at least Town had shown fight and the
desire to score in the second half, which had been lacking throughout the
season. They found a passing rhythm replacing the long balls forward and
with it came the backing of the crowd. The result moved Town up to
17th in the table and it could have been as high as 15th had they found

the goal – a problem Stead had no trouble with, as he netted his first goal for Coventry in their 2-1 victory over Scunthorpe. It reopened debate over his move away from Town, whether a club seeking promotion to the Premier League but instead battling relegation should be loaning out their top scorer, and in turn have to rely on a 16-year-old without a League goal to come off the bench and inspire a side struggling to score goals. For all of Wickham's hustle and bustle, and his obvious potential, he was not finding the net in his cameos.

Financially, the books needed to be balanced, and chief executive Simon Clegg stated that Stead and Alex Bruce had to move on for Town to bring in Daryl Murphy and Healy during the transfer window. He said it would have been 'economic madness' for the club to bring in the Sunderland pair and keep high-earners Bruce, Stead and Tamas Priskin, who was still searching for his first goal at Queens Park Rangers. Clegg confirmed there was still money in the budget if Keane wanted to bring in another player before the end of the season and the Town manager had made it clear there were two areas he wanted to strengthen. These were likely to be centre-half and left-back, although the form of Colback, who was outstanding against Bristol City, weakened the need to fill the left-hand side. Town were no longer being linked with any big names in the footballing world like they were when Marcus Evans first took over. The Giovani Dos Santos's were a thing of the past, replaced by the names of unknown trialists and any player who had previously played under Keane.

Town's lack of a promotion push was costing them in the transfer market, and Keane's name lacked the pull for players around the globe, with the club at the wrong end of the table. Murphy and Healy had come down from the Premier League because they had no future at Sunderland, who themselves were being dragged into a relegation scrap. If Town were to prove attractive once more, they were going to have to spend the last third of the season climbing away from the drop zone and into mid-table, with the look of a side which was going to continue their momentum into the next season.

Chapter Eleven

March 2010

'I THINK SOMETIMES IT'S GOOD TO GO A BIT MAD. I DON'T THROW
TEACUPS, I THINK I'D RATHER THROW PUNCHES!'

As spring began to warm minds and souls chilled by the frosty football served up during winter, Roy Keane's position appeared safe, however bad their season would turn out. Relegation would be a different
matter, of course, but while Town were still in the Championship, Keane
would see them through to the end of the season. His backing from the
club was spoken through his transfer dealings, although their significance,
with players having to leave in order for new ones to come in, represented a clear weakening of his position.

The patience of the fans was extraordinary. It had not just been a bad
season results-wise, the football itself was mundane and the general experience of going to Portman Road or following the club on their travels
was depressing. For Keane to keep the backing of the fans, he needed to
turn his team into a winning machine during the final couple of months.
His public persona was helping to keep the faithful onside and the media
had also warmed to him after the early run-ins. Jim Magilton had found
out that mediocre results and performances led to calls not only from the
terraces but from the local newspapers for him to go. Yet Keane was
being given an easy ride by comparison, despite results having proved
worse than they were under his predecessor.

Keane admitted he was loving life in Suffolk – another view which
went down well with the proud locals – and was understood to be moving from his home in Aldeburgh to a property in the Woodbridge area.
'We love it, really nice, we're settled in,' he said. 'The kids are happy, the
dogs are happy, I'm happy, the wife's happy, results could be better.'

His revelation that Town would be doing very little training between
the beginning of March and the end of the season raised eyebrows in the
build-up to Town's trip to Blackpool. 'There won't be any training over
the next few months, in terms of the lads involved in the first team,' he
said. 'They will be playing Saturday, Tuesday, Saturday, Tuesday, until the
end of the season. Game Tuesday, then Wednesday will be recovery,
Thursday will probably be off, and Friday we might work through a few
set-pieces, and just get ready.'

The modern obsession with match fitness, diet, rest and anything sci-
entifically related to football was one thing, but Town had made it

through to March and were not looking like a team which was at ease with themselves. Keane was pointing at seven forthcoming fixtures in the next 22 days, and his experiences of training as a professional footballer gave him more than enough fuel to back himself up against anyone who questioned his decision.

If there was an area which needed working on, it was Town's finishing, and whether they were practising on the training pitch or not, they were having terrible trouble hitting the target during games. It had left them with just a 0-0 draw against Bristol City. It cost them again at Blackpool, as Town's trip to the seaside was anything but memorable, against a side they had already beaten twice earlier in the season. Jason Euell netted the only goal after half-time. Town lost 0-1 and were left ruing a hatful of missed chances on a bumpy pitch. The visitors gave Blackpool a helping hand in the execution, when Gareth McAuley headed on a long throw straight into Euell's path eight yards out.

Keane had made just one change to the starting line-up, bringing Jaime Peters in for David Healy, which saw Jon Walters, still Town's topscorer along with Stead on six, move up front. Peters ended up featuring at left-back, on the left of midfield, and even up front during the 90 minutes as Keane shuffled his pack throughout, throwing on Pablo Counago, Connor Wickham and Healy to find an equaliser. A mixture of bad finishing and decent goalkeeping from Matthew Gilks kept them out, though. Daryl Murphy, who had missed a number of opportunities since his last goal – at Peterborough four games previously – was the main culprit, with Walters, Healy and Wickham also presented with scoreable chances. To cap a day to forget, Leadbitter picked up his tenth booking of the season (for a foul), meaning he would miss the next two matches, much to the annoyance of Keane, who had spoken of the midfielder's bad habit of picking up bookings for dissent. To make matters worse, Jon Stead had also scored again for Coventry.

The defeat took Town down to 18th in the table, and a point above the relegation zone as Sheffield Wednesday and Crystal Palace both won. Keane said the defeat was like 'Groundhog Day' and lamented his side's poor finishing and habit of giving away a bad goal, saying the combination was 'criminal'. He locked the players in the dressing room for 50 minutes after the final whistle and was bristling with anger when he finally emerged to face the waiting press.

Town's situation was not as desperate as it had been in February when they faced four away games on the trot. The league table was tightening by the week, with three points separating Sheffield Wednesday in 22nd and Queens Park Rangers in 16th. Two more victories and the words

'Town' and 'relegation' would no longer be uttered together in the same sentence. However, they were still to record back-to-back victories in the league and had not scored in 197 minutes of football going into the visit of Cardiff City at Portman Road three days after the Blackpool defeat.

Keane's frustration with Leadbitter failed to blow over. He had warned the former Sunderland player of the risk of being booked again before they headed to the North West. 'Grant's an important player for us, so we're not happy about it,' he said. 'I've no problem with players getting booked for tackling people, particularly in the middle of the park, but three or four for dissent is a lot of bookings. We give players the benefit of the doubt once or twice, but three or four means we'll be missing an important player for a massive part of the season. Grant's got no one to blame but himself and he's getting very little sympathy from me.'

Leadbitter wasn't the only player to earn Keane's wrath, as the Town manager found words of criticism for what seemed like most of his squad. 'You keep persevering, keep working on the training field,' he said. 'We're limited in some positions at the club and certain players will continue to play, but they need to learn and it doesn't look like they're doing that at the moment. We're not making it hard for teams to score against us. Whatever's happening with the strikers – and we're trying to deal with that by bringing in new players and by trying different combinations – the defenders have to take responsibility. We can criticise the defenders for not defending properly, but when our strikers and our midfielders get into shooting positions, they should at least hit the target. To say it is frustrating is an understatement.'

Keane's honesty was to be saluted but defeat to Cardiff would have seen his words wearing thin. He had proved that he could talk the talk, but the paying fans and Marcus Evans were more interested in what was happening on the pitch, not Keane's sound-bites. He had no trouble explaining the reasons for Town's lack of points, but was finding it hard to come up with a way of altering the recurring problems. The constant switching of strikers was getting them only so far and, apart from Brian Murphy in goal, Gareth McAuley and Damien Delaney in the centre of defence and David Norris and Leadbitter in central midfield, the rest of the team was a lottery not worth playing. Keane denied he was 'sticking his head in the sand' and said he 'lived in the real world' as he admitted to feeling the pressure and glare of taking Town through their disastrous campaign.

His performance as Town manager was far from disastrous, according to Cardiff manager Dave Jones, who stuck up for the Irishman before the game. He was convinced Town would be a decent side under Keane, given time. 'Ipswich aren't doing as well as they expected, but in their case they brought in a new manager, new players came in and had to bed in,' he said. 'There were high expectation levels, but things don't happen overnight. When Roy went in, everybody assumed that was it, crash, bang, wallop, here we go, we're going to be fantastic. You've still got to earn the right and get the right players and that takes time. He's basically on the first rung of that ladder. His playing career has nothing to do with his managerial career. His playing career stands him in good stead because of what he's done and the dressing rooms he's been involved with. But it doesn't mean that because you've been a fantastic player that it's all going to fall right. You've still got to earn it and Roy certainly did that at Sunderland. He earned the right as a manager. His team didn't do well at Sunderland because he was a good player, it was because he was a good manager. And that's what he will do at Ipswich – he will prove he's a good manager.'

Jones's assessment did not look wide of the mark after Cardiff were easily beaten 0-2 by Town in what was one of their most accomplished displays of the season. On this kind of form, there was no suggestion of Town being dragged into the relegation zone, or Keane's position coming under threat, as they performed like a side in the top six – which Cardiff were at the time. It begged the question: why could they not play like this more often? The scoreline flattered Cardiff, who relied on the agility of keeper David Marshall, while Town's transfer target Michael Chopra was largely kept quiet and was lucky to stay on the pitch when he landed a boot to the head of Owen Garvan.

The night belonged to Daryl Murphy, the striker Town were able to bring in after attempts to land Chopra failed to get off the ground. Murphy ended his mini goal-drought with two close-range finishes to silence the increasing and repetitive number of post-match callers to radio shows who were saying Town were lacking a 20-goal a season striker. It moved Murphy's tally on to five from eight matches. The night was not so successful for Healy, who lasted an hour before being replaced by Counago. The match was over by then and Keane's tinkering, which featured four changes from the Blackpool line-up, worked. Liam Rosenior was axed from the 18, David Wright was preferred to Peters at right-back, Shane O'Connor made his home debut at left-back, Garvan replaced Leadbitter in midfield and Healy started in place of Edwards. Town were always in control, mainly through the controlled passing of Garvan, who Keane finally entrusted with a berth in the centre of the pitch. The team was balanced with two left-footers on the left side, a left and right-footed centre-half combination, and Walters in his best position on the right of midfield. The victory moved Town back up to 17th in the table and four points away from the relegation zone.

Keane's attitude to his side's performance was a downer on a rare happy night for Town. 'I'm still grumpy,' he said. 'We know what the players are capable of and they haven't done it enough this season.' He then went on to joke that he should not be paid and should just stay at home instead. 'It's nothing to do with me, I've decided that. It's nothing to do with the manager, it's up to the players. I'm telling you now. It's up to the players. They'll decide where we're going as a football club. I shouldn't be getting paid. I should stay at home and come in and watch the games!'

Keane was, naturally, pleased with Murphy. He said the move to Town had given the striker a 'new lease of life' and added that he could have been in double figures already with the number of chances that had come his way.

It was another step in the right direction, but for Town to be considered, at the very least, a reasonable team, they would need to claim the back-to-back victories which had eluded them. The Jekyll and Hyde nature of Keane's tactics and selection was depriving Town of any consistency. They were by no means a dreadful team and their record over the past three months showed they were not whipping boys. It was time to find out if they could step up another level, take six points from a possible six and banish relegation fears for good. The defence was standing strong, Murphy was proving a wise acquisition up front, and if another player could find a regular way to goal, Town would be threatening midtable, unless their habitual affliction of following a good performance and victory with a mundane draw or error-ridden defeat reared its head once more.

It had been a while since Keane picked an argument in public, and when the opportunity arose he refused to back down. Prior to Scunthorpe's visit to Portman Road on 13 March, their manager Nigel Adkins claimed Town were still in with a chance of making the play-offs. Keane saw it as Adkins playing mind games – a tactic he said was being played on a regular basis when Scunthorpe faced sides above them in the table. 'He's talking rubbish,' said Keane. 'He's playing a game, so when Scunthorpe come to Ipswich all the pressure's on us because we 'should be in the play-offs'. He's talking nonsense. It's stupid talk. He should look after his own team. Absolute rubbish. It's just mind games. If he thinks I'm going to fall for that he's mistaken, people shouldn't underestimate my own experiences in football. He plays that every week and it works for him with other clubs, but it won't work against us. I don't mind it the odd time and he can do it with other managers, but to try to do it with me, he's kidding himself. We're down there the same as them, it's not as if he's going off to play Real Madrid.'

Keane had been as subdued as many of his side's performances during the last few months but his rant at Adkins turned out to be the prelude to a feisty clash in which Town finally ended their back-to-back victory hoodoo. And in doing so they avoided notching their 18th draw of the season – a club record. Scunthorpe came for a draw and so very nearly achieved their aim, until a dramatic finale – not quite on the same heart-stopping level as the Coventry game, but exciting nonetheless – saw Town clinch all three points.

Only one change was made to the side which beat Cardiff, with Counago starting in place of David Healy, as Keane exhibited a level of satisfaction in his players. Scunthorpe's time-wasting started in the first few minutes, which wound up the home crowd, who were just as irritated by the bizarre decision-making of referee Pat Miller. Counago hit the bar with a close-range header in what was a forgettable first half. The game came to life when Cliff Byrne was sent off for elbowing Colback off the ball, only for Delaney to follow him down the tunnel ten minutes later when his trip on Jonathan Forte, in full flight on the halfway line, was deemed serious foul play.

What was seen as justice by the neutrals arrived in injury-time when substitute Connor Wickham twisted and turned on the edge of the penalty area and found a hole in the Scunthorpe defence. After worming his way through, he arrived ten yards out with only keeper Joe Murphy to beat, and fired home to send Portman Road wild, with Town's substitutes and coaching staff celebrating in front of the Britannia Stand. It was Wickham's first League goal and it made him the club's second youngest League scorer after Jason Dozzell. It was a goal of true quality and came two weeks before he was due to sign his first professional contract.

It was a scrappy game, the type of which Town had struggled to win throughout the season, yet Keane was not getting carried away afterwards – either by the result or the goalscoring saviour. 'I was surprised by the way it opened up for him and it was a good time to score,' he said. 'But it remains to be seen if he's a natural finisher. We'll know in the next few years. There are pitfalls for lots of players, whether it be other clubs coming in, women, drugs or bad injuries. That's why I've never been one for getting carried away with Connor.'

It was a fairytale moment for the 16-year-old and brought back memories of Dean Bowditch's hat-trick at Portman Road against Watford in March 2004 when he was 17. Wickham's winner took Town up to 17th and six points above the drop zone. Only two goals had been conceded in their last six matches. Scunthorpe's style represented a shift from the mindset of visiting teams of the previous 12 months. Visiting sides believed they had a decent chance of taking all three points and it had been two years since teams had come and parked the proverbial bus in front of the goal. In McAuley and Delaney, whose red card was appealed against, Town had a solid unit, and in O'Connor and Wright, Keane had found faith in a pair of full-backs, both of whom were playing on their natural flank. It was coincidental that Town picked up six points from a possible six while Leadbitter was suspended, but it gave Garvan a chance to re-emerge as a midfield force.

Everyone was left talking about the boy wonder Wickham, not whether Delaney would be cleared to face Watford at Vicarage Road three days later. David Wright talked Wickham up as a future England international and likened him to retired West Ham striker Dean Ashton, for his physique and composure. Keane was having none of it, saying there was almost everything to still be worked on. 'His left foot, his head-ing, his hold-up play, his movement, his awareness of what's around him, but that's only natural for a 16-year-old,' he said. 'I suppose his biggest strength is his strength. He's a strong boy in the gym and if anything he'll probably have to ease off on that side of it because you can get too bulky, you can get too big and as a striker he needs that mobility more than any other player on the pitch.'

Wickham's heroics earned him a starting role at Watford, one of Town's biggest bogey teams, having not beaten them since 2004. And that run was extended from ten to 11 matches on what was one of Town's darkest nights of the season. It was not so much the 1-2 defeat and the end of the two-match winning run which sparked such apathy towards Keane and his side, but the manner in which they turned up and failed to show any intent on winning the game and matching a Watford side below them in the table.

The press waited and waited, and waited a while longer for Keane to leave the dressing room after the game.

'We expected him out within about 15 minutes,' said Matt Plummer, among the waiting contingent. 'There were three or four of us who were allowed right down the end of the tunnel where the changing rooms were and we were waiting and waiting with a steward. For some games we would wait half an hour for him but this time it was past 11 o'clock and at one point he came out of the changing room and went into another room and you could see from the look on his face that he was seething and that strong words had been exchanged. When he did come out he was not in a good mood. It was one of those after-match talks where if there was one question he did not like he would react badly. The steward said pizza had been ordered but they could not take it into the dressing room. I watched the players walk out past us that night and they look quite shell-shocked by what had happened. I spoke to Jack Colback and he was OK but you could tell they were hurt and it was not pleasant in there. I wonder whether some of them, even the experienced players, had seen anything like that before. Peterborough away was similar to that night. Strangely, sometimes at home he was more relaxed after a defeat than he was after a win. We didn't expect Watford to be such a late night, given it's one of the closest grounds.'

Some reporters received ten word answers to their questions, and others were given the honour of just one or two as Keane made no attempt to hide his anger. 'We kicked the ball out of play after three seconds, and it set the tone for the night,' he fumed. 'We'll need to spend hours and hours now on the training pitch just practising kick-offs. It's unbelievable. It's a joke. We were rubbish and it's hard to take with Liam Rosenior committing a silly foul early on that led to their first goal. Both goals we conceded were poor, after I decided to freshen things up by making the changes. But it did not happen and they say that changing a winning team can be wrong and this is what happened tonight.'

The changes were indeed strange, given Town's two victories and clean sheets in their last two games. David Wright was omitted from the 18-man squad, with Rosenior coming back in, having not made the bench against Scunthorpe. Wickham replaced Counago, while midfield battler Norris was dropped to the bench for a rest, with Leadbitter returning. The severity of Town's first-half display was summed up by Keane's decision to make a substitution only 22 minutes into the game. Garvan was the player to get the chop, although it could have been any one of the ten outfield players. 'Owen came off because he was not doing well enough but he was not the only one and I wish I could have changed the rules about using three substitutes and made more changes,' said Keane. 'I called our performance criminal the other week and it was a similar thing tonight and it was the most frustrated I have been this season and there have been some frustrating games.'

Keane's tinkering had brought Town fans back to earth with a bump, just when optimism was reaching a season's high. They were left wondering why he brought on Lee Martin – Town's worst player of the season up to that point, given his transfer fee – in place of Garvan, who, although not renowned for his doggedness, had been part of a winning team and on his day was arguably the club's most influential player. Norris, meanwhile, was left kicking his heels on the bench, when his tenacity would have been ideal in such a rugged away clash. Jaime Peters was not in the 18, despite being the pick of the starting 11 the last time he played, at Blackpool. Further substitutions did not arrive until the 80th minute, by which time Town had gone behind to a long-distance Henri Lansbury free-kick, which had eluded everyone, including keeper Brian Murphy, before Colback equalised from close range, only for Will Hoskins to net the winner with 14 minutes remaining to round off a dismal night. The players' haunted faces said it all when they emerged from their lecture.

Matters on the pitch were not the only concern when it was reported that Marcus Evans was financing the running of the club from his other businesses and if he was to walk away, the club would potentially be in a very deep hole. 'Very few Championship clubs break even and Ipswich Town is no different,' said chief executive Simon Clegg. 'Money is moving across regularly from the owner's other companies into the football club. No one should underestimate what he is doing for this club.'

The defeat kick-started speculation in the national press, with Evans reported to be set for a meeting with Keane before the end of the season. Keane denied such a meeting was due to take place, but did little to quell his profile both in the print media and on television with some colourful remarks before Town lined up at Portman Road against Barnsley. It showed the Town manager was hurt by the result and lame performance and that he demanded and expected so much more from his players.

How many times could they take the hairdryer treatment, though? Their nerve-ridden displays had already cost them many points and the manager's voice had only just stopped ringing in their ears from the last verbal bashing. For Keane, who was once punched by Brian Clough while at Nottingham Forest, there were no problems stemming from his anger. Clough's right-hook was the best thing he did to Keane, according to the Irishman. 'Anger's good,' he said. 'It's good to get angry. It's an emotion, it's part of the game. If people upset you and you don't get angry, then I think you're in the wrong game. I think sometimes it's good to go a bit mad. I don't throw teacups, I think I'd rather throw punches! Obviously, I appreciate those days are gone, you can't be going around assaulting people, but I can understand managers' frustrations when they fall out with players.'

Keane's frustration with a number of his players boiled over in the Portman Road media suite when he launched a tirade at their approach on their travels. Almost 45 minutes had elapsed by the time he came up for air and moved on. 'It's the away games that are the problem,' he said.

'Some of our players don't like travelling, they miss the home comforts of their dressing room. You look at our away record compared with our home record. The results will tell you that we're a home team. It's a comfort zone when you're at home. Strange, but we'll get it sorted out, don't worry. I'd like to chat with the previous manager who was here. There's players here that I believe the previous manager fell out with and I can understand why 100 per cent. I look at some of the senior players who have been here for a number of years because they are the ones who know the ins and outs of the club. I look at Pablo Counago, Gareth McAuley, Jon Walters. These type of players have to lead the way because they know the fabric of the club. They should have an understanding of why the team has not pushed for the play-offs over the last few years. It's clear we have talented players but talent alone won't get you in the top six. There are certain players who are making the same mistakes week in, week out. They're the ones who'll take you nowhere fast and I'm aware of that and we'll sort it out.'

It was no surprise that he picked out Counago, a player Magilton failed to work out when playing away from home. The Spaniard was a bit-part player, a talent who could turn it on in an instant, but not often enough for Keane to appreciate. Walters, meanwhile, was a fading force. Handed the captaincy, his body language told of a player who had lost his mojo. Physically, he looked a wreck. The soaring jumps and endless energy from two seasons ago was gone, replaced by a wounded soldier struggling to make it into scoring positions and seldom running in behind defences. His aerial ability had waned, the image of diagonal balls being arrowed towards him on the right touchline under Jim Magilton a distant memory. Instead of feeding off his knock-downs and aiming deep crosses at him at the far post, the ball was coming back Town's way and possession was being lost. McAuley was found wanting as a leader, but was playing his best football without the weight of the captain's armband. In releasing McAuley from the strain, Walters had taken it on and was floundering, his legs looked exhausted and his heart appeared drained of all of its reserves. He was not a vocal captain, roaring on his team-mates and motivating them if they went behind, and nor was he leading by example. Under Keane, however, he was untouchable and undroppable.

Walters was not among the four players who were dropped for the visit of Barnsley. It was a question of how many changes Keane would make and Rosenior, Leadbitter, Garvan and Wickham all made way, for David Wright, Carlos Edwards, Norris and surprisingly, Counago. For the doubters and speculation to go away again, Keane needed both a result and a performance. Statistically, there were far worse teams in the division than Town over the course of the last few months. The lack of excitement and painfully slow progress was bringing miserable faces to Portman Road, and the lock-ins and embarrassing results were unsettling for all.

The result was the right one for Keane, but Town fans did not see the performance they were asking for. It could have been no worse than at Watford, but scraping to a 1-0 victory over Barnsley was not what was in mind when Keane was appointed. Despite a Counago-inspired first 15 minutes, during which Daryl Murphy netted with the goal at his mercy after the Spaniard robbed keeper Luke Steele on the touchline and saw his shot come back off the post, Town faded and went into their shell. Come the last 20 minutes, they had retreated to the edge of their own penalty area and were pumping long, aimless balls forward at 16-year-old lone striker Wickham.

The result was vitally important as it took Town eight points away from the relegation zone. It left a bad taste in the mouth, because of the manner in which they held on and played the second half as if they were the away team. For Town fans brought up on the goal mania of the 1990s, it was difficult to believe they were watching a side that cost so much to bring together, and was paid so highly.

Keane was relaxed afterwards and pleased with his day's work. He admitted the crowd was treated to an unattractive spectacle but performance came second to the result in their current league position. Town fans expected more, and Keane had ignored the club's principles in his bid to achieve the ultimate goal. He could point to his tactics – taking off Counago and strike partner Daryl Murphy and going with one up front – as a success as Town won. It was a fine margin and one which could easily have backfired, and he had a few words for the media's coverage of all things connected with Roy Keane. 'I think there's been a reaction over the last few days – as there always is regarding myself – really over the top stuff about me locking players in dressing rooms, as if other managers haven't done it. Me pressing panic buttons, a load of nonsense, certain players will never play for the club again, really negative stuff the last few days which has really disappointed me from certain parts of the media, but then again that shouldn't surprise me.'

It was noticed by Keane himself that the tide seemed to be turning against him at a time when Town were actually winning matches, rather than persistently drawing and losing as they had been earlier in the season. The feeling that Keane was not the man to take Town forward was still evident, even after a home victory and Town's fourth clean sheet in six matches.

The panic button was ever closer when Town legend Paul Mariner returned to Portman Road as manager of Plymouth Argyle three days later. With Argyle second from bottom, Town normally would have been expected to ease past their lowly opponents, scoring two, three, maybe four goals in the process and keeping the crowd in the ground for the full 90 minutes. In fact, the only occasion the Town fans applauded was when Mariner walked onto the pitch before kick-off, waving and bowing in front of thousands who regarded him as one of the club's greatest ever strikers. It brought back memories of Town's glory days in the late 1970s and early 1980s when they were feared domestically, and around Europe.

Mariner's appearance provided a stark and disturbing contrast. The Town of today were beaten 0-2 and were booed off at half-time and at full-time when the subdued boos echoed limply around a half-empty stadium. Long-time season-ticket holders who had been staying until the final whistle for decades had left early, while chants of 'what a load of rubbish' spilled out of the Sir Bobby Robson Stand. As the game petered out the criticism of the players, be it for a misplaced pass or general lack of adventure, subsided. It was as though nobody cared. The season was dead and the manager had taken the club nowhere. Delaney and Garvan handed Plymouth their two goals with individual errors. Town forced Argyle keeper David Stockdale into at least four decent saves, yet there was no conviction in their efforts.

As much as the finger was pointed at the players for their contribution to another low point in a season of lows, Keane was also culpable for the new depth to which the club had plunged. He named an unchanged side for only the third time of the season. Come half-time, any one of eight outfield players could have been taken off, such was Town's lack of shape, creativity and alarming lack of an alternative plan to find a way past a Plymouth side big on effort and short on quality. Wide men Carlos Edwards and Walters were tucked in on the flanks, creating a congested midfield that played into Plymouth's hands. Norris and Colback's lack of invention was badly shown up as Town repeatedly passed the ball sideways and backwards before McAuley or Delaney hit it long. Counago produced the pass of the game to put Murphy in on goal and the Spaniard was promptly substituted. His exit was greeted by a chant of his name – aimed at Keane rather than the player.

Amazingly, it was Town's first home defeat since September, a fact Keane was quick to inform the press of, and, this time around, they were able to grab a word with the Town manager before 11pm, even though the display merited an inquest into what had gone wrong. 'There will be the usual over-reaction but we have to remember it was our first home defeat since September,' said Keane. 'We huffed and puffed but became a bit predictable. The word tonight is frustration, rather than anger. Had Plymouth opened us up and scored good goals it would be one thing, but we gave two bad ones away. We had good opportunities but didn't hit the target. That was frustrating and has been a problem all season. We don't score enough goals and are liable to give bad ones away.'

The night began with Mariner as the centre of attention and it ended that way, too. First, he gave away his jacket to a young Town fan, as he made his way back to the tunnel after the final whistle. On arrival back in the dressing room, he realised the garment contained his reading glasses, so an appeal was quickly put out on local radio for the safe return of his spectacles.

Mariner then found himself on the wrong end of Keane's wrath when the Town manager laid into him during an interview three days later. Keane was nothing but praiseworthy for Mariner before his visit, but his failure to go for a drink with the Town manager after the game riled Keane. 'I've no problem with Paul coming back here, but after the game Paul didn't have the decency to come down for a drink with us, to see my staff, to see the opposition manager,' he said. 'He was too busy up here seeing all his mates. You remember these things in football. It's not bad blood because I couldn't have spoken highly enough about Paul before the game, but have the decency to come down for a drink after the game. He found his way up here with Mr Sheepshanks and all them when I invited him for a drink again.'

Town fans were next on Keane's list. He was unhappy with the reaction towards Colback, whose set-pieces repeatedly hit the first defender. Keane said the fans were entitled to their opinions but if they wanted to vent their feelings they had to take them out on him, rather than the club's young players. He felt some of the senior players were given a comparatively easy ride, having their names sung when, in Keane's view, they did not deserve it.

'He [Keane] was almost beginning to dig his own grave by criticising the fans and then Paul Mariner,' said Matt Plummer. 'He was already under pressure, had plenty of doubters and people on his back. Mariner was a legend of the club so it was a real own-goal on Keane's part and an incident which was likely to come back and haunt him.'

Then he turned on the tradition of Ipswich Town Football Club, suggesting it was a soft touch both on and off the pitch. 'The gloves are off,' he told the gathered press pack, who were wondering when he was going to end his selective speeches, and who he was going to target next. 'Maybe we're too nicey nicey. Possibly we are too set in our ways. There's a little bit too much tradition about the place. Tradition is fantastic but maybe we're too polite here. Overall, I think we're too nice.'

Keane was right when he said the club was 'nice'. But being nice and being the Ipswich Town it always had been, built on the tradition of doing things by the book and welcoming all, was how it should remain and how its people, generally, wanted it to remain. It was a club which, up until the arrival of Marcus Evans, had stood the test of time by staying true to its roots, instead of selling itself to the corporate devil eating away at the sport. It had been in touch with the community, the fans and the rest of football, until it became the Roy Keane show. Then it was all about the product, which was propelled around the world thanks to the celebrity at the centre. Keane was knocking the ethos of the club and everything it stood for. His point about it being too nice was not inaccurate. The club's lack of ruthlessness had cost it during the last ten years, be it in the transfer market or on the pitch. Remaining a 'nice club' was going to keep Ipswich Town's identity alive, however. The people of Suffolk resented the stereotypical image of a Leeds United, Millwall or Manchester City, with troublesome fans, constant boardroom unrest and money shipped in via an unknown Arab. They wanted the club to win promotion and be the Ipswich Town they had always been – like when they won promotion to the Premier League, like in 2000-01 when George Burley took them to a fifth-placed finish and back into Europe with largely the same group of players who had won promotion.

Keane was behaving like a man who knew he was in trouble, a man whose managerial career was heading in the wrong direction, and it marked the beginning of a media frenzy. His relationship with the media was about to change, as he put an end to Sky Sports quizzing him on the hot footballing topics of the moment. The decision came prior to Celtic dismissing former Town player and caretaker manager Tony Mowbray, which would have been an obvious subject for Keane, given that he ended his playing career at Celtic and had been linked with the job at Parkhead before.

Keane's role as national football spokesman had done Town few favours. It was Keane's name appearing on Sky Sports News every hour ahead of the weekend rather than the club's name, with Marcus Evans's name in the background on the sponsor boards. It was Keane on tackles in the Premier League, Keane on Premier League managers and Keane on Ireland's World Cup chances, not Keane on Ipswich Town. 'Sky in particular come down here and always focus on what's going on at other football clubs,' he said. 'I think for the next eight games I'm just focusing on what's going on at my own club, because that's the priority for me.

Whatever is going on at other football clubs, I've got enough of my own troubles. I'm a football manager learning my trade and I'm not doing a good enough job at Ipswich and I need to focus on that. I need to focus on my job.'

The banning order on Sky Sports came a day before the strongest hint yet that Keane was about to be sacked. As Town fans made their way to Swansea's Liberty Stadium on Saturday, 27 March, they read widespread reports of Keane's tenure being close to an end. *The Daily Mirror* led the way, reporting that Alan Curbishley was lined up to replace him if Town lost at Swansea. The story, not too dissimilar to reports from a few months previously, claimed Keane's abrasive management style had led to dressing room discontent and senior players were unhappy with his 'savage criticism of youngsters'. It also said Keane's relationship with Evans had soured and that they had stopped communicating – a point no doubt promoted by Keane admitting they rarely spoke, simply because there was no need.

Keane's damning verdict on Paul Mariner's post-match behaviour, for which the Plymouth manager publicly apologised, and his views on the club's tradition and values were expected to bring about a cold reception when he walked out to the touchline on Saturday, March 27. Instead, a small band of Town fans sung his name throughout the goalless draw.

Like on previous occasions, Town followed a disastrous result with an improved showing and were decent value for their point, although it was clear they went to Wales with the intention of stopping their opponents, who were set for a place in the play-offs. Daryl Murphy was selected as a lone striker as Town recorded their 18th draw of the season, equalling the record previously reached in 1990-91. Solid but unspectacular, Town provided little threat going forward. O'Connor, one of Town's best players in recent weeks, was moved forward from left-back to left-wing, allowing Peters to come in at full-back to contend with the pace of Swansea winger Nathan Dyer, while Leadbitter returned to midfield in place of Edwards. Apart from Daryl Murphy, Town's top-scorer on six goals along with Walters, the Town side was full of hard-working but limited players, with the exception of the talented yet out-of-sorts Leadbitter, who, like Walters, had been nowhere near top form for weeks.

The attention was more on Keane than events on the pitch and he gave the travelling support a wave in the second half – his last wave, had Swansea scored, if *The Daily Mirror* was to be believed. The result left Town on 48 points and 16th in the table, nine points above third from bottom Crystal Palace. With six matches left and Town safe, bar a horrendous run-in, Keane had all but succeeded in guiding them away from trouble and up to a more respectable position in the table. The bigger picture was telling a different story, though. At the beginning of the month his position looked safe despite the slow progress. Thirty days on, his team was playing worse than it was back in February, the loan signing of David Healy, predicted to make more of an impact than the out-going Jon Stead, had made no difference as he stayed on the bench, and off the pitch Keane was making all the wrong headlines.

When he spoke after the game, he sounded as though he was ready for the bullet. 'Better managers than me have lost their jobs and if the board want to move me on then that is the name of the game, but I have a wife and five kids and I will be all right. I'm very proud to be manager of Ipswich and, please God that will continue. I'm certainly not fearful of losing my job. I've got a good life but football is massively important to me. I came down to Ipswich to do a job and I don't think I've really started yet. I appreciate that people do get impatient, particularly supporters, but I was pleased with the supporters who travelled down here. They got behind the team and got behind myself and that is very much appreciated.'

The furore surrounding Keane strengthened on Sunday. The clean sheet and merits of a back line containing McAuley, Delaney, and consistency of Murphy in goal were of secondary importance when *The Guardian* revealed it had grounds for stating Keane would be sacked in the next seven days. It said the club's board had run out of patience and an announcement would be forthcoming from the club. Keane had already been linked with the Celtic job, and with his position at Town unstable, a straight swap with Tony Mowbray was on the cards, according to the tabloids.

It took a call from *The East Anglian Daily Times* on Sunday evening for the club to comment, and when chief executive Simon Clegg responded, it was hardly a comforting statement for Keane and the supporters who wanted him to stay and see out what he had started. 'I'm still fully committed to Roy Keane,' said Clegg. 'It has been a disappointing season, but Roy is still building his team. I understand there have been some speculation stories, but Roy is just starting out to get us where we want to be.' Clegg may have been committed to Keane, but what about Evans? The silence was deafening.

Throughout Monday, Town fans were waiting for either the club to make a reassuring statement, or to confirm Keane had indeed been sacked. He still had the backing of a large percentage of fans, who did not want to see the club go down the route of hiring and firing managers as often as the players changed into and out of their kit, a habit other clubs had fallen into without success. They liked Keane's attitude towards winning, his own personal success as a player and his ambition for the club. However, he was dragging the club down and, as all chairmen and owners insisted, any club was bigger than the manager, especially Roy Keane. As loyal as many were, no tears would be shed on the terraces if Keane was not in the dugout.

Clegg eventually reiterated his desire and the club's stance on Keane by Monday evening when a statement was posted on the club's website. 'I'm aware of the media speculation around Roy but the club's stance is the same as it has always been,' he said. 'We remain fully behind the manager and he will be in charge as usual against Reading on Saturday. Some of the stories I have seen over the weekend are complete rubbish, like talk of Roy and Marcus falling out and not talking to each other. Marcus travels the world with his business commitments and speaks to Roy as and when they need to, but it's part of my job to liaise with the manager and we meet or talk two or three times a week, every week. Obviously we are disappointed with the season we have had so far and no one is more disappointed than Roy. Clearly results have to improve but everyone at Ipswich Town is fully focused on achieving that.'

What about beyond the Reading match on Saturday? The suspicion was that Evans was manouvering behind the scenes in the way he did when Jim Magilton was sacked – a new manager was being lined up and the changeover would be swift.

Tuesday brought fresh stories in the papers, which were bombarded by emails and letters from fans wishing to put across their view. The Irish media were also following every cough and splutter in the latest saga in Roy Keane's box-office life. The most damning story came from *The Daily Mirror*, which claimed Keane was 'hanging by a thread' and described Evans as being 'thoroughly disillusioned' with him. It then quoted an unnamed former board member as saying Keane was 'ruining the club' and that the 'mess he left at Sunderland was only just being cleared up'. The players were described as 'frightened' by Keane and after the Watford lock-in an unnamed player was quoted as saying 'You wouldn't treat dogs like it'. It did not end there, as Tony Loughlan, Keane's assistant, came in for criticism, his training sessions branded 'tedious'.

Chapter Twelve

April 2010

'ATTEMPTS ON GOALS IS LIKE GOING TO A NIGHTCLUB. YOU COULD SPEAK TO 50 GIRLS BUT IF YOU'RE GOING HOME ON YOUR OWN IT'S NO GOOD, IS IT? YOU COULD ONLY SPEAK TO ONE AND GO HOME WITH HER!'

Instead of stewing over what may or may not happen in the future, be that immediately or 12 months down the line, Keane went away for a few days with his family after the 0-0 draw at Swansea, and by the time he returned he was, contrary to media predictions, still in a job. He said the 'speculation' was more disturbing for the players and other members of staff whose futures were also on the line, than for him. The chances of him passing up the opportunity to respond to the damning verdicts on his tenure and the impending end of it were slim.

'I've been down this road before,' he explained as he came face to face with those questioning his suitability to lead the club. 'I had it just before I left Manchester United with a lot of media building up a head of steam about stuff I was supposed to have said, stuff I was supposed to have done. Lies after lies. I had it just before I left Sunderland, more lies there and unfortunately a lot of people got sucked into them and believed them. I've got two years to try and turn the club around and that's my intention.'

Keane's PR skills were in full force when venting his views on a week that saw his face and name fill both national and local press. The Suffolk traditionalists were offended by his comments about the club being 'too nice' because many preferred a club which held on to its values rather than following the likes of others in trying to buy success and whoring themselves to corporate greed.

Although Town possessed the wealthy owner who had spent a considerable sum on new players and an expensive manager, the experience of going to Portman Road was the same as ten years previously, apart from a swipe card entry system at the turnstiles and different goal-celebration music. The team was still playing Championship-class football and the players, although well paid, were not conducting the prima-donna style walkouts as seen in the Premier League. Although the club's roots were slowly being pulled from underneath them, with the owner rarely addressing the fans, they were yet to be subjected to outlandish ticket price rises and the club continued to be at the heart of the community, albeit with a business-orientated edge.

'There's nothing wrong with being nice, my dad always said it's nice to be nice, but you've got to have that nasty streak,' Keane said, rebuilding bridges which would be broken again in future months. 'The nasty streak I meant was at certain times of the game. I don't mean the club or the area or the supporters, because they've been brilliant, but in terms of concentration [on the pitch], we've conceded a lot of late goals and that's when you need a nasty streak. Knowing when to foul somebody, time waste, we see clubs doing it all day, but I think we're generally a naïve team. That's why I say the team's probably lacked one or two characters. I've seen it with other teams and other clubs. It gets to injury time, I wouldn't say [it's] cheating, but there are times when you can take your time with the throw-in. We've had it here a couple of times when clubs have come here and players have been down for four or five minutes and they get up and there's nothing wrong with them. There's a cuteness to it, that's what I meant. I didn't mean the people at the club, but I mean the players need to be more streetwise.'

Keane put across the impression that the future of Connor Wickham was of greater importance than his own after describing talk of a break-down in his own relationship with Evans as 'nonsense'. The young strik-er had netted his second goal in two games for England Under-17s against Slovakia. He left for England duty as a 16-year-old but returned to Ipswich Town aged 17 and able to sign his first professional contract, having been chased by a host of Premier League clubs. Keane confirmed the situation would be revealed during the Easter weekend during which Town would face Reading at home and Derby away and it was announced that Wickham had indeed signed a two-year contract, which, he said after victory over Reading, was 'never in doubt'.

The 2-1 win was the perfect response for Keane, whose side were up to 14th place on 51 points – eight clear of the relegation zone and seem-ingly safe from relegation. Gareth McAuley and Jon Walters scored immediately after Reading's Matt Mills was sent off in the first half for a two-footed tackle on David Norris, before Gylfi Sigurdsson netted a last-minute consolation.

Easter Monday saw an even better performance at Derby County, as Town returned home with a 3-1 victory, taking them up to 13th in the table – respectable considering the depths they had plunged to. Keane avoided the temptation to name an unchanged side from the successful 11 who beat Reading, dropping David Wright and David Healy for Shane O'Connor and Wickham. Two games in the space of three days was chal-lenging physically, but not beyond footballers of 20 years earlier, who were yet to be subjected to squad rotation and buzz words such as 'match fitness' and 'recovery' – a term more likely to represent the time it took to drain the previous night's beer from their system.

The result, thanks to goals from McAuley, Carlos Edwards and a late finish by Wickham after he broke from the halfway line, and the general display were what Keane had been demanding from his team all season. Against an average Derby side, who were reduced to ten men when Stephen Pearson was sent off along with manager Nigel Clough for foul and abusive language, Town were the more threatening side in the first half, held firm when put under increasing pressure after half-time and then caught their opponents on the break at the death. It was the perfect recipe to pick up points away from home, but so often, one or more of the ingredients went missing.

'These are the kind of performances we need,' said Keane. 'We are trying to change the mindset of what Ipswich is seen to be, particularly away from home where we are probably seen as a soft touch and we have got to change that. We need to start turning in performances like that on a regular basis if we are to progress. There was lots going on. Decisions to be made but going away from home and scoring three goals is something we have not done very often this season and it's very rewarding.'

The Easter double and extinction of the threat of relegation cheered Keane up as all talk of him being dismissed had dried up. Now it was a case of seeing out the remainder of the season without disaster and working out how Town could start the following campaign without a record-breaking winless run and hopefully put themselves in the promotion running.

Keane was full of sound-bites ahead of his return to Forest's City Ground, where he expected a few boos because of the fickle nature of football, but was looking forward to rekindling memories of Brian Clough. Asked if he would repeat Clough's habit of kissing people, Keane responded: 'I only kiss my dogs.' He continued to pucker up to the media as he produced an Ian Holloway-esque explanation for Town's lack of firepower, even though Football League statistics showed they had unleashed the most shots in the whole division (347), 31 ahead of second-placed West Brom. 'Attempts on goals is like going to a nightclub, you could speak to 50 girls but if you're going home on your own it's no good, is it? You could only speak to one and go home with her!' said Keane to a gathered media impressed with his analogy. Angry man turned comedian.

The smirk was quickly wiped off the faces of Keane and Town fans, as Nottingham Forest powered to a 3-0 victory after a goalless first half. Keane named an unchanged side for only the fourth time this season, with Pablo Counago and Owen Garvan failing to make the bench. But the players passed up their opportunity to reward his faith after half-time. There was a peculiar tactical switch in the line-up which saw Walters start centrally in midfield, with Leadbitter moved to the right, but it failed to work as Town lacked ideas in the final third and Forest took advantage with goals from Luke Chambers, Guy Moussi and Robert Earnshaw to confirm their place in the play-offs.

While Keane felt the scoreline was 'harsh', he again bemoaned the lack of goals in his team and would have to do without Damien Delaney for the remainder of the season after he suffered a serious ankle injury in the game. At least Town were beaten by a decent side and although the scoreline showed the gap between the side in the top six and Keane's out-fit in the bottom half, it did not leave the bitter taste of the defeats against Watford and Plymouth.

The season was winding down with Town having nothing but pride to play for. Having handed one-year professional contracts to seven academy scholars, Keane was expected to give youth its head before the last ball was kicked. Defender Tom Eastman, from Clacton, had already made the bench. Goalkeeper Brian Murphy was struggling to make the country, let alone the home game against Doncaster on 17 April as he was trapped in Ireland because of the closure of UK airspace due to the ash cloud produced by the Icelandic volcano. 'Last I heard he was in Carlisle at half-nine last night driving with his missus, God help her,' said Keane the day before the game.

Murphy made it back to Suffolk by kick-off but was unable to stop Town setting a new club record with their 19th draw of the season. Wickham's strike was cancelled out ten minutes from the end when Dean Shiels converted a disputed penalty, given against Shane O'Connor for an infringement on the eventual goalscorer. At 1-1, neither side went hell for leather to claim all three points, with both assured of their Championship status. Keane's promise of bringing the youngsters in was preserved, as Tommy Smith replaced the injured Delaney at centre half and Billy Clark made his debut in the final minutes, after being selected on a bench which also included Troy Brown, Eastman and Luke Hyam, alongside Richard Wright who was fit again after his knee injury.

Keane said he was 'not proud' of the new club record and was frustrated by his side's predictability, he also admitted there was a lack of quality on show but these problems would not be rectified until he found a settled side playing in a fluent formation.

Jack Colback had played his part and was named Players' Player of the Year for his contribution from midfield while on loan from Sunderland.

Keane had made no secret of his desire to keep Colback on a more permanent basis. Jaime Peters was named Most Improved Player, while Gareth McAuley won the sponsors and boxholders award and Eastman the Academy prize. Keane put a slight downer on Colback's award despite regarding the red-head 'outstanding', when he went on to say: 'While it was nice for Jack, his contribution to the team has been excellent and I'm sure he enjoyed it, individual awards should mean very little to players, it's all about the team.'

McAuley and Colback were two of a selected few who had been 'carrying the load' according to Kean. He felt the need to publicly voice his disapproval at the contributions of certain members of his squad. 'I think we look back on the season and there have been several players who have done more than their fair share of carrying the load,' he said. 'I look at other players and say 'we need more from you'. I dread to think where we'd be without Jon Walters, Grant, Damien and Gareth. Despite disappointments in certain parts of games, they've been a big part of things. I think David Wright has done well coming in, scoring that goal against Derby, showing good experience, playing left-back and playing right-back. Young Connor Wickham's done more than his share, Brian Murphy was a big boost when he came in, young Jack Colback and David Norris when he came back from his injury. I look at those players and wonder where we might be without them. It's no coincidence that when certain players play in my team the chances of us winning are a lot, lot higher than when other players play in the team.'

It was noticeable that Keane picked out those players noted for their work ethic and tenacity on the pitch – those who were selected week in week out for the reliability of attitude rather than their end product. McAuley had enjoyed an outstanding season and deserved any praise which came his way, but Leadbitter and Walters, for all the hype and reputed value in the transfer marker, had been unable to drive Town into play-off contenders.

Wickham remained in the national press on an almost daily basis, with a merry-go-round of Premier League clubs linked with Town's outstanding young talent, who was blossoming in the final weeks of the season. Sunderland manager Steve Bruce admitted his interest in the 17-year-old, should he become available, but Keane's response was that he would be 'lynched' should Wickham be sold while he was manager. Keane also moved to quash reports of him heading back to Scotland to take the vacant Celtic job. He said his family were happy in Suffolk and they were about to move into a new house, which was almost ready, in Woodbridge. Keane's first year at the club was over, and ahead of Town's trip north to the division's champions Newcastle, he reflected on the ups and down of his first 12 months in charge. He said he should have made changes during the summer and brought in more experience – a feature which he felt had worked for Newcastle. He hoped he was 'a better manager' after enduring the winless run at the start of the season and then hoisting Town up the table to safety, although he admitted anything other than a top-six place next time around would not do.

The visit to a celebrating Newcastle riled him, as he let it be known what he thought of a club which classified itself as one of English football's top names partying as a result of success in the second tier. 'I don't think Newcastle should be having a party, I don't think there's anything to celebrate,' he said. 'At Sunderland they asked us about an open-top bus and I nearly threw up! For clubs like Newcastle and Sunderland, with the type of crowds they get, I honestly think they shouldn't be celebrating anything.'

A Championship record crowd of 52,181 saw Newcastle lift the trophy and retain their unbeaten home record at St James' Park, but they were given a stiff test by Town, and Walters's eighth goal of the season clinched a share of the 2-2 spoils in injury-time. Rising star Andy Carroll had put Newcastle in front in the first half, only for his Suffolk equivalent, Wickham, to claim his sixth goal of the season to draw Town level. It looked like game over in the 82nd minute when Leadbitter tripped Nicky Butt after a Liam Rosenior pass sold him short and Shola Ameobi netted from the spot.

There had been a lack of intensity to the game, though Town came away with renewed hope, having matched the best side in the division on their own turf. Wickham was a constant threat and scoring regularly, making Town fans wonder just how good he could be in one or two years, should the club be able to keep hold of him.

There was good news for Keane when he received the public backing of the club, as confirmed by Simon Clegg. 'There is a timescale to everything and as far as the manager is concerned it is acute with his contract ending in 14 months' time,' said Clegg. 'We are working for an owner who is an extremely successful businessman and one that is not used to failure. Roy will be here next season. He is committed to the club and the club is committed to him.'

April was about to close when news filtered through that the two Wrights, David and Richard, were not in Keane's plans for the following season and would be released once their contracts expired in the summer. Richard's exit was on the cards after his injury problems and the signing of Brian Murphy, who had performed well enough to be considered number one for the future. The end to David's Town career did not go down well with Town fans, who admired the full-back for his low-maintenance attitude and whole-heartedness on the pitch, as well as his goals which seemed to arrive in dramatic circumstances. He had proved reliable and versatile, switching between right and left-back and, although his pace was on the wane, he was a useful squad member, who was also well-respected for his charity work in the local community. He said he did not agree with the decision to release him but 'had to respect it'.

He was joined on the released list by Dutchman Pim Balkestein, while Rosenior's loan was due to end, along with that of David Healy – out injured for the final few weeks of the season – Daryl Murphy, who the club were reported to be interested in signing on a permanent deal, and Colback, who was heading back to Sunderland. Jon Stead was also expected to be on his way, with his loan switch to Coventry reportedly set to become a permanent deal.

'Daryl Murphy turned out to be a very good signing,' said Matthew Mehen. 'If we had managed to sign him permanently the squad would have looked a lot stronger and he would have been one of the first names on the team-sheet. I think Keane came to realise that he didn't have many contacts in the game so [the player] could only come from one of two places – Manchester United or Sunderland. Whoever was on the bench at Sunderland he would go for. Like Stern John I was not exactly over the moon to find out we had signed David Healy. There was no real imagination to these loan signings and it didn't appear he was working overly hard to create contacts anywhere else. Healy was a test to see if Keane could get anything out of a player who had had a setback or two, but it was always a case of one strike and you are out with Keane and there are few good memories of Healy's spell.'

Changes off the field were to follow as well, with Keane looking to bring in an assistant manager – reported to be former Reading and Watford manager Brendan Rodgers, who he met while they studied for their UEFA Pro Licences. Coach Steve Foley's contract was not renewed as Town ended the season in a state of flux.

There was no happy ending to a campaign which would for ever be remembered as an unmitigated disaster. Sheffield United were the visitors to Portman Road on 2 May for the season's final fixture. Keane gave 18-year-old Eastman his full debut in the centre of defence, in place of David Wright, who was dropped from the squad, as Smith moved across to left-back. It was a day Eastman would never forget – for the wrong reasons, as Town's refereeing nemesis, Andy D'Urso, sent him off for two bookable offences in the second half. The Blades were two goals up by that point through Mark Yeates and Ched Evans. Richard Cresswell then made sure the stadium emptied well before the final whistle and the obligatory lap of honour. Town lost 0-3.

'That game just summed up the season and typified all that had gone wrong – leaking goals, not scoring enough, bad performance,' said Matt Plummer. 'It was a flat day when so many people wanted to get it out of the way and draw a line under the season. It was one to write off.'

The negative end to the season left Town fans, thousands of whom had already streamed away and decided against giving the players a farewell, wondering just how bad their side was. It was a season of two halves – the embarrassing, record-breaking mess of the first half, and the gradual improvement littered with depressing lows in the second. What was certainly clear was that for Town to trouble the play-offs or higher next time around, they needed reinforcements to the squad which fin-ished the season under Keane. 'No one likes losing but imagine if we'd won today,' said Keane, facing the press for the final time until after the summer break. 'I might have thought "maybe we're not that bad". You always have doubts in the back of your mind – shoes, cars, holidays, your marriage – but this has confirmed it in my mind, especially those last 20 minutes. I'll be bringing in characters. Forget stats, ages, the country they're from or what size boot they wear. It's all about characters.'

It was character which was called into question again as Keane made one final dig at two of his players when he admitted the two Wrights, unavailable for the chance to say farewell to the Portman Road crowd, were absent through their own choice. 'They didn't make themselves available for today, and they would have been involved, most definitely,' he said. 'Strangely they turned in for training yesterday not 100% fit. One trained and then walked in after half an hour saying he wasn't right. But there you go.'

Was it a lack of characters which resulted in Town's final placing of 15th (their lowest since 1966, with the exception of 2005-06 when they also finished 15th)? Keane had had the previous summer and the January transfer window to mould his squad as he wanted it and was afforded the money to buy Lee Martin, Tamas Priskin, Grant Leadbitter and Carlos Edwards, plus loan deals for Daryl Muprhy, David Healy, Stern John, Jack Colback, Liam Rosenior and Asmir Begovic.

Town fans and Marcus Evans could only hope – should he stay true to his pledge to give Keane another chance – that the manager would have more success in the transfer market second time round. A total of 50 goals in 46 league games backed up Keane's yearning for a striker who could find a way to goal. Murphy and Wickham helped in the latter months and Walters, who top-scored with eight in 43 appearances, had been supplemented in mid-season by Stead, who would probably have added considerably to his six in 13 starts before falling out of favour. Town conceded 61 goals and were considerably harder to break down in the second half of the season once the McAuley/Delaney partnership settled down, but the lack of attacking impetus saw the ball coming back towards their own goal all too often.

'I was really deflated come the end of the season and lost a lot of interest in football,' said Town fan Oliver Procter. 'Had there been a worse season in modern times? It was bad under Mick McGiven in the Premier League when he was sacked and George Burley took over, but I have to concede this had been one of the most boring seasons I had seen since supporting the club, with hardly anything to cheer about.'

Town finished 14 points off the play-offs, and 35 behind second-placed West Brom. Newcastle swept to the title with a mammoth 102 points, conceding just 35 goals. Sheffield Wednesday, Plymouth and Peterborough were relegated – Town avoiding the drop by nine points. The draws had crippled Town's season but so did the desperate defeats which lived long in the memory for their horror and the questions they raised each time. Keane used 37 players during the season – some experienced, some youngsters, loanees, his own transfers, and a few of Jim Magilton's signings, and come May it was still nigh impossible to predict his starting 11 on a game-to-game basis. He got it wrong in his first full season but was not the first to do so. The support of the owner remained and the fans wanted him to succeed. For all of the huff-and-puff football served up by the manager and his team, they generally liked Keane the man and were prepared to give him another chance – his last chance.

Chapter Thirteen

Pre-Season 2010 – May to August

'IF MANCHESTER UNITED HAVE TO SELL CRISTIANO RONALDO, I DON'T THINK WE'RE IN A POSITION THAT WE CAN TURN DOWN AN OFFER FOR A PLAYER.'

The season had only just ended when Tottenham Hotspur offered £5 million for Connor Wickham. The deal was reported to include a season-long loan back to Town, but the club refused to comment. His flurry of goals towards the end of the season ensured that he remained in the spotlight after he had finally signed a professional contract with Town. Now hard cash was offered for a Town commodity, the lack of comment from the club was a worry for fans, who were used to seeing the crown jewels being sold off at reduced prices. Insiders were insistent the bid was on the table, and there was an argument for selling Wickham and spending the money on an experienced striker, or even two, depending on availability. However, Wickham's value was likely to soar, possibly by two or even three times the amount quoted as the fee offered by Tottenham, if he was to have a fruitful second season in the Championship.

One player who would not return was Liam Rosenior, who was no great loss to Town. The full-back always had something outlandish to say when it was his turn to face the press. After departing Town after his loan spell from Reading ended, he said he might not have wanted to stay even if they offered a contract. 'I came to Ipswich to get them into the top flight, but as it didn't happen there is no certainty I would have signed a new contract if offered one,' he said. Rosenior made 28 starts and three sub appearances while with Town, scoring one goal, and felt there was no problem with his performances, despite being out of favour in the final month of the season. 'Before the game at Vicarage Road I was being sick and I can't think of another off-day that I had.' Peters offered more as a full-back and if they were to get back into the Premier League they were going to need better players than the former Fulham defender.

Brighter news came with the announcement of New Zealand's World Cup squad, which included defender Tommy Smith. The first Town player to play in the World Cup since Matt Holland (Republic of Ireland) and Amir Karic (Slovenia) in 2002, Smith had won only one international cap before his call-up. Keane was also offered the chance to attend the tournament in South Africa, as a number of television punditry offers came his way. He subsequently turned the offers down, instead preferring to concentrate on getting it right at Town. 'There were a couple of offers but I've decided not to take them up. I need to concentrate on getting things right at Ipswich,' he said. 'This is a very important summer for me. The most important I've had in my time in management – and that's because of the poor season we had last year. It's a vital period for me in terms of getting the club in shape. While we've obviously not got the intensity of matches to prepare for, it will be a busy time. There is a lot of hard work to be done and I want to get on with it. Like all managers I will be watching the World Cup and, while you'd expect the players from the likes of Italy, Brazil, Argentina and the other top teams to be out of our reach, you never know what the smaller nations might bring.'

Instead of sharing his views with the world via their television screens, Keane was scouring the transfer market for the type of players he felt would transform Town into a force. He had spoken on numerous occasion of the need to have the right characters in his side if they were to progress and become a winning outfit. 'There are certain positions in the team where we are lacking the right characters,' he said. 'Last season we lacked that streetwise player who would tell players it's time to shut up shop, calm everyone down a bit. We'd still be going gung-ho at the end of a game when we needed a player to take his time over a free-kick, to slow the game down – collect a booking if need be. When I'm talking about the right characters – I'm talking about someone who knows the Championship, someone who is vocal in the dressing room, someone who has a big physical presence about them, has got vast experience behind them. We are lacking that sort of player in two or three areas.'

'There was this whole thing about Ipswich being too nice and there being too many players who were comfortable at the club who had been there for a while – mainly those who came in under Jim Magilton,' said Phil Ham. 'Keane maybe thought they had had an easy ride and were in a comfort zone and it had to change. There was certainly a preference for players who were like Roy Keane himself – wearing their heart on their sleeve, the battling type – rather than those with natural talent, people like Owen Garvan and Pablo [Counago]. I perhaps expected to see more of the kind used by the managers Keane played under. Some great players who become managers find it difficult to deal with players of a lesser ability.'

One of Keane's wanted 'characters' was Crystal Palace's Shaun Derry, who, at 32, was not going to boost season-ticket sales. Cardiff's failure to beat Blackpool in the play-off final sparked reports of a renewed Town bid for striker Michael Chopra – linked as many times with Town as Daryl Murphy and many other Sunderland players since Keane took over.

As May ended, there were no new additions to the Town squad, on or off the pitch, with Brendan Rogers reported to have held talks with the club with a view to becoming Keane's assistant. Come June and reports of Keane's demise were once again rife in the national press, with Marcus Evans, whose helicopter was spotted at the Playford Road training ground, reported to have met with the manager to reassure him of his future at the club. Steve Cotterill, close to being named Portsmouth manager, and Tony Mowbray were also reported to have met Evans but there was very little proof to back up the claims. Town were linked with players up and down the country but Cardiff brought disappointment to many Town fans when they admitted Chopra was not for sale and they were in no position to sell their leading striker.

Former Town manager George Burley was unveiled at Crystal Palace just before Smith made his World Cup bow in New Zealand's 1-1 draw with Slovakia. The World Cup was making a noise around the globe, but for its choice of musical instrument rather than the quality of football and Town issued a statement saying the maligned 'Vuvuzela' would not be allowed inside Portman Road.

Derry, who was out of contract, signed a two-year deal with Queens Park Rangers. Heading out of Town was Liam Trotter, who was a free agent after his contract expired and he decided a two-year deal at newly promoted Millwall was a better option for his career ahead of a one-year extension under Keane at Portman Road. Trotter was a regular in Keane's side during the early part of the season but as their winless run grew and grew, Trotter was one of a number of players who fell out of the side and was unable to find a way back in. At 21 he was at an age where he wanted to be playing regularly and, with Leadbitter and Norris in front of him, he was always likely to be playing a bit-part at Town. Richard Wright and David Wright had also moved on and were searching for new clubs, with the full-back becoming Burley's first signing in south London. Smith's New Zealand picked up an impressive 1-1 draw with Italy, in which the Ipswich defender gave away a penalty for a foul on Daniele De Rossi which was converted by Vincenzo Iaquinta, and then a goalless stalemate with Paraguay, but bowed out of the competition.

The Town squad were back for pre-season training at Playford Road on 28 June, without any new additions. However, Luciano Civelli trained with the first-team squad for the first time in 15 months after his knee injury, and the make-up of Keane's squad come the August kick-off was clearer when it was revealed eight first-team players had been made available for transfer. The list consisted of Alex Bruce, Owen Garvan, Alan Quinn, Colin Healy, Jon Stead, Lee Martin, Pablo Counago and Kevin

Lisbie. That Keane wanted to off-load a number of his under-performing players before the season was to be expected as he tried to free up space and funds to bring in new faces. A few on the list could consider that they had unfinished business. Stead would probably have finished as top-scorer had he not been suspended just as he found form and was then loaned out, while the treatment of Garvan was a mystery to all but his harshest critics. One significant name not on the list was Tamas Priskin, whose two goals for Town were scant repayment for the £1.7 million fee shelled out for the Hungarian.

It was ironic that Town started their pre-season action with a goal-glut courtesy of the 'unwanted eight'. Ridgeons League side Newmarket Town were beaten 9-1, with Counago netting a hat-trick, Garvan twice and Martin, Leadbitter, Quinn and Healy once each. It was certainly an effective way of putting them in the shop window for any possible suitors in attendance. The scoreline and scorers were of less significance than the appearance of Civelli. 'We've got an important player back for us again,' Keane said. 'We've not seen too much of him at the club. He's been out for 16 months and that's a long, long time, so it's great for him to have half an hour. Sixteen months is a long, long time out and it's not just about the physical side of recovering from that injury but the mental side as well.'

The new assistant manager failed to materialise as Brendan Rogers became the new Swansea manager, but Keane did make alterations to his coaching staff with former Liverpool and Everton defender Gary Ablett joining the backroom team, as Ian McParland decided not to return to the club for family reasons. Ablett would later undergo treatment for cancer and McParland would return to the club.

Changes continued with the release of the squad numbers for the season ahead, which confirmed who was and was not likely to feature for Keane in the forthcoming campaign. Wickham took over the number nine shirt from the unwanted Counago, while Bruce and Garvan were also shunted out of the first 11. Youngsters Jack Ainsley, Reggie Lambe, Ian McLoughlin and Troy Brown all signed one-year contract extentions allowing them to be granted numbers, while Shane O'Connor signed a two-year deal after showing the potential to become a first-team regular during the second half of his first season at the club. The first official signing of the summer was 19-year-old Conor Hourihane from Sunderland, who arrived without any fanfare, having yet to make a first-team appearance for the Premier League club.

Histon were beaten 6-0 in the next friendly before a more accurate gauge of how Town were shaping up came in the form of a visit to

Dutch giants PSV Eindhoven. Keane made plenty of changes during the match and his side were fortunate to lose by the game's only goal. More worrying was a training ground injury to Damien Delaney, who underwent two emergency operations on his thigh. He picked up what he thought was a dead leg, but was rushed to hospital for surgery when it quickly became clear the problem was far worse than initially thought. 'It was just a tackle in training, but he carried on the session and it was only afterwards he started feeling the discomfort,' said Keane. 'The doctor was called and he went straight to the hospital. He's a very lucky boy. He was very lucky our medical staff got him to the hospital very quickly and they operated very quickly. There was a lot of bleeding and they had to open up his leg, but we believe the surgery went very well. It could have been the end of his career, very much so. It's a big blow to us, a big blow.'

Come mid-July and Town's own squad were reported to be the subject of bids from other Championship clubs. Bruce looked set for a switch to Sheffield United for a fee in the region of £200,000 before the deal fell through, while Garvan was on Burley's radar, although a bid of £100,000 – a laughably low figure just two years earlier – was turned down and Jon Walters was said to be worth £2.5 million in the eyes of mega-rich QPR. Keane confirmed three offers had been received and Priskin was linked with Swansea and Lisbie with Millwall, so until confirmation of any finalised deals went through, it was anyone's guess as to who would be departing Portman Road.

The speculation rumbled on for more than a week until the club finally admitted that Lisbie had joined Millwall, on a season-long loan, Bruce had gone to Leeds United, and Town had signed Cardiff City's Mark Kennedy. The 34-year-old Irish international left-back, who cost £75,000, would add experience, according to Keane, who did not want to rely on O'Connor as his only out-and-out left-sided full-back. 'Players have done good jobs for me there, young Shane's come in as a young player but it's unfair to expect him to play 40-odd games for us,' said Keane. 'Wrighty [David] did a good job for us last year, but obviously being right-footed it wasn't ideal for the balance of the team.'

Jon Stead was in talks with Premier League new boys Blackpool. He had already turned down the chance to move to Bristol City when a strong Town side beat Bury Town 1-0. Stead's move broke down despite the chance to play top-flight football again, because Ian Holloway's club chose to avoid the risk of financial meltdown, as had happened to so many newly promoted clubs who tried to retain their Premier League status by investing heavily in new talent. Stead was left out as Town were beaten 0-1 by West Ham at Portman Road – Carlton Cole scoring the only goal – in the flagship pre-season friendly. Town saw plenty of the ball and were not outclassed by their Premier League opponents but a lack of firepower was unmistakeable, with Priskin starting up front on his own, and Counago, Garvan and Martin failing to make the bench.

There were no more additions or departures before the end of July, but as the new season drew ever closer Town's revolving door started to open. The onset of August saw the eventual departure of Garvan to Crystal Palace for £225,000. The transfer made sense in that Garvan was moving to play under a manager whose passing style was well known and cherished by Town fans, and which suited Garvan's own attributes. The Irishman was leaving behind an unfulfilled start to his professional career, having promised so much as a teenager in the first team. But he was unlikely to become a 'Keane-style' player, mixing his undoubted ability on the ball with brawn and blood for the cause.

Walters's long-term future always felt as though it would be away from Portman Road, from the moment he became an integral part of the first-team under Jim Magilton. Premier League sides had been watching him and stories circulated of his family's wish to move back to the North West. Walters had insisted he was happy at Town and, having been hand-ed the captaincy by Keane, the summit of his career up to that point had been reached in Suffolk. But Keane revealed on 5 August that talks with Stoke City had been continuing throughout the summer and he expected Walters to be on his way if the two clubs could agree a fee, with Town understood to be holding out for £3 million. Town had turned down a bid of £3.5 million from Wigan Athletic two years previously, according to Keane, who denied Walters had asked for a transfer. 'If Manchester United have to sell Cristiano Ronaldo, I don't think we're in a position that we can turn down an offer for a player,' he said. 'I've had a number of conversations with Jon about different aspects of the club and the players, and he knows that if an offer comes in and the club sees it as acceptable, then it's very hard to stand in the boy's way. I understand that, I live in the real world. But at this moment in time Jon's an Ipswich play-er, he's under contract and he's on a decent wage, let me tell you.'

The selling of one of the club's most important players echoed the days when their young starlets were cherry-picked by the hungry hordes of the Premier League, making bids for the likes of Richard Wright, Kieron Dyer and Titus Bramble in the knowledge that the club needed to sell to balance the books. The power had shifted since the 1990s – the players now held all the cards, and should they wish to leave, there was very little the club could do to stop them. From the moment Evans walked into the club, it was never envisaged Town would have to sell their prize assets to stay afloat like in years gone by. But now, if a bid came in and Walters wanted to move on, move on he would.

While Town followers wondered who would be the next to walk away, the club softened the blow by announcing the signing of goalkeeper Marton Fulop from Sunderland for £750,000 and he was unveiled alongside Kennedy. The giant Hungarian said Keane had been trying to persuade him to move south throughout the close season, having worked together for two years on Wearside, and he was willing to swap the Premier League for the Championship in order to play regularly.

'Keane knew the personalities of players like Fulop and Kennedy and there was something in the make-up of the squad he inherited which he did not like, saying it was "'like a cancer",' said Matt Plummer. 'It was all about characters and the right type of people, who were not necessarily the right type of players on the pitch. Not too many people were excited about Kennedy, though, and Brian Murphy did well in goal [at the back end of the previous season], so another goalkeeper arriving in Fulop was unexpected.

'There were other areas of the team which needed strengthening. All of the popular players, like Garvan, Stead and Pablo, left under a cloud. Garvan dropped off the radar completely and from the outside it was hard to understand why. We all knew what a good player he could be and he was someone who just needed a manager to tap into his talent and get the best out of him. He was the kind of player Keane's team needed – he could pick a pass and unlock defences and there were so many occasions when he could have solved a problem for them but was not even on the bench.'

Chapter Fourteen

New Season 2010-11

'PLAYERS GET THEIR HEADS TURNED AND WE ALL LIVE IN THE REAL WORLD, WELL I KNOW I DO.'

The anticipation felt at the beginning of Roy Keane's second full season in charge was in low supply when he prepared to take his team – for it was now definitely his team and not one he had inherited – to Middlesbrough for the first game on 6 August. The belief that Keane brought with him a magic wand had dissipated to the extent that not even the most ardent optimist would vouch for Town's promotion chances. The last 12 months was a sobering experience and quiet fears were held that it could get worse, that Town could start the season on another winless run and become embroiled in a relegation scrap. It seemed anything was possible under Keane.

The raft of new acquisitions was yet to arrive, although Town fans were now used to Marcus Evans's funds failing to stretch beyond mid-range Championship purchases and Premier League cast-offs. The squad selected for the trip to Middlesbrough, on paper at least, was arguably weaker than the one which started the 2009-10 campaign. Lee Martin moved to League One side Charlton Athletic on a season-long loan deal after proving Keane's biggest flop in the transfer market. Pablo Counago was not in Keane's plans, or thoughts, after the manager confirmed the player would not be making the trip to the Riverside because of a 'lack of heart and desire' shown in training. It signalled the end of Counago's Town career under Keane.

Six of the side which had started the opening match of the 2009-10 season at Coventry were in the squad for the Middlesbrough fixture – Gareth McAuley, Jon Walters, David Norris, Jaime Peters, Tamas Priskin and Jon Stead, who was expected to depart in the coming weeks. However, from the insistence that major changes were needed during the summer, with 'characters' necessary for Town to move forwards and upwards, the side which started at the Riverside was largely the same as the one which finished the season with the comprehensive defeat by Sheffield United at Portman Road. Marton Fulop replaced Murphy in goal, Tommy Smith and McAuley were in the back four along with Peters, while Mark Kennedy was a new addition at left-back. Ahead of them, Grant Leadbitter, Norris, Walters, and Carlos Edwards were mainstays of the good and bad times of 2009-10, while Priskin had not played for

Town for nearly eight months. The substitutes' bench, like in May, featured inexperienced youngsters such as Reggie Lambe, Jack Ainsley, Troy Brown – who Keane felt could step up and replace the departed Alex Bruce in the first-team squad – and Conor Hourihane. Damien Delaney and Connor Wickham were both out injured but it showed the paucity of the squad, with Keane deciding Town would be fine without replacing those from the 'listed eight' who had not been replaced.

The intention was to have Shaun Derry bossing the midfield, or if not him, a player of similar experience and know-how. Instead, Keane turned to former Northgate High School pupil Luke Hyam, just 18-years-old. Hyam played in a central midfield three with Norris and Leadbitter during pre-season, showing bite in the tackle and mature positioning. Chances to impress during pre-season had been few and far between because of a lack of first-team fixtures arranged, but Keane denied his side were 'undercooked' going into the season. Hyam had done enough, and while the fans would have liked to have seen a big signing lining up in blue, the next best option was a home-grown youngster.

Keane told the media that his and his staff's target for the season was to be 'competing in the top six', which was hopeful given the lack of squad strengthening and improvement since he took over. 'We want to give the fans something to shout about as, whichever way you look at it, we let them down last year and we want to make up for that,' he said. 'The Championship is going to be as competitive as ever but we want to be in the mix and if we get one or two new faces in we'll have a good chance. But we've got to go out there and do it week-in, week-out, Saturday, Tuesday, Saturday, Tuesday and be consistent, something we weren't last year.'

Middlesbrough were favourites to claim the title come May, of what was now named the npower Championship. Gordon Strachan had spent plenty of the club's parachute payment following relegation in 2008-09 on prolific Rangers striker Kris Boyd, midfielder Nicky Bailey and rumoured Town target Stephen McManus. It was a dream start for Town, however, who wasted no time in chalking up their first victory of the season, months earlier than last time around, with a 3-1 victory. Town even fell a goal behind when Scott McDonald finished from close range in the first half but they turned possession into meaningful attempts on goal after the break when Tommy Smith, upfield for a free-kick, saw his shot from the edge of the penalty area deflect in off former Town loanee Matthew Bates. Town were in front a minute later when Priskin, back in favour following his forgettable first season, headed home an Edwards cross from six yards. Lambe and Ainsley made their debuts late in the game as substitute Stead put the result beyond doubt, volleying in from Leadbitter's lob forward.

The relief was there to see on the faces of the Town players and among the Town following, who felt justified in thinking they were about to begin the slide down another slippery slope towards the nightmare that was the 14-game winless run. The opposing managers even agreed that Town deserved to win and Keane spoke afterwards of the 'good spirit' among the squad and those who had played a leading role on the pitch. He said the difference on this occasion to the previous season's struggles on the road (Town won only four times away from home) was the chances-to-goals ratio. 'What we didn't do last year was take the chances we had, but today we did, with Tamas and Steady scoring two very good goals. That will be the difference as to whether we are going to be competing near the top half of the table.'

'We knew who Keane wanted to sign during the summer: Shaun Derry, Kevin Kilbane and John Eustace and a right-back after David Wright left,' said Phil Ham. 'It was telling that Keane did not receive the budget he wanted. The expectations before the first game could not have been any lower. There was scepticism towards Keane. The club's supporters still wanted him to succeed but most were giving him until October and I thought Marcus Evans would do the same. They had done relatively well against PSV and West Ham during pre-season and then played Middlesbrough off the park. Everyone looked fit and refreshed and they made the most of what they had.'

Indeed, work was going on behind the scenes to make sure that Town had a fully supplemented forward line. Stead's days were numbered despite his effective cameo and decent goals to starts ratio since his arrival under Jim Magilton, while the club would admit in the ensuing days that Walters had asked for a transfer in light of the negotiations between Town and Stoke City. Priskin's display suggested he had wiped the slate clean and was reinvigorated and ready to make something of his Town career, but Counago was well out of the picture and stories were doing the rounds of an alleged bust-up which had resulted in the Spaniard training with the club's youngsters. 'Pablo is behind these [young] players at the moment from what I see on the training pitch,' said Keane. 'Our training ground is open to anybody, anybody can come and watch us train.'

Keane played down suggestions that Wigan Athletic striker Jason Scotland was on his way, only for Wigan manager Roberto Martinez to contradict him and admit a move was in the pipeline. Cardiff's Ross McCormack was another attacking player reported to be close to signing in a deal involving Stead. But there was no progress in time for the first round of the Carling Cup on 10 August which saw Town on their long-distance travels again, this time to the South West and Exeter City.

A growing injury-list contained Civelli (fresh knee injury), Connor Wickham (ankle), Delaney (thigh), Alan Quinn (groin) and, after the weekend, McAuley (back), Edwards (groin) and Kennedy (hamstring). Meanwhile, Fulop and Priskin were away on international duty with Hungary, which meant Keane, on his 39th birthday, was given no choice but to turn to the youngsters who featured heavily in pre-season. There was no expectation on Keane to find a winning formula with a smatter-ing of teenagers playing each week, but questions were asked of why they were so threadbare going into the new season after a summer which was filled with the World Cup in South Africa. The world transfer market was slow until the tournament, won by Spain, was completed, but the level of the market Town were working at should not have been overly affected, although there may have been a knock-on effect with Premier League clubs refusing to release their fringe players until their own new signings were complete.

'I knew over the summer with the changes we were making we need-ed a little bit of luck to get through the season, let alone the first few weeks,' Keane said. 'I think we're just having a difficult spell and we need to get through it.' Wickham and Kennedy were long-term absentees according to Keane who was waiting for news from the chief executive on negotiations with the possible signings.

Leadbitter, Norris and Hyam were the only players considered first choice who made the starting line-up and the young players did them-selves justice in what turned out to be an epic encounter. The game was goalless when Irishman Ronan Murray came on for his debut in the 52nd minute, and no sooner had he entered the fray than Town went behind. Twelve minutes later he was celebrating after looping a header under the bar from Shane O'Connor's cross. Murray's impact continued to grow as he fed Norris who put Town in front, but Exeter drew level through Ryan Harley's spectacular strike with ten minutes of normal time remaining. The youngsters showed they had the stamina to keep Exeter at bay and Norris sealed their place in the second round when he buried a rebound from close range.

Keane was pleased with both his senior players and the youngsters, especially Stead, who he described as 'outstanding' up front on his own towards the end, and Murray who he described as 'the most natural fin-isher at the club' and able to 'sniff out a chance'. The two victories on the trot gave Town the perfect impetus and helped the younger players to believe that they belonged in the first team and could live up to Keane's demands. Six goals in two games was also a surprise and if more signings could be made to strengthen an injury-hit squad, the future looked bright.

A flurry of activity saw Andros Townsend the first to arrive, on a season-long loan from Tottenham Hotspur. A product of their academy, the 19-year-old winger had been involved in the Premier League club's pre-season action and was linked with a move to Town in May by the TWTD website. The left side of midfield was a weakness, as Luciano Civelli was yet to return to the matchday squad after his setback, and Colback, who filled the role on occasions during the previous season had left, while Quinn, another to have been moved out wide, was out injured and Edwards and Peters had also been asked to swap sides from the right.

The club's interest in Jason Scotland was finally admitted on 12 August when Keane said talks had taken place with the 31-year-old and a fee in the region of £750,000 was understood to have been agreed, although two other Championship clubs were tracking the Trinidad & Tobago international, according to Roberto Martinez. McCormack was also in talks, although that deal was made more complicated by the inclusion of Stead, whose start to the season made fans wonder why he was being sold, especially as the fees reported to have been accepted were down in the region of £250,000.

The imminent arrival of a proven striker at Championship level – Scotland's form with Swansea City earned him his move to Wigan in the Premier League – was overshadowed by the announcement that Walters had asked to leave the club. The Town captain was absent from the matchday squad at Exeter after reporting ill and it was the beginning of an ugly departure from the club. 'Jon came to me and said he was aware of interest in him and that he wanted out of Ipswich,' said Keane. 'These were his exact words and you can quote me on that. Players get their heads turned and we all live in the real world, well I know I do. Do players get tapped up? Absolutely, 100 per cent.'

Keane said he would not be able to prove that Walters was tapped up and accepted that player power was now a part of the modern game, although not one he was in agreement with. The praise Keane had reserved for Walters since he had taken over was lavish and extreme, even when his performances failed to merit it. Keane said Walters had been informed he could leave the club when 'the figure was right' and then stuck the knife in when he questioned Walters's illness on the day of the Exeter game, which left Town with just six substitutes. 'Jon said he had a virus but when you miss a game you are opening yourself up for criticism. We have to take his word for it. Simple as that,' said Keane, who added that he wanted 11 players who were 100 per cent committed, not 99 per cent, and that he would prefer to lose ten of the next ten games with the youngsters than include a player who did not want to be a part of the club. In Keane's eyes there had been too many players at Town who were not committed, who 'have talked a good game, signed new contracts, got the pay rise, then they want another pay rise. Then the wife's not happy, the dog's not happy, the cat's not happy. You can only play that card so many times.'

The extension to Town's unbeaten start to the season, due to a 1-1 draw with Burnley at Portman Road, played second fiddle to the Walters drama. He was in Keane's side on the Friday morning, but on Saturday he was only to be seen in the directors' box and Norris wore the captain's armband instead.

A blunt but full explanation came from Keane after the match: 'I spoke to Jon on Friday … I had been thinking a lot about the captaincy side of things and I just felt that it isn't right that a player who has a clear desire to leave the club should be captain. I thought it was a straightforward one but Jon's reaction was unbelievably overboard, he's been disciplined and as long as I am manager of the football club he will never kick a ball for us.'

Another offer had come in for Walters, reported to be from Queens Park Rangers, on the Friday night and Keane wondered if that was just a coincidence or not. He said their disagreement was not a 'ruck', more an 'exchange of views'. 'I've had heated exchanges with many a person, the wife, players, team-mates, managers,' he said. 'I've crossed the line a few times myself and you have to take your punishment. But I think Jon was going to be leaving next week anyway, no secret there because his agent was speaking to every Tom, Dick and Harry, why should I hide behind anything?'

In time Walters would not hide either, and the soon-to-be Stoke City player would have the last word in his spat with the Town manager, who had drawn first blood by taking the moral high ground.

It was a spectacular fall out,' said Matt Plummer. 'Like David Wright, we got to know him quite well as he was one of the handful of players put forward for press duties, along with McAuley and Richard Wright when he was at the club. Walters seemed like a good professional and a decent man. Keane thought so as well – publicly – saying he would like a team of 11 Jon Walters and that he was the second best player in the Championship after Blackpool's Charlie Adam. With hindsight you look back and wonder if it was brinkmanship, with Keane raising Walters's stock a bit but at the time I thought he was simply full of admiration for him. They appeared to have a strong relationship but then there was the major issue and, like some of the other players who left, what a sad way for that chapter to end. Walters never recaptured the form of his first full season under Magilton, when he was deployed on the right of midfield. There was obviously something Keane liked about him, maybe that he worked hard and even though he was not pulling up many trees on the pitch Keane admired his effort and wanted the other players to replicate that.'

Walters's place in the team was taken by Townsend, who started on the left of a front three which also included Stead and Priskin. O'Connor, Smith and Hyam added further youth to the side, while the bench was made up of teenagers with the exception of Colin Healy, who replaced Leadbitter at half-time after he was forced off with a suspected chipped ankle bone, and substitute goalkeeper Murphy. Townsend showed flashes of genuine skill in an even contest which only truly came alive in the final quarter-of-an-hour when, first, Burnley defender David Edgar was sent off for a second yellow card, and then, with four minutes left on the clock, Norris back-heeled from close range following a corner for what he, and the vast majority in the ground, thought was the winner. However, the visitors condemned Town to a customary draw in injury-time when Clarke Carlisle met Graham Alexander's corner.

Keane was a little carried away in saying his side's display was 'brilliant' but certainly four points from two league games was encouraging. 'A lot of our players had played 120 minutes on Tuesday night. We travelled back carrying injuries, were missing important players and we get a performance like that. Give me that all day,' he said.

Disciplinarian Keane gave his players a few days off and warned himself that he would need to be careful with the likes of Hyam. 'You can't expect these young players to play 46 games in the Championship,' he said. 'We could do that but these boys will be crippled when they're 24 or 25 like a lot of other players have been … we want these boys to be playing for the next 10 or 15 years, not two or three and having knee operations, hip operations and taking pain killers.'

Help was on hand with the loan signing of 23-year-old defender Darren O'Dea – another Irishman, who had two full international caps to his name – from Celtic. However, it was Walters stealing the headlines again with a story in *The Daily Mail* claiming the former captain refused to take part in a pre-season Sky Sports interview along with two teammates because he did not want to be filmed in an Ipswich strip. The article then alleged that Walters complained to club hierarchy that he was being bullied by Keane – a claim which was dismissed by the club.

Walters's protracted move to Stoke finally went through on 18 August, with the two clubs agreeing a fee of £2.75 million rising to £3.25 million after a certain number of appearances. Stoke manager Tony Pulis said he was looking to bring more goals to his squad and Walters fitted the bill. He saw the 26-year-old as 'one of the outstanding performers in the Championship' during the past year.

'Walters was not worth £2.75m in my eyes,' said Matthew Mehen. 'To see him go to the Premier League for that fee and Jon Stead go to Bristol City for £200,000 was a joke. I agree with the way Keane ended up speaking about him and treating him. He had played under Sir Alex Ferguson and Brian Clough – two of the best man-managers in the game and if that was going to be the way Keane dealt with players [who wanted to leave] then I had no problem with it. Walters never excelled again to the standard of his "wonder season" under Jim Magilton. He was often played up front by Keane, having been moulded into a winger by Magilton and I did feel for him in that respect because he would then be switched back out wide and I think he had lost touch with his role out there.'

The saga appeared to be over and Town could concentrate on continuing their unbeaten start without their former captain, and without Counago, who moved on a season-long loan to Crystal Palace, Town's next opponents, two days after the exit of Walters. The Spaniard's contract was to expire at the end of the season and his Town career appeared to have come to a rather tame end, following 147 starts, 92 substitute appearances and 62 goals, many of them memorable.

Opinion from the stands on how useful Counago could be to Keane, who had just Priskin and Stead as fit strikers, was split firmly down the middle. On one side were the crowd calling for fresh blood up front and pointing towards Counago's declining goal output, while on the other side they argued that he was still the purest footballer on the Town staff, who could have an impact if given a regular opportunity in the side. Counago encouraged Town to keep the ball on the ground, therefore producing the kind of free-flowing football that the crowd was hankering for.

Four new signings were on Keane's wish-list and he was hopeful of being able to spend the money acquired from the sale of Walters, and the impending departure of Stead, who was talking to clubs despite being involved in first-team action. The only new face in the Town side at Palace was O'Dea, who replaced O'Connor at left-back in what was a feisty affair at Selhurst Park. Counago was ineligible but Palace included Garvan and former Town striker Alan Lee.

The game sprung into life just after half-time when Stead, in the thick of the action again, was hauled down inside the box by Claude Davis, who was subsequently sent off. Leadbitter, having made a miraculous recovery from the ankle injury which had resulted in him leaving Portman Road on crutches after the Burnley match, netted from the spot. Town went 2-0 up after 55 minutes when Leadbitter's cross from the left was met by Edwards, who fizzed the ball into the roof of the net. The visitors themselves were reduced to ten men with 20 minutes to go when Townsend caught goalkeeper Julian Speroni in the face with a high boot and referee Jon Moss was quick to even the game up. Both Keane and Palace manager Burley agreed afterwards that a red card was harsh. There was time for Neil Danns to pull a goal back in injury-time but Town were comfortable 2-1 winners, making it three league games unbeaten and seven points from a possible nine.

'Having been glad the previous season came to an end, I was hoping Keane would sit down and look at his squad and try and figure out how to get the best out of them,' said Town fan Andrew McGarry. 'It was clear that Evans did not want to back him in the transfer market, though, and you could see what was going to happen in terms of him getting the boot when things started to go wrong ... but the most surprising thing was how well we started the season.'

Stead's imminent departure prompted reports of a final £4 million bid for Cardiff's Michael Chopra, but a deal never got off the ground. With Walters gone, Counago and Kevin Lisbie sent out on loan and Wickham injured, it could have been Stead's opportunity to cement his place in the side and enjoy a prolonged run as first choice. However, at a time when he was playing well, and more importantly Town were playing reasonably well, he signed for Bristol City for a measly £225,000. Sure to be a high wage earner, as was Walters, his exit from the club signalled a further shift in the club's transfer policy and its ever-shrinking budget. Nevertheless, Keane thought he would get better value for money from Scotland, who joined Town on the same day for £750,000 and undoubtedly considerable wages considering he was dropping down from the Premier League, where his goals had completely dried up – only a single strike in the top flight in 32 appearances.

Keane said Stead was leaving with his 'best wishes' because he had 'done well for us in recent weeks when we've had a lot of injuries and one or two other strikers leaving the club'. He added: 'We're disappointed to lose him, but that's the situation we face at the moment.' Stead was a victim, as much of Evans's tightening of the purse strings, as his own heavy first touch and inconsistency.

Jason Scotland, meanwhile, was seen by Keane as a 'poacher', who would 'work the channels' and was different to the other strikers at the club – which amounted to 17-year-old Wickham and Priskin, plus the youthful Murray. 'We are always going on to our front players about being in and around the six-yard box and Jason will do that,' said Keane. 'He had proved he can score goals at this level but we have to be patient with him and give him time to settle in.'

Town fans had already been subjected to Priskin's settling in period, which commenced a year previously and was yet to end and, having seen Keane cast aside the majority of the club's other strikers, it was not unreasonable for them to expect an awful lot from Scotland, and whoever else might be brought in. They were also wondering where the money had gone and why 'Operation Premier League' was no longer the message coming from the club, particularly with its fading voice in the transfer market.

Throughout the summer Keane did not try to hide his frustration at the club's inability to sign the players he wanted, but chief executive Clegg allayed suggestions that he and the manager were on collision course. 'People can read into it what they like,' he said. 'We have a very open, close relationship and there are frustrations all round. We are looking to try and run this on the right sort of economic model. We can only go back to the owner so many times, he's only prepared to commit so far on a season basis.' Clegg reiterated his and the club's desire to win promotion, though his words felt hollow given the lack of financial backing. Keane himself then spoke out to let everyone know he was not banging on Clegg's door each morning demanding more money for signings.

'The important thing for me as a manager is to know where I stand and I've always been like that,' he said. 'If I have to sell ten players next week, as long as I know where I stand, I'm OK with that. I know there's been decent money spent over the last few years, people tend to forget that. We've brought Marton Fulop in and Mark Kennedy, these lads are on decent wages. Darren O'Dea came in from Celtic. They're not on £400.'

Scotland's debut came a day after he signed at Crewe Alexandra for the second round of the Carling Cup. He was left out of the starting 11 as Town featured a more experienced line up than at Exeter, with Brown, Smith – now a fully-fledged part of the first-team picture, O'Connor and Hyam the youngsters involved from the first whistle. In view of the lack of numbers and inexperience, the last thing Town needed was for the game to go to extra-time yet again. It would have been avoided, had Edwards's first-half shot had not come back out off a post. Scotland was brought on at half-time but Town made little headway and Keane gave them a stern talking to on the pitch before extra-time began. It worked because in the 102nd minute Norris smacked home a loose ball from a corner for his fourth goal of the season and third in the competition to take Town into the third round.

Keane's new-look side was functional rather than spectacular but it was reaping the rewards from being resolute in defence, due to McAuley in the main, and had found a way to goal, without threatening to beat anyone heavily. Keane saw this potentially exciting start to the season as the result of weeding out certain members of the squad and moving them on because of their 'negative' influence. 'If you've got players moaning all the time, thinking the world's against them and not even able to get in for a quarter-to-ten, get them out the door, I say,' he said. 'I don't see any negative energy, I don't see any players coming in feeling like it's a chore to train or play for Ipswich Town. I think the difference from last year would be that there were players whose attitude to training I wasn't particularly comfortable with. Deep down they knew that and that if I had half the chance I'd get shot of them. Maybe that's the difference now with the players we've got at the club. I'm not including everyone with that. Don't think Garvs [Owen Garvan], Steady or Jon Walters are among them ... there were one or two players who have left the club because when they were out of the team they weren't really good for the club.'

The fall-outs between Keane and his playing staff were not affecting the manager's relationship with the owner, according to Simon Clegg, who said discussions would take place before the end of the season regarding Keane's contract. He was making a decent case, on current form, for an extension but doubts remained whether Town could maintain it.

Discussions had already started according to one Sunday newspaper after Town beat Bristol City 2-0 at Portman Road on 28 August. The transfer window was to close in a few days' time and Keane was looking to use the loan market which he felt had 'saved them from relegation' six months earlier. But those selected to play against Stead, making his debut for his new club, did the business. Town could have given their visitors a hiding, similar to the 6-0 thrashing in November 2007.

Town were up to third ahead of the international break and all appeared to be rosy, with Scotland scoring on his full debut. The cross-bar had been rattled three times – by Leadbitter, Priskin and Scotland – before Town finally took the lead just before the hour. Keane switched from his preferred 4-3-3, which saw Priskin on left, to a 4-4-2, with him moving inside to partner Scotland. Priskin's impact was instant, closing down England goalkeeper David James, who had been sold short on a back-pass, before tackling him, getting back on his feet and netting from a tight angle for his first goal at Portman Road. Scotland then scored his first goal Town goal, also from a tight angle after James saved Priskin's shot. The Hungarian was a different player to the uncomfortable confidence-shorn striker of 12 months previously. He had begun to show his international credentials and was proving an increasing handful for defenders, working opportunities for himself to pull the trigger with his powerful right foot.

Priskin admitted that the 2-0 win was his 'best game' in a Town shirt. Keane agreed that he was 'more settled', especially with fellow Hungarian Marton Fulop at the club. 'Tamas is a talented boy,' explained Keane. 'Sometimes, particularly strikers, need a bit of luck and let's be honest, when he came to the club last year, we weren't exactly flying or playing with loads of confidence.'

Priskin may have been playing better and improving by the game, but as the first month of the season drew to a close Keane warned that his side were not performing at a level much higher than last time around. The difference, he said, was simple: they were taking their chances.

Chapter Fifteen

September 2010

'I EVEN TOOK A PICTURE OF MY SICK AND SENT IT TO THE PHYSIO BECAUSE I KNEW ROY WOULDN'T BELIEVE ME …'

Three wins and a draw, plus two Carling Cup victories were sufficient for Roy Keane to be nominated for the Manager of the Month Award for August, although he would eventually lose out to Queens Park Rangers manager, Neil Warnock. The transfer window closed without addition. Stephen McPhail, the Cardiff City midfielder, and Luke Moore, the West Brom striker were both mentioned in connection with Town but no deal was forthcoming. The loan market was probed and former loanee Jack Colback was revealed as a player Keane was set to hold talks with.

The unbeaten run continued at Portsmouth where Town held firm to claim a point in a 0-0 draw, keeping them third in the table. David Norris, who was due to begin talks on a new contract, with his existing one expiring at the end of the season, struck the post and Darren O'Dea squandered the best chance for a Town side which was stronger in depth – Connor Wickham, Mark Kennedy and Damien Delaney having returned to a bench which was no longer reliant on young members of the reserve team. Marton Fulop produced the save of the match to deny David Nugent, earning his weighty wage in the process according to Keane: 'He's on a decent pay packet – that's why we brought him in, to make saves.'

Successive home games against the top two sides in the division – Queens Park Rangers and leaders Cardiff City – followed. Keane expected both opponents to be near the top of the table because of the number of goalscorers in their ranks – Cardiff boasting Town target Michael Chopra, Jay Bothroyd and Town fans' enemy, Craig Bellamy, who chose to drop down from Manchester City in the Premier League where his relationship with manager Roberto Mancini had soured. Bellamy was still a top Premier League player who was not short of offers from top-flight clubs but his heart was in his native Wales.

QPR arrived first, for a Tuesday night fixture under the Portman Road lights and it was a duel on the pitch and in the dugout area where two of the feistier managers in English football were going head-to-head. Neil Warnock, however, gave Keane a glowing appraisal prior to the game. 'I've always had time for Roy,' he said. 'He tells it like it is and is an easy target when asked about Manchester United and Ireland, but he doesn't duck away from anything. Now he's got his team undefeated they are looking like one of the outfits to beat if you want to get promotion.'

Town were swept aside for their first defeat of the season. The 0-3 scoreline was no exaggeration, as they subsided against a team led by the mercurial skills of Adel Taarabt and eye for goal from the in-form Jamie Mackie, who scored twice before Heider Helguson netted a penalty after a foul by Smith on Mackie.

Keane had tinkered again, dropping Tamas Priskin to the bench and replacing him with Andros Townsend, whose three-game suspension was over. O'Dea aggravated a knee injury picked up on international duty, his place taken by Kennedy. Priskin and Wickham were both on at half-time as Townsend and Luke Hyam had found the going tough against such a strong and experienced side. The second half saw Town run out of ideas and the crowd grew agitated at the return of long, high balls pumped towards strikers whose strength was the ball to feet. Keane said he saw the performance coming, having been unimpressed with his side's display in the straightforward victory over Bristol City. He felt the players had a 'night off' and were given a reminder that they would have to match the level of performance shown by QPR to expect promotion.

The reality check gave Keane plenty to think about before Town faced their next major hurdle in Cardiff City. His side were yet to score a goal in the first half all season and had fired blanks in their last two matches. Changes up front were frequent even when the side and its strikers were scoring and Wickham was pushing for a start after a couple of substitute appearances. The lack of goals was underlined by Keane in his pre-game media briefing, when he admitted the profligacy in front of goal stemmed back into pre-season against the likes of Tottenham, West Ham and PSV, though goal-gluts could hardly be expected when facing opposition of such repute and grandeur.

There were mixed feelings for Town fans at confirmation that Bellamy would miss out through injury. He was sure to be a thorn in Town's side, as he always had been in his Norwich City days, but his inclusion would have given the match an extra edge and bite to it and the fans were looking forward to goading Bellamy for the first time in years. Chopra also missed out and Town took full advantage, producing a much livelier display than the surrender to QPR. Tom Eastman replaced Jaime Peters at right-back, while Hyam dropped out so that Wickham could partner Scotland upfront as Town returned to a more conventional 4-4-2, and it worked a treat.

The unwanted trend of failing to score in the first half continued but like so often in the new campaign, Town found a way through after the break when Carlos Edwards's cross was headed into his own net by Adam Matthews, leaving his team-mates bemused and Town thankful for the generous gift. The second goal arrived after 74 minutes when Scotland finished clinically from eight yards after controlling an Eastman cross. The 2-0 win took Town up to second behind QPR, and the fans in a crowd of 22,599 went home satisfied, having seen Wickham produce an outstanding display and his strike partner Scotland look good value for his transfer fee.

Keane was pleased to have weathered a Cardiff storm in the first ten minutes but thought his side were well worth the result come the end. He said the foundations were laid by the strikers' 'work-rate and hold-up play'. The promise shown by Wickham after his injury lay-off was bringing a feel-good factor back to Portman Road after the quiet summer. However, any chance of Keane staying in the weekend headlines for the right reasons were vanquished by Jon Walters, who had bedded in at Stoke having scored his first goal for the Potters, and the dirt-digging was set to begin.

The national press knew Walters had fallen out with Keane before leaving Town, but his side of the story was yet to be brought to public attention – until *The News of the World* came asking. 'We had Exeter away and all during the week everybody in my family had a vomiting bug. So I quarantined myself from the wife and kids to try to avoid it,' he was quoted as saying. 'But at 3am on the Tuesday morning I was throwing up. I even took a picture of my sick and sent it to the physio because I knew Roy wouldn't believe me, what with it being a cup-tie, clubs being interested in me and all that sort of thing.' And still, it would not be the end of Walters versus Keane.

'There were never the fallings out under Sir Alf [Ramsey] which have been reported to have happened under Keane,' said Town legend Ted Phillips. 'Alf spoke to us on a Friday after a light bit of training. He would come into the dressing room and we would all be showered and sat there ready to listen to him. He would then spend two hours chatting to us about what he wanted. Then on the Saturday we would go out and play and he would just sit in the Directors' Box. When Alf spoke to us he spoke the truth.

'It was a friendly team, we had our laughs, and we used to travel to places like Manchester and Liverpool on the train. He was such a good man. There was one time I was catching the train from London to Colchester when Alf was England manager and he said we should sit together. I got up to get us some drinks and Alf told me to sit down and he disappeared off and came back with a couple of beers for me and a scotch for him. Then when we reached Chelmsford he went and got us a couple more drinks each. The next morning, I was on the 6.45am train to London, found a seat and sat down with my paper and read that Alf had been sacked by England. It was only hours since we had been chatting about the old days together and he did not say a thing about being sacked.'

Keane breached the subject of Walters only briefly when responding to another story which had left him miffed. Reports had emanated from the Irish press of the death of his dog, Triggs, who was brought to the world's attention after Keane's walkout from the 2002 World Cup when he was filmed taking the Labrador for a walk. 'It's not true. My dog is still alive,' said Keane. 'Lies, lies and lies. Unbelievable. Stories about my dog or Jon Walters, nothing surprises me.'

What was a surprise to all, though, was Town lying second in the league and, with a break in the league fixtures because of the continued involvement in the Carling Cup, Keane took stock and praised the players for their early season endeavour and success. 'They've done the club well so far, but we know there are only seven games gone and there's a long way to go yet,' he said. 'But we've given ourselves a chance of having a better season than last year. We were dead and buried this time last year. They're [the players] all buckling down. I'm more than pleased with them.'

Keane was quick to give praise where it was deserved and even quicker to criticise individuals when he felt necessary. His words cut deeper to the heart than those of his predecessor, Jim Magilton, who one felt was conscious of what he was saying appearing in print, not that it stopped him from venting his true feelings. It was just Keane could not help himself, as if he would be punished for withholding certain views and sharing opinions.

The unpredictable team selection was back in force for the Carling Cup third-round tie at Millwall on 21 September. Only Tom Eastman, Gareth McAuley and Andros Townsend held on to their places from the victory over Cardiff, as Damien Delaney made his comeback from the career-threatening thigh injury suffered in training, while Reggie Lambe and Colin Healy were afforded rare starts.

Tamas Priskin, unlucky to have been dropped in recent matches in the eyes of Keane, gave Town, playing in the previous season's red strip, the lead with their first goal in the first half all season. McAuley volleyed a second before half-time, leaving Millwall, beaten 1-6 by Watford the previous weekend, demoralised going into the break. Millwall, however, came out reinvigorated and Steve Morison pulled a goal back when

Delaney should have been stronger in the tackle on the edge of the penalty area. With McAuley dealing with everything which came his way, Town played out time to book their place in the fourth round – the first time they had reached that stage since 2002-03.

The performances of the fringe players meant they were in contention for the next League match, at Scunthorpe. It was the kind of headache Keane wanted, having been shorn of so many senior players at the beginning of the season, but with Connor Wickham, Delaney and Mark Kennedy all fit again, concern at Town's strength in depth was ebbing away, even more so after the manner in which Eastman and Luke Hyam had proven they were competent enough to cope with the Championship.

The strength in numbers did not stop Keane from bringing in Jake Livermore, on loan from Tottenham Hotspur. The 20-year-old signed initially until 13 November, but was expected to stay at Portman Road until January. He brought with him the experience of loan spells in the Championship with Derby County and Peterborough United and started Tottenham's Carling Cup defeat by Arsenal days earlier – his second appearance for the Premier League club. Despite the availability and fitness of Norris, Grant Leadbitter, Hyam and Healy, plus the versatility of Peters, who had been asked to play centrally by Keane on previous occasions, the Town manager said it was an area he felt his squad was short of competition for places. Norris was on four bookings so another would trigger a suspension, but until then, Keane said the squad was at its 'strongest since I've been at the club'.

Such strength in depth had its merits and its drawbacks. Keeping everyone happy would be a problem Keane had been forced to deal with before, but it would also mean increased squad rotation and less opportunity for a best 11 to gel and then excel. It was an issue which had blighted Jim Magilton's latter days in charge and Keane suffered from the same compulsive need to change the team on a game-by-game basis in his first season. Of course, players would have to earn their places and make sure they made the most of their time on the pitch. Some players would have quiet days, though, and then turn it on the following week, while others only found consistency by playing in every match – Gareth McAuley, whose form during the opening games of the previous two seasons was disappointing before slowly improving and becoming arguably the side's most important player, a prime example.

There was good news before kick-off at Scunthorpe when Town were drawn at home to Northampton Town in the last 16 of the Carling Cup. For those who had started in the victory over Cardiff, the day improved further, when Keane retained the same 11 players, although it meant a host of changes from the midweek cup game. His faith went unrewarded as Town spluttered and stuttered their way through the opening half an hour. Hyam was waiting to come on when David Mirfin lifted a header over Marton Fulop and by this stage Town were lucky to be just one goal behind. Wickham, like Owen Garvan on that devilish night at Watford, was the chosen one to have the ignominy of being hauled off before half-time. It had to be bad for the club's most prized and valuable asset to be taken off during the first half, though it could have been any number of the Town side whose number was up. Hyam went into the middle of midfield behind Norris and Leadbitter as 4-4-2 became 4-3-3 or, more accurately, 4-5-1 with Carlos Edwards and Townsend out wide and Scotland alone up front. Some managers would go for broke when they went behind – a feature of Joe Royle's management – but Keane's response tended to be the opposite – he would regroup, hold on, and hope the flow of the game would sway his way with an extra man in midfield or by going like-for-like with the opposition.

For those shivering on the antiquated terraces of Glanford Park, it was a wake-up call, that the horrors of nights like Watford away and Plymouth at home were still in the blood, a disease generally under control but able to flare up at unwanted times. Thankfully, Keane administered the correct medication, although the dosage was just on the light side, as Town arose from their malaise and equalised after 58 minutes through Peters, a half-time replacement for the ineffectual Townsend. The Canadian was fortunate when a tackle on the edge of the penalty area bounced back off him, in similar vein to Steve Morison's recent goal against Town goal for Millwall, providing a clear run on goal, and he finished emphatically. Both sides went on to miss golden chances, Peters saw his header cleared off the line and Darren O'Dea hit the bar, as a point apiece in the 1-1 draw proved a fair result.

Keane held his hands up afterwards and said his team selection was wrong, with Peters, Hyam, Healy and Mark Kennedy all unfortunate to miss out from the start. The alarming first-half display did not avoid censure and Keane confirmed there were eight or nine players who were not up to scratch and deserving of an early exit as he wondered 'when they were going to get going'.

Playing badly and gaining a draw away from home was a decent trait, provided it did not happen too often. While this Town side was far from the venerable juggernaut of Sir Bobby Robson's finest, or George Burley's free-flowing machine at the turn of the millennium, the sum of its parts was sufficient to suggest that Keane would enjoy an improved season. But while Scotland, Townsend, Priskin and Edwards were show-ing flashes of match-winning quality and putting the odd goal away, there was no comic-book continuation of Wickham's rise towards stardom. Of course, it was unfair to pin grand hopes on such young shoulders, how-ever broad they may be, but Wickham was expected to continue his rise to the top, scoring goals in a league in which he could expect plenty of chances. If there was a potential positive from his humiliating substitu-tion, it was that the vultures could see he was not ready for the top flight and possibly not worthy of the hefty transfer fees being bandied about. It was ironic, then, that reports were appearing of Tottenham renewing their interest, with an £8 million deal including Townsend and Livermore, on the cards. Keane described it as 'nonsense' and remained unflustered when queried on Wickham's future – an almost weekly occurrence.

The rollercoaster at Scunthorpe prompted Keane to revert to 4-5-1 at Reading on Tuesday, 28 September, where he dropped Wickham, as well as Tommy Smith and Eastman. It meant Town fielded a new full-back pairing of Troy Brown on the right and Peters on the left to deal with the pacy Jimmy Kebe. Scotland squandered a one-on-one in the first half to keep up Town's record of having yet to score in the first 45 minutes in the league since their trip to Newcastle in April.

The evening went downhill for Town shortly after half-time when Hyam was flashed a second yellow card for kicking the ball away, and even though the game was evened up numerically when Matthew Mills was also shown a second yellow, Town failed to take advantage of the extra space on the field. Wickham and Reggie Lambe were introduced but it was Reading who found a way through with four minutes remain-ing. A corner was cleared to Jem Karacan and his shot from outside the area was diverted home, perhaps fortunately, by substitute Simon Church, who was played onside by a lost-looking Lambe.

The first away defeat of the season was compounded by suspensions earned by Hyam and Norris, though the image which stuck in the mind was Scotland missing when clean through and Keane reminded his strik-ers of what was expected of them. 'If you don't score goals you're going to go nowhere fast,' he said. 'We had the same last year and we don't want to go down the same road. Our leading scorer scored eight last year [Walters] and if our leading scorer gets eight this year we will be in the bottom half.'

The lack of goals was an obvious issue during Keane's reign and, hav-ing generally become harder to beat since overcoming the record winless run, the Town manager was expected to inject more flair at the other end of the pitch. Townsend and Edwards were earning decent marks in the local press and, more so in Townsend's case, were popular among the fans, but neither was likely to hit double figures. And playing either side of a midfield comprising Norris, Leadbitter and Hyam meant Town, statistically at least, carried only a modest goal threat. Norris started the season with a flurry but most of his work was done in between the two boxes and the single striker system saw whoever it was, be it Scotland, Priskin or Wickham, isolated. Scotland's mobility was one of his weaker attributes, but he had shown technique in front of goal, despite the glaring miss at Reading. Priskin, meanwhile, was back out of the side, having spent time on the left wing rather than his preferred central role, and Wickham was still to hit top gear.

Town were more fluent than during Keane's first few months in charge and the extra man in midfield gave them more possession. Problems arose when they went behind and their opponents sat back on their lead, stifling Town by defending in numbers. It led to the 'get out ball' which bypassed the midfield and led to groans from the stands as it immediately returned to where it came from, without a target man to hold it up. A risk-taker was also lacking – a jack-in-the-box who influenced maybe one game a month, earning an extra 10-15 points a season in the process. Without such a player, Town would advance only so far, as shown by one league victory during September.

Chapter Sixteen

October 2010

'A LOT OF SUPPORTERS OUT THERE, NOT JUST AT THIS CLUB, DON'T KNOW
TOO MUCH ABOUT THE GAME.'

The league table had settled down after the unpredictability of the
opening couple of months when the clubs relegated from the Premier
League were emerging from their hangover, both financially and emo-
tionally, while the previous season's also-rans were finding out if a summer of transfer activity and squad reshaping was bringing desired results.
For Town, it was a period of convincing all that they were not in a false
position and could retain consistency – an achievement generally beyond
all Championship sides apart from those in the top three.

Bottom of the table Leicester sacked Paulo Sousa after nine matches,
displaying a ruthlessness absent from Portman Road [since the sacking of
Jim Magilton two matches before the end of a season], where Roy Keane
had been afforded time to turn the club around. His management was put
to the test when Leeds came to Portman Road on 2 October. David
Norris and Luke Hyam were suspended and Town needed livening up
from their dozy display at Reading. Leeds featured two Town cast-offs in
Richard Naylor and Alex Bruce – the latter selected at right-back, where
he had performed to luke-warm reviews during his Portman Road career.

Keane was aware of Bruce's hot-headedness and taste for a tackle, be
it on time or late, and ensured that Andros Townsend gave him a torrid
time. With Tom Eastman recalled to the back line, Jaime Peters and Jake
Livermore – making his full Town debut – paired in midfield in front of
Grant Leadbitter and Tommy Smith called up, literally, at the last minute
for Darren O'Dea, who pulled up lame in the warm-up, it was a young
side chosen by Keane to face a Leeds team beaten 4-6 by Watford at
Elland Road during midweek – a scoreline made more incredible by the
fact that Leeds had been 4-1 up.

Those expecting the round of applause given to the returning Naylor
and Bruce to be the only cheer in the first 45 minutes, having waited two
months to see a first-half goal scored by Town, were thankfully wrong
when Livermore's precise pass released Jason Scotland to work his way
around Leeds goalkeeper Shane Higgs and finish. Bruce's inevitable
booking arrived after 55 minutes, for a foul on Townsend. And his second yellow came 25 minutes later, for another foul on Townsend, but by
that time Leeds were level through Robert Snodgrass. The red card gave

Town hope and with eight minutes left Carlos Edwards returned the ball back into the box after a poor corner to the waiting Smith, whose header put Town fifth in the table going into another international break.

'All the players had been telling me before the match about Brucey,' said Townsend afterwards. 'They told me to keep getting at him as it would lead him to dive in.' It was plan well-worked and a rare example of Town out-thinking their opponents. Bruce's red mist enveloped a group of 30-40 Leeds fans after the game when they attempted to storm their way back on to Portman Road from coaches parked in the Cattle Market car park, before they were eventually stopped by police. Twenty-seven supporters from both sets of fans were ejected from the stadium during the match.

Tamas Priskin and Marton Fulop were away with Hungary, Gareth McAuley joined up with Northern Ireland, and Connor Wickham with England Under-19s. Brian Murphy was a late call-up for the Republic of Ireland. Keane was happy for his players to win international recognition, though the flip side of an extra match during midweek was felt by Darren O'Dea, whose knee injury sustained with Ireland in September was refusing to clear up and required surgery – he was expected to be sidelined for six weeks. Keane himself went to watch Scotland host Spain in a European Championships qualifier, which the European and World champions won 3-2. 'You have to watch these good teams if you get the opportunity. Outstanding. Brilliant to watch,' he said on his return to the Portman Road.

Keane's quest to bring in another Premier League loanee before Coventry came to Portman Road on 16 October resulted in Jack Colback returning to the club, swelling Town's midfield options together with Norris and Hyam, whose suspensions were over. Young, hungry loanees from the Premier League, such as Colback, Townsend and Livermore, were a popular option among Championship clubs because of the inability to tempt senior players who preferred to sit on high wages, wait for a chance in the first team or run down lucrative contracts rather than drop down a division. The Championship had a stigma attached to it – players dropping out of the Premier League were perceived to lack the technical and physical attributes needed for the top flight and a career in the second tier, where the 'triers' belonged, beckoned. Town's three loanees from Premier League clubs still had a chance as time was on their side.

Colback was predicted to feature in Sunderland's first team by manager Steve Bruce, but after a solitary eight-minute substitute appearance in the Carling Cup against Colchester United, he was allowed to sign for Town until January. Normally, the return of a former Player of the Year would bring a ripple of excitement, but Colback was a similar type of player to Town's other midfielders – comfortable on the ball, hard-working and able to score the occasional goal. His versatility was of benefit, though it left Town fans wondering where he would fit into a midfield already featuring Norris, Leadbitter, Hyam, Livermore, Healy, Edwards, Townsend and Peters, plus the hope that Luciano Civelli may one day step foot on the pitch in a competitive first-team game.

'Keane never seemed to work out what tactics he wanted to play, as hardly a game went by without major changes to the starting 11,' said Andrew McGarry. 'Then it was odd that when all he wanted to do was sign midfielders, he spent most matches watching his back four lump the ball over the top of them to strikers who could not head it!'

Civelli became a myth to Ipswich Town fans. He existed only in the sense that his name was mentioned at press conferences – when journalists asked week after week if there was a chance he could make a first-team comeback. For those attending the sporadic reserve-team matches, they could see Civelli had indeed recovered from his near career-ending injury, though he was no longer the purveyor of Argentine artistry, a player with a luscious left foot and Town's equivalent to Tottenham's Gareth Bale, who was in the process of rewriting the role of the modern left-sided player.

Civelli was medically fit, according to Keane, but mentally he was struggling to overcome the scars associated with 18 months out of action. Still, there was hope he would one day return as good as hew, especially as Keane had yet to write him off and, should Town enter a rough trot, there was the thought that Civelli might miraculously come galloping to the rescue. Until then, he was just Civelli, the injured Argentine who was unlikely to ever be seen again, except by training attendees and hardcore reserve-team followers.

Even with Norris and Hyam back from suspension and Colback in the mix, Civelli's name cropped up ahead of Coventry's visit. Keane felt his side was harder to get into than at any previous point in his reign and the members of his squad would have to work incredibly hard to dislodge those in the team – Civelli included. 'It's straightforward, the team will pick itself – the players who are on good form are chomping at the bit and are training properly,' he said. 'That's why when people like Luke [Hyam] and Chuck [Norris] get suspended and we win a game, they've no argument if they don't get in the team. I don't have to put these boys straight back in the team. The bar has been raised, that's what we want to do. We want to try and raise the bar every single day, and that's a credit to the players at the club. Luca's [Civelli] had a decent run in terms of games [in the reserves] and just as importantly has got training sessions under his belt. Enough of talk about injuries and comebacks. Whether he wins a place in the team will be up to the boy himself. Who should I put Luca in front of? Andros [Townsend]? Carlos [Edwards]? He'll have to do a bit more to get in ahead of those lads.'

'It made you wonder whether Keane actually communicated with Civelli,' said Town fan Matthew Mehen. 'We knew some of his rehab was done in Argentina and you wonder how long Keane spent talking to him and how much of a say Civelli had on whether he was fit or not. Civelli himself said he was fit, he was playing in the reserves, so why was he not at the very least on the bench for the first team earlier? It was baffling. The fans had warmed to him quickly when he first arrived and it was easy to see why.

'We may never know why Keane was so reluctant to play him – there were so many times Keane said Civelli was fit and then didn't pick him. How could he prove himself if he wasn't given a go? Maybe it was a cultural thing where Keane saw Civelli as another Pablo or Priskin – a risk. Maybe Keane needed an assistant alongside him to provide another opinion on players. Is he ever going to be able to work alongside an assistant or does he always have to be the main man, his own man? I think that could be his downfall long-term.'

Civelli's name was in the matchday programme but not in the matchday squad as Keane chose to bring back Hyam, leave Norris on the bench, and move Peters to right-back in place of Eastman. Colback was not included after signing the day before the game, as Keane stayed with the lone striker system which started in the victory over Leeds before the two-week break.

Coventry were renowned for their direct style of play, which was the brainchild of manager Aidy Boothroyd who had earned the nickname Aidy 'Hoofroyd' while managing a short journey down the A12 at Colchester United. Colchester had been used to playing on a pitch resembling a paddy field, though, and avoiding the lush Portman Road turf would seem a waste. An awkward afternoon was forecast and that was exactly what Town experienced, going behind in the first half to Clive Platt's header from close range, and it could have been two when Lukas Jutkiewicz crashed a shot against the underside of the bar, down on to the line and out. Referee Rob Shoebridge and his assistant deemed the ball had not crossed the line, although it was an incident requiring video technology.

Hyam was sacrificed at half-time as Keane sought more incision and cutting edge, bringing on Wickham to partner Scotland. Coventry increased their lead, when Jutkiewicz tangled legs with McAuley in the box and calmly placed the resultant penalty. Less than two minutes later Town were back in the game when Scotland met Peters's cross sweetly for his fourth goal of the season but, even with Priskin forming a three-man front line, domination and possession provided no end product and the 1-2 defeat meant Keane's side were down to sixth.

A succession of poor set-pieces and lack of invention had led to growing frustration in the stands where the Town fans expected to beat a middle-of-the-road side such as Coventry. They were also annoyed with Keane's growing insistence on playing a lone striker at home, believing that it gave the wrong impression to the opposition and went against the ethos of the club, which historically set out to attack and entertain.

The atmosphere at Portman Road was hardly acerbic and, compared to matches on the Continent where all manner of missiles were thrown onto the pitch and at underperforming players, it could be considered tame. The white hankies stayed in pockets, unlike at the Bernabeu, while the pig heads stayed at the butchers and the snooker balls at Riley's.

The reaction upset Keane, who did not take kindly to being told how to run his football team. He said he did not mind people having opinions but felt a lot of people 'do not have a clue what they're talking about' when it came to football. Instead of stopping there, Keane, as so often before, let his tongue continue:

'I think a lot of people, particularly in this area and our supporters, are probably set in their ways. Instead of worrying about tactics and systems and moaning and groaning, I'd say get behind the players, particularly the younger boys. Not many teams in the Championship are playing with two or three players from last year's youth team. Get behind them and don't get bogged down by tactics and systems, that's up to me to sort out. A lot of supporters out there, not just at this club, don't know too much about the game. They come and pay their money, they come in and they watch, but they get brainwashed by the 'experts' out there. They all have their favourite players that they think should be playing, or they think we should be playing with two strikers, whatever it might be, which is no problem. But the players we've been putting out every week have been doing a good job.'

Keane displayed his thick skin by urging the crowd to take out its frustrations on him – not the players, because if he was to get it all wrong, with less than a season to run on his contract, he would pay the ultimate price for his failures. The club, its staff and players, were anything but 'doom and gloom' as they attempted to put the Coventry defeat to the back of their minds three days' later when they travelled to Watford. The glass half-empty brigade were those paying for season tickets and writing in the local media, according to Keane, who said neither would play a big part should the club win promotion.

There were a few wry smiles among the crowd at Vicarage Road when Town lined up with a front two of Scotland and Priskin, although it meant a wingless-wonders 11 featuring Norris and Colback – making his second Town debut – playing either side of Livermore and Leadbitter in midfield, as Keane made six changes, including Brian Murphy replacing the injured Marton Fulop in goal.

Despite his barbed comments aimed at Town supporters, Keane was given a smooth ride when he made his way to the dugout, and during the majority of the first half. The mood changed when Watford scored twice in a five-minute spell before half-time, through Stephen McGinn and Marvin Sordell, leading to the vocal message 'sort it out' from a travelling contingent of more than 1,200. Substitute Norris looped a header under the bar and into a vacant net midway through the second half but Town, with Delaney, Scotland, Wickham and Ronan Murray all in advanced positions by the end of the match, succumbed to their third defeat in four matches, 1-2, and dropped to eighth place.

Fortunately for the local press, prepared for a repeat of the previous season's post-match lock-in, there was no need for the sleeping bag in the car or the deck of cards to pass the time. Keane was not too despondent and said Town were going through a 'little sticky patch' but there was no inquest into systems and tactics.

Short of knocking at the front door with a bouquet of flowers, Keane went some way to patching up his relationship with the Town fans. 'I can understand the moaning and groaning, I have no problem with that, but sometimes just encourage the younger players just that little bit more because we have inexperienced players in important parts of the pitch,' he said a couple of days after the Watford defeat. He had had time to reflect on two defeats in a week, which was about to become three at Nottingham Forest. 'I hope they're not too upset, I hope they're fine and I hope they will agree with me in terms of getting behind the younger players. The senior boys will be fine because they've played 300, 400 or 500 games, but the younger players, who might not have played ten games yet, sometimes need that little bit more encouragement, particularly after they've made a mistake. That was all I was asking and I'm sure fans will understand that.'

The media were not let off the hook. There was no hugs, handshakes, pats on the back, on or off camera, as Keane blamed 'lazy journalists' for depicting his views as 'blasts' each time he challenged anyone or anything.

'If people think I was blasting anybody, I wasn't,' he said. 'It was just a case of getting behind the younger players.'

Town's chances of making the top two by the end of the season were written off by their own manager, as if he could see the rocks ahead which would ultimately spring not just a leak but bring about a full on capsize and journey towards the bottom of the ocean. 'I think the two teams that have the best chance of promotion will be QPR and Cardiff and then there'll be a battle between all the others,' he said. Portsmouth and Middlesbrough, both relegated from the Premier League in recent years, were also predicted by Keane to do well, despite slow starts to the season. Forest, Swansea, Watford and Norwich were also predicted to be in running.

The difference between QPR and Cardiff and the rest of the division, and in particular Town, was their ability to attract players of a high calibre – the likes of Craig Bellamy and Jason Koumas (who had struggled to get into Cardiff's starting 11), and Adel Taarabt at QPR, who was regarded as the top talent in the division. Neil Warnock was building a squad chock full of strikers to ensure his side was never short of firepower if injuries or lack of form struck. If Jamie Mackie, Heider Helguson and Tommy Smith were unavailable, Rob Hulse, Patrick Agyemang or Leon Clarke could step in, plus Rowan Vine, who had commanded a transfer fee of £2.5 million in the past, but was out on loan. Warnock would later add West Bromwich Albion's Ishmael Miller and Newcastle United's Wayne Routledge on loan. Handsomely bankrolled, the Loftus Road club were doing everything in their power to make sure they won promotion. It was the scenario Ipswich Town fans envisaged when Marcus Evans took over the club, but he was unable to sustain the level of financial investment that would help put Keane's side up near QPR at the summit.

Having created his own team since April 2009, there were few excuses for Keane, even though the transfer funds had dried up. Only Norris, Peters and the injured Alan Quinn remained from the first matchday squad he had selected at Cardiff, when Town had won 3-0. He refused to complain and instead pointed the finger at himself before Town's run of defeats was extended at the City Ground. 'After a couple of defeats, I haven't been getting out my black book and phoning people who I think can come and help us,' he said. 'There's no panic or emergency. We don't like losing football matches, but I think it's the first time in a long while that we've lost two in a row. We don't like it, but I've got great faith in the staff I have with me and we need to do a slightly better job. It's not just about the players doing their jobs properly, it's about the manager doing his job properly and I'd have to say looking at the last week, I haven't done it well enough.'

His tactics were questioned once again, as he had reverted to the lone striker system, which reaped no reward, and furthered Town's measly total of one goal in the first half so far in the season. Keane's idea of a 4-3-3 was nothing like that of Barcelona or Arsenal – purveyors of the beautiful game in its most beautiful form. Apart from the switching of the two wide front players, Keane's system was set in concrete, the lone striker gamely soldiering on without the benefit of a playmaker tucked in, as coaches would say, 'between the lines' of midfield and strikeforce, in the mould of Cesc Fabregas, creating space and angles, and threading inviting passes through the defence.

'Keane was only interested in the hard-working players who ran around a lot, but possession was key,' said Town fan Andrew McGarry. 'The players he had, failed to keep the ball long enough as they were not of sufficient quality. In Counago we got rid of a forward who could hold the ball up and link play with others in the final third, something we lacked massively when he was not in the team. Garvan was the best pass-er of the ball in the squad and while he may not have been someone who threw himself into tackles and got himself dirty, he was a key player in terms of providing the side with attacking options.'

David McGoldrick gave Forest the lead in the 13th minute when he latched onto a low cross and Lewis McGugan's thunderbolt free-kick from 35 yards put the game out of Town's reach two minutes before the break. Colback came closest for Town, hitting the bar, but, like at Watford, they held their own in terms of possession but did very little with it in losing 0-2.

Town were sliding down the table and this was the first time they had lost three league matches in a row under Keane. Four points from six games was a worrying trend and the noises coming from the Town man-ager hardly provided reassurance for fans thinking that they had turned the corner and would compete for a play-off place – the minimum expec-tation at a club the size of Ipswich Town. 'We're asking young players to do men's jobs,' he said, after making four changes to the side. 'We saw that at Forest, and it's not me writing things off, but they're physically big-ger than us and they're more experienced than us. We were up against a team who weren't far from getting in the Premier League last year. We know where we're at and I learned a lot about the team at Forest and there's a lot of hard work ahead.'

The Carling Cup fourth round tie against Northampton at Portman Road gave a break from the league, and Keane's relationship with Town fans surfaced again beforehand. He had received a mixed reception from travelling Town supporters at the City Ground and he reiterated his plea for the players to be backed – even at his own expense. 'The supporters have been fine since I walked through the doors,' he said 'They've been very good, particularly last year when they were unbelievably patient, but that's one of the reasons I took the job. I don't know if I was ever their best pal. The fans no doubt are frustrated at the moment. I live in the real world and when you're losing football matches it creates tension and frustration, which we all have.'

Some of the frustration lifted as Town booked their place in the quarter-final for the first time in ten years with a 3-1 victory. Northampton took a fortuitous 16th minute lead when Liam Davis's 25-yard shot clipped Tommy Smith's boot and looped over the head of Brian Murphy. Town were having no trouble scoring in the first half in the cup and Edwards and Delaney put them in front before half-time. Priskin's glancing header from a Leadbitter free-kick ensured a safe passage through in the final few minutes.

Further goals from Priskin was a requisite for Town to regain their league form, as Scotland could not be expected to carry the burden alone. Wickham's on-off season due to injury was hampering his development and, although his cameos were delivering proof of his ability, the goals were not in rich supply.

Keane said he understood the contrasting opinions on Priskin, who like so many of Town's strikers in recent years, had been written off by some fans as a waste of money and rated by others who backed him to come good eventually. 'I know he has his critics, but you have to give the boy a chance,' said Keane. 'I think he's the type of player who can frustrate fans because of the way he sometimes runs and his body shape and because he will try stuff. Even against Northampton he was trying stuff on the edge of the box and that takes bravery, particularly from an attacking player. I thought he deserved his goal and he earned it with his workrate.'

On the resumption of league action, the message from Portman Road was one of positivity. There was no reason to push the panic button after three defeats on the trot, according to Keane, who felt the media were being over-critical of him and his side. 'I didn't come here with my own PR people, I don't have pals in the media,' he said. 'When I or certain other managers lose certain matches it's "pressure", it's "jobs at stake", you've "got to turn things around" blah, blah, blah. Let's see how things turn out. Other managers can go through spells where they don't win for two or three months and nothing's ever written, but that's the name of the game. As I've said before, our intelligent supporters understand where we're at.'

Keane thought he maybe deserved more credit for getting Sunderland promoted, having seen other managers getting a 'pat on the back' for taking clubs up and then keeping them in the top flight. He added: 'I don't all of a sudden think that because we lost one or two games I haven't got a clue what I'm doing … It doesn't mean that I went home the other night [after the Northampton win] thinking that I'm the new Bobby Robson. I'm 39 years of age, I've got a lot to learn.'

The doubters were answered on Saturday, 30 October when Town ended the month on a high and a return to form with a 2-0 victory over Millwall at Portman Road. In a game littered with chances, Scotland continued his run of goals in front of the home crowd and Leadbitter scored from the penalty spot after Priskin was fouled by Danny Shittu. The four-man midfield of Leadbitter, Norris, Colback and Edwards predictably lacked width and invention, but with Keane utilising two strikers there could be few complaints and his system was a success to help Town to within a point of the play-offs in 11th place. Centre-halves McAuley and Delaney came in for praise from Millwall manager Kenny Jackett after the visitors asked thorough questions of the Town backline.

Two league wins and three defeats represented an inconsistent month and Keane spent most of it trying to calm talk of a crisis. Following the victory over Millwall he asked people to 'relax and chill out', telling the world that the club was in a sound position and that there was no need for the over-reaction to some of the defeats.

However, those who did know their football – few and far between in Keane's eyes – were sceptical of the merits of the squad Keane had assembled and of the manager's ability to take it forward. It was crucial that the run of defeats be merely a blip. Otherwise, Keane's future would be questioned for what felt like the umpteenth time – the prudence of keeping a manager in the last year of his contract who was yet to fulfil his and the club's ambition, instead taking them to the no-man's land of mid-table mediocrity.

Chapter Seventeen

November 2010

'THEY CAN BOO ME ALL THEY WANT. I NEVER WENT INTO FOOTBALL TO BE POPULAR, IN FACT IT DRIVES ME ON AND I BLOODY ENJOY IT.'

'Lies lies and lies' was Roy Keane's view of many of the stories published in the press. A new month, a new story, this time even more far-fetched in his opinion. Connor Wickham's appearances had been mainly from the bench since his return from the injury suffered during pre-season. The refusal to start the highly rated youngster every week had caused a rumpus, according to *The Mail on Sunday*, with the 17-year-old and the manager falling out over his lack of playing time.

'Some of the stuff I read is quite extraordinary,' chief executive Simon Clegg said at the Supporters' Club AGM. 'If something like that happened it would be in the local press, it wouldn't be in the national press. You guys would have heard about it sooner than them and I thought you killed the story brilliantly locally. There was no substance to it.' Coach Tony Loughlan was also present and dismissed the story out of hand, saying it was 'total nonsense'.

Town were allegedly going to have to choose between Keane and Wickham, with one of them leaving in January. The story said Keane had used 'tough love' with Wickham to keep his feet grounded, but this had led to the striker becoming 'confused' by his bit-part role.

Carl Marston, writing in *The East Anglian Daily Times*, said there was no chance of an 'either, or, situation' and that 'results' would determine Keane's future, while 'economics' would decide whether Wickham was to stay at Portman Road. 'On current form, Connor Wickham has no divine right to be starting games for Ipswich Town,' wrote Marston. 'Wickham's presence on the bench has more to do with a struggle for form rather than any alleged row with his manager.'

A classic Keane response to the story came on 5 November, the day before Town faced Sheffield United at Bramhall Lane. 'The only concern was when we were go-karting on Monday, Connor was trying to get me off the track, I know that. He was pushing me,' he said. 'Unless he's upset about the go-karting, it's rubbish. I don't have bust-ups, I've told you before. I had to bump a few out of the way! That's why Connor's unhappy, he finished third!'

Twenty-one members of the Town squad were due to become free agents at the end of the season and while most were fringe players and youngsters, a few – like David Norris, Gareth McAuley and Carlos Edwards – were key figures in the first-team dressing room and on the pitch. Keane said he was 'dead relaxed' about his own position but concern was growing over the future of McAuley, the kingpin in Town's back line, of whom 'loads' of offers had come in, according to Keane, who was hopeful the 30-year-old would agree fresh terms.

A colossal performance by McAuley on his 100th appearance for the club, including the winning goal, put the rest of the Championship and a few Premier League clubs on high alert, as Town overcame Sheffield United 2-1 to make it two successive league victories and three in a row including the Carling Cup. Richard Wright watched from the Sheffield United substitutes' bench as Tamas Priskin took his tally for the season to five with Town's first attempt, when he nudged in from close range after United failed to deal with a long Edwards throw into the box. The Hungarian hit the post ten minutes later but Stephen Quinn, brother of Town's Alan, drove in from the edge of the box to equalise. Town were not to be stopped, and went into the break ahead when McAuley headed a Grant Leadbitter cross up in the air and, when it dropped, he buried a shot past goalkeeper Steve Simonsen. Marton Fulop kept the Blades at bay in the second half as Town rode their luck to hang on and move up to sixth place.

Just as he refused to get carried away when Town were losing, Keane declined the opportunity to bask in the glory of sitting in a play-off place just weeks after he was being told to 'sort it out' by the club's supporters. He knew his side were fortunate to come away with victory and admitted that on another day they could have lost, and possibly by a substantial margin.

If the cracks for Town were beginning to appear at Sheffield United, they opened up like a crevasse when Derby County came to Portman Road on Tuesday, 9 November, leaving Keane to tell already disappointed Town fans that the side was not ready to stay in the top six, as they dropped to seventh as a consequence of a 0-2 defeat.

Keane spoke beforehand of his squad's strength in depth and of how difficult it was to pick a starting line-up, but the lack of star quality was the lingering feeling by the end of 90 fruitless minutes. With Jason Scotland, Jaime Peters, Andros Townsend, Mark Kennedy and Darren O'Dea to call on from the bench, Keane had experienced cover at hand. Nevertheless, nobody provided either the killer touch in the first half when Town were on top, or the ambition and bravery to change the game when they went behind to two strikes from Kris Commons, the first a free-kick which took a fortuitous deflection.

The upshot of the defeat was more than just failure to win three successive league matches under Keane for the first time. Leadbitter picked up his fifth booking of the season and a subsequent one-match ban, while McAuley was forced off in the second half with a worrying Achilles problem. Norris was already sidelined with an ankle injury picked up in the win over Millwall.

The players were kept in the dressing room for over an hour and the airwaves were filled with doom-mongers. When Keane surfaced he was just as downbeat, painting a picture of a team he was struggling to cajole into the perfect package. 'We've lost to QPR at home, Coventry, at Watford, at Reading. We're losing lots of games,' he said. 'We're winning a lot more than we were last year but we're losing more as well. As much as we were disappointed with the run last year, a lot of those matches were draws.

'We're a mixed bag at the moment. I think what we've got to learn as a group is that when we're not quite at it, like tonight when I don't think we were, we have to grind out a result. And we've not done that.'

Then the next episode of the 'Walters and Keane Show' aired, via the *Irish Independent*. It was the most revealing insight into the inner sanctum since Keane took over, as Walters, fresh from his first Republic of Ireland call-up, told of an empty relationship between manager and player. Walters claimed there were few words exchanged between Keane and the squad 'on the playing side' and described the state of affairs as 'strange' and Keane as a 'one-off'.

Walters said the fall-out prior to his departure to Stoke came as a surprise as he was one of the players who had escaped an 'earful'. A name picked out who was regularly on the receiving end was Owen Garvan. 'He didn't get much of a chance and, when he did, he got an earful all the time,' said Walters.

The sympathy extended to the coaching staff whose Town careers were ended after Keane took over: 'Bryan [Klug] had been at the club for probably 20 to 25 years,' said Walters, 'and there was Charlie Woods, who was Bobby Robson's number two. Good coaches and good people to have around who were all let go for one reason or another under Roy. That was disappointing. They were good people to work for and part of what the club is about. Ipswich is a bit unique, it's in the middle of nowhere and it means so much to everyone in the town. When they got let go . . . all the lads respected them quite well . . . and that was Roy's decision.'

And then came the comment for which Keane's reign would forever be remembered: 'As soon as I got here, everyone asked what I had done,' said Walters. 'Liam Lawrence [who played under Keane at Sunderland] was here before he went to Portsmouth as well. They were laughing because they knew exactly what I'd been through. Even now I speak to the lads at Ipswich and when they get beat, well, we know what's been said before we even speak to anyone. We guess, 'Aye, this is what's been said this week,' and we ring all the lads and that's what happened. It's eggshells all the time.'

Eggshells. The performances were such that the players looked as though they were afraid of the consequences should they lose. The panicky long balls, lack of composure in possession in the defensive third, refusal of the midfield to run with the ball and choosing to play safe by passing sideways and backwards, and strikers feeding on scraps and high balls, and then being told in public they were scoring too few.

Captain Norris was the first player to publically defend Keane after Walters's latest outburst, saying that he had 'never had a problem' with the boss. Then Damien Delaney followed suit, although he first admitted that words were exchanged in the dressing room after the defeat to Derby before explaining it was part of Keane's ambition and the defender would be concerned if the players were not challenged to step up a level.

Keane's response was delivered at the press conference the day before Barnsley visited Portman Road. He refused to respond specifically to Walters' comments but made it clear he was fed up with the reports of unrest at the club. 'I shouldn't have to come on every week and defend the spirit of the players,' he said. 'It's wrong and it's boring. Last week it was about Connor Wickham. If you think I'm going to defend the group of players or the spirit in the group every week … what's the point? I'm not getting bogged down with it. It's for another day. People can have their say, and it's cheap and it's lazy. I've had it before with ex-players I've worked with those who have done books, [Dwight] Yorke, [Niall] Quinn, good luck to them. Today is a day for me to focus on my job. There might be another day for that, as obviously I'm no pussy cat myself and if I have to defend myself I will.'

The mood at Portman Road changed on Saturday, 13 November. A second depressing home defeat in the space of a few days created a bitter atmosphere, with the acrimony aimed at both Keane and his underperforming players. The attendance squeezed over 18,000 – well down on the 22,000 who witnessed victory over Cardiff and 23,000 against Leeds, but more than the 17,500 against Derby – and included owner Marcus Evans.

The day turned sour when Goran Lovre and an own-goal by Town goalkeeper Marton Fulop gave Barnsley a two-goal lead at half-time. The second goal was unfortunate, Adam Hammill's shot hit the inside of the post and ricocheted off the back of Fulop into the net. A chorus of boos greeted the half-time whistle as Town, without the injured McAuley and Norris, and the suspended Leadbitter, had exhibited the same weaknesses as against Derby – little cutting edge except for the willing Priskin, and a defence leaking avoidable goals.

'Barnsley were a team who could play better away from home, having been used to playing on their horrible pitch at Oakwell,' said Matthew Mehen. 'They thrived on the Portman Road carpet and were not the first to do so. We had no answer to them. Sitting in the lower section of the Sir Bobby Robson Stand, when the crowd turn against the team or the manager, you knew about it.'

The response to falling two goals behind had been to withdraw Scotland and Townsend and bring on teenagers Luke Hyam and Ronan Murray, and revert to 4-5-1. Five minutes later it was 0-3 when Garry O'Conner slipped away from marker Tommy Smith and met a low cross, generating calls from the stands of 'We're supposed to be at home'. The derision grew louder after a further five minutes when Priskin, Town's most dangerous player, was substituted to a background of 'You don't know what you're doing'. The introduction of Wickham left Town with an attacking force consisting of a 17-year-old with six career goals to his name and 19-year-old Murray, yet to score at first-team level, or even start a match. Town had used eight players aged 21 or under during the 90 minutes.

'Barnsley was the game when you knew something had to give and it was only a matter of time,' said Matt Plummer. 'Derby was disappointing but then the Barnsley game coming so soon afterwards and them [Town] playing so badly exacerbated it. Patience literally snapped. The fans just thought that after all the talk and all the hype of when Keane took over there was nothing to show for it on the pitch. When Priskin came off it was a ferocious reaction borne out of frustration. From the press box I looked around the ground and there was real anger in the fans' faces. Priskin was Town's best player without a doubt. The fans were thinking 'this can't be right'. So many had stuck by Keane up until then but he lost a lot of support on that day. Reflecting afterwards it confirmed what a lot of people thought – that the squad was weaker and the team was going backwards. There were so few options on the bench and the lack of marquee signings spoke volumes in terms of the trust coming from the boardroom. It cemented the belief that he was on borrowed time.'

Smith nodded in Edwards's corner with ten minutes left but it failed to weaken the predictable booing at the final whistle as Town fans were left in no doubt where their season was heading after a 1-3 defeat. Fed up with Keane's tactics and the lack of entertainment at Portman Road, the still lofty league position was of small value to most.

'When you don't win matches every decision is going to be analysed and criticised, that's the nature of football,' said Keane, trying to stay calm in spite of the home crowd cheering each Barnsley touch of the ball during the second half.

'Any fan cheering Barnsley should have been dragged out by the stewards,' said Oliver Procter, watching the match from the Sir Bobby Robson Stand. 'This was the most frustrating thing – the crowd not supporting the team. I was even more infuriated at Carrow Road [in a few weeks' time] when people started singing "Keane out" with the Norwich fans ... of all the times to be negative, it was disgraceful. Our role was to support the players and manager – Liverpool do this exceptionally well, even when times are bad.'

Keane kept a lid on the behaviour of the home crowd but it would be in his thoughts in the coming days. 'They [the fans] were pretty supportive last year when we went 14 games without a victory – the Watford game I'll never forget – they were very, very good to us,' he added. 'But at this moment in time, you're still hoping that fans would understand where we're at. Don't underestimate the loss of Gareth McAuley, David Norris and Grant Leadbitter. I don't want to use that as an excuse but they are important players for us. We just have to get on with it.'

According to Phil Ham, Town's season started to go wrong as the fixtures became harder and opportunities to impress a crowd eager for entertainment were few. 'Whereas at the start of the season teams like Middlesbrough and Crystal Palace were being beaten – and were being beaten by most other teams – Town were then coming up against the likes of QPR,' he said. 'Keane started changing things around, although there were injuries. The cohesion they had at the start of the season just started to ebb away. Barnsley, Doncaster, Swansea are all sides who have not got huge amounts of money but had managers who had got them playing attractive football, while Ipswich, during the same two years, had been through two managers and spent millions of pounds and were no better off. The crowd were fed up as Barnsley looked a class above. The club hadn't been in the play-offs since 2005 and the discontent just manifested. Has there been a lower point in the last 10 or 20 years? The Portman Road crowd cheered the away side in 2003 when Wimbledon beat Town 5-1 so it wasn't the first time.'

Just when it seemed everything was going wrong for Town, it grew worse, and quickly. Mark Kennedy, captain for the day against Barnsley, suffered a hamstring injury, as did Hyam. Then the club announced a loss of more than £14 million for the year up to June 2010. During that period £7.2 million had been spent on players, with £1.1 million brought in from player sales. Next came the suspension of the club's under-18 manager Mike Pejic. Reports in the press said it was due to a 'falling out with players amid allegations of bullying'. The club released a statement simply stating that internal procedures meant they would not comment.

Having had nearly a week to stew over the calamities of the two home matches, one of Keane's turbulent press conferences was expected on Thursday, 18 November and sure enough there were a few harsh words – aimed at the Town fans for once, as well as freelance journalist Dave Allard. Keane's fan-related speech led to the type of headlines the Town manager loved to hate – 'Keane blasts Town fans', 'Keane slams disloyal supporters' etc. It was manager's death-wish time, though, and Keane, as was his way, had something he needed to get off his chest, whatever the consequences.

He accused the fans of failing to be the team's '12th man', using clubs such as Celtic and Stoke as examples. Then he likened Town fans to sheep when the subject of home fans cheering Barnsley at Portman Road arose. 'You always remember these things,' he said. 'I remember when I played for Ireland I got booed against Iceland because one reporter, who was an idiot and was pals with the manager, did a piece saying the fans should boo me. And guess what? They all booed. Sheep. One or two boo and the rest follow. As I've said before, I remember after the Watford game [at home last season] when I thought the fans were brilliant and they cheered us off the pitch even though we drew the match and were in the difficult run. You don't forget these things and you don't forget the fans last weekend either.'

Next Keane told the gathered press, excited by his golden quote-laden speech, that it was for the best that the club's next two fixtures were away from home '... the players can go out and relax a little bit and enjoy what they're trying to do, which is learning their trade. And they should be applauded for that, not jeered. I think it's too easy now. We see it with other games, we saw it with international matches on Wednesday night. There's this mentality of booing teams all the time. They can boo me all they want. I never went into football to be popular, in fact it drives me on and I bloody enjoy it. Get behind the players, get behind the young players that we've got. We're two points off the play-offs and players who are 18 or 19 years of age are getting jeered and booed. Young Connor Wickham's coming on and the fans are booing because I'm taking Tamas Priskin off. We're 0-2 or 0-3 down at that stage and they should be applauding Connor coming on. Two weeks ago they wanted Priskin out of the club.'

'The fans had been really supportive,' said Matt Plummer. 'If the situation Town found themselves in was mirrored at a big city club the board and fans would have reacted differently and he would have been out either during the first season or in the summer. But the fans did stick by him and, especially at the away games, where they sung his name. Up until this week they had done so at home as well. Having a go at the fans underlined all the problems and tensions and we knew it could not go on like this.'

Keane was not finished there. Having criticised the fans for the umpteenth time, he then took the bold move of claiming that Town were 'making progress' despite being 12th in the table and in no obvious way much better off than when he had taken over. 'I know people have said I'm a bit mad before and they'll think I'm even madder after that statement,' he said. 'I see a manager who is making progress, a manager that will make mistakes, like everyone else, and a manager who is learning. But given the right support and respect, I will do a good job, if it's not at Ipswich it will be somewhere else, simple as that. I will be a successful manager, guaranteed.'

Allard felt Keane had said enough and the time was right to inform the Town manager of his own view. 'I like Roy Keane and saw him as a challenge when he first arrived,' said Allard, who had covered Town for *The Evening Star* for 30 years and was at the press conference on behalf of *The Daily Mirror*. '*The Star* had a tape recording of the incident and they put a phone number on the back of the paper for people to call and listen to it. It came about when Roy was saying the supporters knew nothing about football and it was affecting the young players. I interjected and asked if I could make a point. I said "the fans are booing you and your coaches for your tactics". He went spare! He started to have a go at me and said he did not have to listen to this, etc. He had a moan and a groan but I remained indignant and told him he was "treated like royalty at this club". He was astounded by this. He was getting angrier and angrier and the club press officer, Steve Pearce, tried to intervene but I was not prepared to back down. I said "you might intimidate some people but you do not intimidate me".

'His [Keane's] reputation goes before him and there were a lot of people intimidated by him – coaches, players, press. You could see some of the press were frightened of him in the press conferences and I had listened to so many of his unfair comments about supporters and just snapped. Playing one up front at home when you are 0-3 down does not go down well anywhere. Then he brought on Ronan Murray and stuck him out on the left and I told him how unfair it was on the young boy. He replied that Sir Alex Ferguson does it with Wayne Rooney and we had a good argument. Roy was out of order and he knew it and I think he went away and thought about it.

'I felt as if I was getting hero status among my peers for telling the truth and I am proud of it. I do not know of any other press man who has challenged him like that. The Irish press were ringing me up and the phone never stopped. I have not met anyone so revered or as intimidating in football – you could see the fear on people's faces when he walked in and you can only imagine what he was like in the dressing room. He never knew anyone in the media on first name terms – we were a blob of inconvenience.'

Phil Ham was also present when Allard took on Keane. He thought the comments about the supporters not knowing anything about football related to the fans phoning in to a radio show earlier in the season when they were saying he should not be using 4-5-1 at home and away all the time. 'It all came out that Keane was moaning at the fans which was a bit distorted from what he was actually saying and, at the time, all the best teams in the world were using 4-5-1 home and away,' Ham said. 'I think deep down the majority of fans agreed with what Keane said that day.

'As for Dave, he was baiting Roy who took a bite and fell for it. Generally, Roy was very good with the local media – he felt more comfortable talking to them than the national press, who he was not so familiar with, and one of whom came in and asked about the Pope on one occasion!'

Town fans who made their way to Hull on 20 November witnessed no sign of the progress Keane was talking about. Although his name was chanted, as was the norm away from home, it was a typical display under his leadership and a typical outcome – a dour 0-1 defeat. His team selection failed to set pulses racing and smacked of going to the KC Stadium for a draw, with Scotland deployed as the lone striker in front of a midfield consisting of four central players – Norris, Leadbitter, Jake Livermore and Colback – plus winger Edwards, and a back four of natural centre-halves – Tom Eastman, Delaney, Smith and Darren O'Dea.

Hull struck the woodwork twice in the space of a minute just before half-time and the only goal of the game arrived in the 77th minute when Robert Koren's 25-yard effort beat Brian Murphy – recalled in place of Fulop – to end the home side's two-month wait for a victory in front of their own supporters. It was Town's third loss in a row and sixth in eight league games, dropping them to 13th place. Keane said the 'pressure was building within' and that he and his players would 'lick their wounds' ahead of the season's first instalment of the East Anglian Derby.

During the next seven days Keane attempted to halt the slide, which was gathering pace by the week, by dipping into the loan market. On paper, the signing of Rory Fallon from League One club Plymouth, with a view to a permanent deal, was more evidence that Keane's success in the transfer market was severely lacking and the club were no longer backing him with significant funds. Fallon's goalscoring record in English football was pitiful and gave fans little hope of him firing Town to a play-off place with a burst of five goals in as many appearances. Statistics of 143 appearances and 19 goals for Plymouth suggested his career was set to be played out in the lower leagues, despite playing in all three of New Zealand's matches at the World Cup.

On the pitch, Fallon was a physical nuisance able to provide knock-downs for a strike partner and the type of striker Town were lacking. In theory at least, Fallon could help one of Scotland, Priskin or Wickham find a more regular way to the back of the net. 'I think sometimes when balls come into the box we don't have anyone available who goes and attacks the ball, whether that's in the starting 11 or on the bench,' said Keane. 'Rory will hopefully give us that, but we want to be fair to the boy as well and not expect miracles from him. It's up to the other players to try and help him out.'

'All of a sudden the league position was a worry and the season was becoming desperate,' said Matt Plummer. 'There had to be some kind of reaction to the defeats and bad run of form. That Rory Fallon was seen as the saviour showed how far they had fallen. It was a desperate signing.'

The troublesome right-back role, which had been filled by one of Peters, Eastman or Troy Brown, none of whom were natural full-backs, was solved by the arrival of Dutchman Gianni Zuiverloon from West Brom for a month, taking Town's loanee contingent to six (rules stated five loanees were permitted in a matchday squad but because Darren O'Dea was on loan from an overseas club he could feature too).

Zuiverloon's pedigree was more promising than Fallon's, having cost West Brom £2.3 million, although he had featured in just Carling Cup fixtures since their promotion to the Premier League. 'We've persevered with Jaime Peters at right-back, he's done reasonably well for us when you consider that he's more of an attacking player, and Tom Eastman's done well for us, but he picked up a groin injury last weekend so we've needed a recognised right-back,' said Keane. 'It has been shown up particularly away from home when we've not been able to get up the park, so he'll give us that.'

Both new signings would be required to make their debut at Norwich, with Wickham's injury problems resurfacing, McAuley undergoing surgery on his Achilles tendon, and Eastman, Kennedy and Hyam also out. 'We're looking at him [McAuley] being out for a couple of months, maybe a bit less, bemoaned Keane. 'It's a big blow to us, particularly when you consider we lost Darren O'Dea for six or seven weeks and we lost Damien Delaney for a couple of months at the start of the season. Luke Hyam's out for five weeks, Connor Wickham at the start of the season, Connor a few weeks ago and again on Wednesday. It's been stop-start for a lot of our players. Our plan was to have more of a settled squad and team, and of course we lost Steady and Jon Walters on top of that, so we've had to deal with a few setbacks. For us to lose Gareth for a couple of months is a big blow, but it's a case of just getting on with it. Every team will suffer injuries, I never thought for one minute we wouldn't have that, but I think that the players we've lost are important players. I think what we've had is too many young players in our team and they've been depending on one another. I've no problem with playing the younger players, but in the Championship to be going in with four, five or six in a starting 11 is hard going.'

It was to be Keane's first, and last, East Anglian derby and he admitted it was about time Town fans were given something to shout about. The irony of his comment was that there was no end of targets for supporters to aim some noise at come 3pm on Sunday, 28 November.

First there was cheer, for Luciano Civelli was included on the bench, marking his first inclusion in the matchday squad for 20 months. He took up his place alongside Fallon, while Zuiverloon was in the starting 11. Keane had spoken of his side's need to spend more time attacking to give the defence a breather and the time had come again to revert to a strike pairing of Scotland and Priskin. However, Peters and Townsend were excluded completely and Murphy was dropped for Fulop in goal.

Fans hoping to see a blood and thunder encounter waited just three minutes for the first flare-up when Norwich striker Grant Holt produced a late tackle on Colback, leading to a melee which required diplomacy to calm. Twelve minutes later Norwich went in front when O'Dea hesitated and was dispossessed by the maverick Holt, who was in on goal. Town hit back and showed the kind of character so badly missing in previous weeks. Leadbitter's free-kick was headed back across goal by Priskin and Delaney stormed in to nod home from in front of the line.

Delaney's – and Town's – day was about to turn traumatic, however, leaving them 'deep in the manure' according to *The Sun*. Holt evaded marker Delaney to run onto an inch-perfect pass from Arsenal loanee

Henri Lansbury to put Norwich ahead. Two minutes later Delaney's conversion from hero to villain was complete when he hauled down Holt, who was heading goalwards. Keane's immediate reshuffle saw Scotland sacrificed for Colin Healy, with Colback moving to left-back and O'Dea to centre-half.

Town's spirit stayed intact until the 76th minute when Holt became the first scorer of an East Anglian derby hat-trick since 1998, when Alex Mathie netted a first-half triple in the famous 5-0 victory at Portman Road. As Town tried to push as many players forward as they dared, they were caught on the break and Wes Hoolahan chipped over the advancing Fulop to make it 1-4 and mark Town's heaviest ever derby defeat.

The embarrassment for Town fans extended beyond the result. They were the club in East Anglia with the wealthy owner, the history and the big-name manager. Norwich, meanwhile, were going about their business quietly, yet efficiently under Paul Lambert – a manager working his way up the ladder – and moved up to fifth in their first season back in the Championship after a brief stay in League One.

The home fans, the vast majority of the 26,532 at Carrow Road (the ground's highest attendance since 1984), spent an hour telling Keane he was going to be 'sacked in the morning' and, in truth, it was a Sunday roasting for Town. They made Holt, who Lambert was honest enough afterwards to say 'lacked finesse', look like a world-beater and one of the finest strikers in the country, rather than the burly lower-league goal-poacher of previous years.

Keane then gave a bizarre post-match appraisal of where Town's season was heading. Instead of rallying the troops and insisting they could find a way to revive a campaign which was heading towards ruin, he played the opposite card and said it was likely to grow even worse in forthcoming weeks. 'At the moment I don't think we're capable of going on a run like we've seen from other teams, Burnley and Derby for example,' he said. 'I've been saying for a month now that we're only a few points off the play-offs, but if anything that gap's going to get wider because we've got a tough run of games. 'We've got injuries and we don't look like we're going to score many goals, so we're a long way off the play-offs yet. I think we've heard that from clubs before about managers [who are told they're staying] and the next day they're gone. I take any comments that might come with a pinch of salt.'

Whatever the psychology of his words, the doubt surrounding his position was mounting by the game and defeat to West Brom in the Carling Cup quarter-final was expected to have major consequences, despite Simon Clegg having given Keane his backing a week previously.

Sitting 16th in the table, Town were a mere six points from the play-offs, but everyone was now looking down – even the manager. He knew what was coming.

Chapter Eighteen

December 2010

'AN OLD IRISH FRIEND TOLD ME NOT LONG AGO, "SOME DAYS ARE ABOUT SURVIVING, YOU'VE JUST GOT TO HANG IN THERE".'

The dreaded phone call never came. Marcus Evans left Roy Keane in charge – for the Carling Cup-tie at least, Town's biggest home match of the season up until that point – and there was no conversation between the two after the Norwich defeat. There was logic in keeping Keane at this point, for the transfer window was closed and a new manager coming in would inherit the same squad – made up of injured players, a plethora of willing youngsters and a core without an ounce of confidence. But on the flip side, leaving it any later would put the club at risk of falling even lower in the table, and potentially into a relegation scrap come the second half of the season.

Keane changed his tune two days after conceding that his side were destined for a winter of deep discontent. He defiantly insisted he was capable of turning Town's season around but said it could be any day that he changed his mind and had to sit down with the owner. 'I'm surviving. Just about! It's part of the job and part of life,' he said. 'An old Irish friend told me not long ago, "some days are about surviving, you've just got to hang in there". I've seen other coaches and managers going through difficult spells and it's about hanging in there and hopefully things will turn. You might get that bit of luck – someone might score from 30 yards and turn the season around.'

The attendance at Portman Road for the quarter-final was an accurate gauge of which way the fanbase was leaning – either towards the Keane camp or towards a change of manager and a fresh start. Weakened by injury, suspension and ineligibility, it was hard to see how Town were going to put up a fight against Premier League opposition. The fans were wounded, the players were wounded and the manager was hurting. Keane said Town would have to be at their 'very, very best' to get a result and at the least bring the fans some cheer and replenish what he described as a 'rollercoaster relationship' between the paying public and himself.

His patched up side, which included Bermudan youngster Reggie Lambe and an inexperienced back line of Jaime Peters, Troy Brown, Tommy Smith and Darren O'Dea, were greeted by a crowd of little more than 11,000. Looking ahead from the time Keane was appointed, nobody would have predicted so few would be present for a cup quarter-final 19 months down the line. Nearly 13 years previously Portman Road had been full as Chelsea beat Town after extra-time in a thrilling League Cup quarter-final. True, West Brom featured names such as Giles Barnes and Simon Cox compared to Chelsea's Ruud Gullit and Gianfranco Zola, but that Town side had also been an attraction. The fans were in attendance to cheer on 20-year-old Richard Wright in goal, the long-serving Mick Stockwell, the theatrical and skilful full-back Mauricio Taricco, characters like Tony Mowbray and Mark Venus, homegrown star Kieron Dyer, club-man Matt Holland and derby day hat-trick hero Alex Mathie. Youngsters wanted the names of these players on the back of their shirts. More than a decade on, Tommy Smith, Colin Healy or Jason Scotland were nowhere to be seen on the replica strips making their way around the ground. It was so difficult to identify with Keane's team of 2010 – both pre and post summer.

Cup football threw up an upset every season, like it did in October 1997 when Town's march to the quarter-finals included a 2-0 victory over Manchester United at Portman Road – a Manchester United which included Paul Scholes, Andy Cole, Jordi Cryuff, Karel Poborsky and Phil Neville. West Brom went into this tie on the back of a 4-1 victory over Everton but made nine changes to their side. From the first few minutes, when David Norris could easily have given Town the lead, another Town scalp was on the cards.

This was a rare day when Town matched commitment with quality and should have been well in front by half-time. Two decent penalty appeals were turned down, the calls aimed at referee Mike Jones echoing around the near two-thirds empty stadium. Those who decided to turn out, on what was a freezing night with the lines on the pitch painted blue to help visibility, gave Keane a reminder that his tactics were baffling even though Town were dominating Premier League opponents when he removed Andros Townsend and sent on Shane O'Connor. Four minutes later, the 69th minute, Keane could rest a little easier as Carlos Edwards was brought down inside the penalty area and Grant Leadbitter stepped up to put Town into their first cup semi-final for ten years, and two games away from Wembley. Keane learnt of their semi-final opponents when handed a piece of paper during his post-match press conference. 'Good news, it's Arsenal! There's always a downside, isn't there?' he joked. 'We've got Chelsea around that time as well. 'Hopefully, I'll be here in January. I might be gone at the end of January though!' His words would become more poignant in a month's time.

Possibly enjoying the scarce feeling of success, the poor turnout escaped Keane's wrath and instead he was philosophical, pointing at the low attendances in cup-ties up and down the country and the plummeting mercury. 'Hopefully a few more might come back for the semi-final. If the first leg's at home!' he quipped.

'The cup run was fairly low key – they were expected to beat Exeter, Crewe, Millwall away, Northampton, and then West Brom had such a poor crowd that it showed it was not catching the fans' imagination,' said Matt Plummer. 'However, it must have bought Keane a little more time. It always used to be unusual when the crowd was under 20,000 at Portman Road, it tended to be early 20s, mid-20 or late 20s for a big game. Now it dipped to 18-19,000 in the league and a lot of that came down to the way the team was playing.'

A few more came back to Portman Road on 4 December for the return to league action against Swansea. Still the ground was almost half empty, though, proving that the cup run was a hollow attraction and the damage to Keane's reputation and standing had already been done. There were three reasons why Town should fear the worst: the game was screened live on Sky Sports and their record in front of a television audience had been awful in recent years, nemesis Andy D'Urso was referee, and Town were going into the game on the back of four straight league defeats.

It soon became five, as Swansea came from behind to win 3-1. Townsend headed his first Town goal from an Edwards cross after 51 minutes but Craig Beattie then netted with his head and Smith was caught dribbling inside his own six-yard box by Joe Allen who took full advantage. D'Urso lived up to his reputation among Town fans by failing to award what they felt was a clear penalty four minutes from time when Edwards was sent sprawling by Mark Gower. Instead of equalising, Town went further behind as Beattie curled a beautiful 25-yard effort over Brian Murphy, leading to calls from the Sir Bobby Robson Stand for Keane to 'knock out' D'Urso.

A touch of class was displayed afterwards when Keane refused to blame the Billericay official, who had sent off Tom Eastman on his debut, for the defeat. Keane preferred to rule out excuses for Town's inability to halt the losing run, or reproduce the effervescence of the midweek cup success. 'It's a bit like Groundhog Day [Town losing] – doing the same thing over and over again,' he said. 'You've all seen that movie, it's quite good I know, but we're doing the same thing over and over again and I keep coming up here saying the same stuff. You've got to draw the line somewhere on it. It's unacceptable and we'd had two or three before that, then we had a couple of wins in between. But it's eight defeats in ten, which is unacceptable.'

Town were missing Norris against Swansea because of illness. Gareth McAuley was also absent and Damien Delaney was left to watch from the stands, with Keane deciding not to recall him following his suspension for the red card at Norwich. This meant the spine of the team was weak, from the lack of experience and leadership in defence, to the absence of drive and protection in midfield, which was apparent whenever Norris was out of the side. Edwards told the media the goals they were giving away were 'laughable' and said the defenders seemed to think they were 'Franz Beckenbauer', no doubt referring to Smith's misguided composure inside his own six-yard box and O'Dea's effort to deal with a bouncing ball at Norwich.

The club's PLC AGM on 8 December was expected to produce an insight into the future of the club and the direction owner Marcus Evans was going to take. Chief executive Simon Clegg played down reports that the next match, at Preston, was set to be Keane's last at the club and said the club could still achieve a place in the play-offs. 'I have spent quite a lot of time reading stuff which is nothing more than pure speculation and it causes me much hilarity and amusement,' he said. 'If we lose the next 20 games without taking a point, if you take that eventuality, of course the manager won't be here. But there really is no mark in the sand when the owner and I have agreed that we are going to address this issue one way or another. It's just not there.' Keane was in attendance but was handed an easy ride by shareholders as his quick wit and knack of satisfying those asking the questions saw him leave with his head held high and without any tirades or arguments to report in the next day's news.

It was a week when managers and their relationship with club owners came under the microscope because of Chris Hughton's sacking at Newcastle United. Respected by the fans, by the media and within the football world, not to mention liked by the club's players, Hughton had won the Championship and then taken Newcastle to 11th in the Premier League. It was inadequate for owner Mike Ashley, who preposterously decided he wanted a manager with more experience. What would Ashley have done with Keane in the position Town found themselves in?

Keane brought in a sports psychologist to avert the losing run from becoming a habit, though that appeared to be a month too late. He considered the Championship a 'mental challenge' and was looking at every angle to stop Town's downward trend, which had left them in 17th place before the Preston encounter. He reiterated the need for dressing-room leaders, noting that the senior players in the squad lacked a natural commanding presence, so without the guidance of a Shaun Derry or a Lee Carsley, a psychologist was the next best option.

Salvation was not to be found by dipping into the pool of reserve-team players, who were criticised and about to experience a 'reality check' over the coming months. 'The reserves haven't come on,' said Keane. 'We rewarded six or seven scholars last year when we gave them the deals and told them that they were now in the big league and wouldn't be getting arms wrapped around them by academy coaches Sammy Morgan and Gerard Nash, and have people like that baby-sitting them. They're in the real world now and they've got to earn a living.'

Instant wonders failed to materialise as Town's tendency to lose without much of a fight continued. The return of Norris to the midfield and Mark Kennedy to left-back brought Town a small step closer to full strength and Keane gave Rory Fallon a first start up front alongside Jason Scotland, while Delaney was again left out of the squad.

But against a Preston side which was bottom of the table and without a victory in seven games themselves, a 0-1 defeat extended Town's losing sequence to six matches and took them a step closer to the relegation zone. The manner of the defeat was of as much concern as the result itself – like so many of the recent games. Town offered only a modest threat and Keane played his standard hand of introducing all three sub-stitutes in the second half. However, none of the 14 players who spent time on the pitch was able to find the accuracy of Preston's Iain Hume, who fired in a low shot for the winner in the 50th minute.

Sir Alex Ferguson was in the crowd to see his son Darren, the Preston manager, lift some of the pressure on himself, but Keane's outward appearance showed how badly the losing run was weighing on him. Sporting the beard which was iconic in his final days at Sunderland, Keane said there was no problem with his side's application or commit-ment, just their goalscoring prowess.

'You wouldn't believe how much it's hurting, but you could try and guess,' said Keane. 'I'm a proud man and I don't like getting beaten.' At least the players were publically behind him, playing the PR game far bet-ter than they were the game which mattered on the pitch. Their stance was that they were to blame rather than the manager, but was he helping them with the way the side was set up and the considerable game-by-game changes to personnel and system?

The exclusion of Delaney since his sending off at Norwich led to rumours of a fall-out between the Irish defender and Keane – some of the stories embellished to the extent that the pair were alleged to have been pulled apart in training. The club moved swiftly to deny it, saying it 'categorically refutes the malicious suggestion'. Delaney himself then backed it up with a statement describing the story as 'total rubbish' and

Keane would later have his own say on the matter. 'If I have a bust-up with Damo I am in trouble because I have a lot of time for Damo. It's the usual rubbish,' said Keane. 'If there's one player I am not going to fall out with then it's probably Damien because he's a fellow Cork man.'

As much as Keane's position was under scrutiny, the future of Marcus Evans was also questionable. The lack of serious funds and public backing of Keane caused fans to wonder if he still believed it possible to deliver Premier League football to Portman Road. After all, he had spent millions of pounds of his own money for absolutely no reward, and at this point it was hard to see how and when Town were going to turn a corner. On 16 December he released a short statement to try to reassure the weakening Town support, though it included nothing on the manager's future. 'I remain as committed to Ipswich Town now as I did when I first became involved with the club three years ago and the target remains the same – to take ITFC back to where it belongs – the Premier League,' it read. 'I have always looked long term as a businessman and that's certainly the case at Ipswich Town as well.'

With the beard gone after a few days away in Manchester, Keane admitted he needed to take a step back and look at the situation from a 'different angle' but he said there were no thoughts of walking away. Ten defeats in the last 13 matches was the worst run he had known in his career – playing and management – since the age of eight and he was not envisaging 'everything in the garden to be rosy' if Town beat Leicester on 20 December at Portman Road.

Keane was hoping to make it to January, when the transfer window would reopen, and then to be handed funds to galvanise the squad and, at the least, find a regular goalscorer or a creative player to assist the strikers. It was an unsettling time for everyone at the club, with 21 players out of contract in the summer and talks ongoing with key senior players McAuley and Norris.

Keane was not about to go easy on the players just because his own performance as manager was receiving widespread criticism in the media – including polls in the local press which showed the majority wanted a new manager in place. Tamas Priskin was picked out as a member of the squad failing to do the business, although he could consider himself unfortunate, given the general improvement in his performances since the start of the season and the considerable goal-threat he carried when Keane showed faith in him. His latest crime was his substitute appearance at Preston, which lasted 16 minutes of normal time and contributed next to nothing. That was the view of his manager, who knew all about impact substitutes, having played alongside master substitute Ole Gunnar

Solskjaer at Manchester United. 'Some people in this modern game – and we saw it last weekend – some players don't like or want to be sub, which is crazy,' said Keane in reference to Priskin. 'They go on the pitch and they show you that they're upset by their body language, not just at our club, it goes on at lots of clubs. It was an important learning weekend for me in terms of the players I'm working with. Lads who want to play and lads who certainly don't want to be sub. You don't mind a player being grumpy but they seem to bring that grumpiness onto the pitch with them instead of going out there and doing the business.'

An opposition injury jinx, suspensions, deflected goals, dodgy refereeing decisions, beach balls on the pitch; there are many ways a club in despair can find some luck. For Town, with six defeats in a row, their Christmas present was an extreme winter blast. Heavy snow started to fall at Portman Road on 18 December around an hour before the scheduled 5.20pm kick-off (the match was screened live on Sky Sports, hence the unusual kick-off time for a Saturday). Some supporters were forced to turn back for home when the snow set in and made progress towards the stadium nigh impossible, but 16,278 made it.

The match lasted through to the final whistle, and probably just as well for referee Stuart Attwell, infamous for awarding a 'ghost-goal' in a game between Watford and Reading in 2008 when players, management and the crowd were bemused to see him award a goal when the ball, in fact, went yards wide. The snow fell throughout the 90 minutes and settled on the Portman Road turf – a couple of inches deep in some places, covering the lines which were painted blue again. The layering of snow saved the match from postponement by preventing the players from skating around on the hard surface underneath. Captain Norris said it was the worst conditions he had ever played in, while Town groundsman Alan Ferguson confirmed the match was half a degree from being called off and felt Attwell was 'unbelievably brave' for letting it go ahead.

Brave, or weak, knowing the referee would have to face a visit from Keane? Somehow, Town found solace in their bitter surroundings, whereas Leicester, managed by Sven-Goran Eriksson, stumbled around like camels in the snow.

Priskin paid for his display at Preston by being left out completely, as was Andros Townsend, who was said to be suffering from a virus but was later revealed to have left the club and returned to Tottenham. Delaney, Marton Fulop and Shane O'Connor were drafted in. Whether it was Keane's selection, tactics or simply the weather which helped Town into a 3-0 lead was open to opinion. But whatever the virtues of Town's setup, they certainly fancied it more on the snow than Leicester. The colour of the ball, lines and pitch made no difference to Town as they took the lead through Norris with their first sight of goal. Scotland drove in a second and poked a close-range effort to make it 3-0 before half-time when the groundsmen did their best to clear the pitch and fend off the worsening conditions.

Attwell, however, threatened to throw a major spanner in the works when he decided to take the teams off after an hour so the pitch could again be cleared and conditions judged to see if the game could at the least continue. As the referee made his way to the warmth of the dressing room Keane was in his ear with a few words of advice. Fourteen minutes later the teams emerged and the final half an hour was played out, bringing Keane and Town fans momentary joy as the losing run was brought to a shuddering end.

Keane, who feared the worst when Attwell brought the match to a halt, said Town 'played to their strengths', using the height of Fallon, and later the returning Connor Wickham, to avoid the roulette of playing the ball on the unpredictable surface. Eriksson, unsurprisingly for a manager who had just seen his side beaten 0-3, felt the match should either have been postponed beforehand or cancelled when the teams were taken off and said it was a 'bad advert' for football. The Leicester players were in the ear of Attwell as soon as they went behind, according to Norris.

As the snow continued to settle around the country, Town breathed a colossal sigh of relief and Keane could enjoy the taste of his Christmas dinner that little bit more. For goalkeeper Brian Murphy, Christmas was made painful by a broken ankle suffered in training, which was expected to keep him out of action for three months, and a similar fate befell O'Connor, who dislocated a shoulder.

As good as the result was against Leicester, Town remained in the thick of a crisis. A snow-affected victory after six defeats was simply a break from the norm, like moving under the eye of a hurricane when you can look up and see blue skies for a short while before the storm returns at full gusto.

'I would have liked to have seen him [Keane] gone before the Leicester match,' said Andrew McGarry. 'It would have given the new manager a couple of weeks to look at his squad and work out what he needed to do in January. I think being a big name, though, the fans had expected too much of him, despite winning promotion with Sunderland (plus, although he took over when they were bottom, they had a strong squad for the division). He was an inexperienced manager who was out of his depth, but often these great players fail to be great managers because they have no concept of dealing with players who are not able to perform the same skills as they could, and also do not know how to deal with players who are lacking in confidence and going through a run of comparative failure.'

Keane denied it was 'make or break' time for the club but he and the rest of the staff were given a chance to recharge and reassess where they were at, when a frozen Portman Road was deemed unfit for the Boxing Day visit of Watford. The hot air blowers and inflatable tent did their best to keep the game on, and the tent was up until 90 minutes before kick-off when referee Grant Hegley deemed certain areas of the pitch too hard. Many fans were already at the ground and, on seeing a pitch clear of snow and visibly more playable than against Leicester, were perplexed when the announcement was made. The trip to Doncaster's Keepmoat Stadium on 28 December also fell to the big freeze but the postponement was finalised 24 hours in advance.

The transfer window was just days away and Clegg confirmed Keane would have money to spend as there was 'no axe hanging over the manager's head'. The signs were pointing towards the club retaining Keane until the end of the season and the end of his contract – possibly with the opportunity to rebuild and prove himself one last time, as long as Town escaped relegation and deep embarrassment in the second half of the season.

It was the end of a desperately disappointing year for the club and its supporters. The promising form of August and September was a false dawn, as injuries highlighted the flimsiness of the squad and a lack of vision on Keane's part after his decision to stock up on carbon-copy midfielders when they needed flair and a right-back. Zuiverloon briefly filled the void but was called back to West Brom before the New Year and Town were again facing up to the reality of using square pegs in round holes. For the fans, the Portman Road experience was a cold affair. With the country still feeling the pinch financially, it was a huge ask to expect the paying public to back Keane's side, knowing that the quality of football was at its poorest for a decade. The beauty of football is its unpredictability, but even Keane had admitted watching Town was like Groundhog Day.

The New Year would bring Marcus Evans and Ipswich Town to a crossroads and Keane was well aware that the writing was on the wall for him should the purse strings stay shut. It was interesting that he was able to spell out so many of the problems associated with the side he built but was unable to do anything about them. He knew they were predictable and one-paced going forwards – so he sent Townsend back to Tottenham citing the player's 'potential lack of game time' and expressing a desire for a more 'defensive minded' player on the wing. He knew the club could not be dependent on players who were contracted to other clubs, yet he continued to bring in loanees who were arguably no better than the players he either sent out on loan or banished to the reserves for a few weeks at a time. 'It [bringing in loan players] catches up with you and I think it's caught up with us now and will over the next few weeks,' he said. And he knew his side needed to play with more freedom to take the pressure off the defence, to avoid the need to keep a clean sheet to win a match. But still they were shackled.

'Will the club invest in players when the manager's contract expires in about four or five months' time? Who knows? There are lots of question marks that we need to look at over the next few days,' he said.

Chapter Nineteen

January 2011 – The Final Stand

'I'VE BEEN KEEN TO STRENGTHEN OVER THE LAST 16 MONTHS, SO A FEW DAYS WON'T MAKE A DIFFERENCE. I WON'T BE ON THE PHONE TONIGHT.'

1 January 2011. A New Year brought with it with a fresh purge on managers in English football. Preston's Darren Ferguson and Burnley's Brian Laws failed to see out 2010, but George Burley made it as far as 2011, only to be relieved of his duties at Crystal Palace, wallowing in 23rd place in the Championship after a three-goal defeat at Millwall.

Roy Keane was waiting to see if his New Year wish would be granted – three signings in the transfer window, and a few victories to go with them. The increasing regularity of managerial changes was 'nature of the game' in his view, having accepted publicly that his job had been on the line for some time.

Town's 1-1 draw at Coventry City – their first in 17 games – represented an improvement upon their three previous away matches which all ended in defeat, although it would have done nothing to alter Marcus Evans's thinking towards the manager and his January strategy, especially as Town, boosted by the return of Gareth McAuley, took the lead through Rory Fallon two minutes before half-time and spent most of the second half playing against ten men. Freddy Eastwood equalised three minutes after the break when Marton Fulop failed to keep out his saveable effort after a lay-off from Marlon King, whose ugly challenge on Darren O'Dea then brought him a red card.

The substitutions followed – Troy Brown, Connor Wickham and Ronan Murray – but none of the youngsters could change the pattern of play and Town were left facing questions of why they were unable to break down ten men and, at the least, create clear-cut chances. 'The hardest part of the game is putting the ball in the back of the net, but we haven't got six strikers like Cardiff, Forest and teams like that, experienced strikers,' said Keane. 'We're bringing young boys off the bench in Connor, who has just come back from injury, and young Ronan, who got a good shot away.'

3 January 2011. 'What is bugging Keane the most is the stalemate he finds himself in over a player he would love to have permanently – Jack Colback,' wrote Elvin King in the *Evening Star*. Colback's loan spell at Town was nearly up and he told Keane that a further loan deal was not his preferred option as he wanted the security of a permanent move if

Sunderland manager Steve Bruce would be willing to let him go. The sticking point was the potential transfer fee. 'We might not be able to agree a fee with Sunderland and we might not have any money to spend on Jack,' Keane said. The January window was now open and Keane had already spoken to Evans about the funds available. The drawstrings appeared to be closing on the transfer kitty after Keane revealed they were 'playing it by ear'.

Four changes at Coventry were followed by five changes for the first match at Portman Road in 2011 when Nottingham Forest visited. A Damien Delaney own-goal late in the first half gave Forest victory on a day when nothing went right for Town or Keane. Grant Leadbitter was sent off for a high lunge late on, but by that time, even though Forest were only one goal ahead, enough was seen to know that there was no way back for Town – or Keane.

Chants calling for his removal came from the Sir Bobby Robson stand and, as he made his way along the touchline towards the tunnel after the final whistle, he made a gesture in the shape of a mouth with his hand, aimed at disgruntled fans in the Britannia Stand, who were voicing their disapproval of the state of the club and Keane's management. Season-ticket holder Mervyn Collen was reported in the *Evening Star* as the recipient of Keane's gesture after he asked the Irishman 'how much longer is this going to go on for?' 'I was confronted by one of the stewards but I told him that I hadn't done anything wrong,' Collen told the paper. 'It's not as if I ran on to the pitch or anything like that. I've been watching Ipswich for over 20 years now. In my opinion if you pay your money you're entitled to have your say and people should take that on the chin. I have nothing personal against Mr Keane. I just don't think he's the man for the job. What happened on Monday was the result of me seeing a series of poor performances.'

There was no comment from the club on the incident, nor did Keane add anything on the matter which was seen by the few yet to leave the stadium. Instead, he was asked, predictably, about his future and transfers. 'It is not important whether or not I keep my job,' he said. 'My job is not important, what we have to do is get the best out of this football club. It's not about me, the club is bigger. I'm doing my best, but if the best is not good enough, then I will pay the consequences … I've been keen to strengthen over the last 16 months, so a few days won't make a difference. I won't be on the phone tonight.'

6 January 2011. Word started to spread of Keane's departure from Ipswich Town late in the afternoon, first of all on internet message boards, and with bookmakers suspending betting on his successor. The deed had indeed been done – Evans contacted Keane by phone and brought an end to one of the most tumultuous periods in the club's history. The news was then confirmed in the press, though not by the club. By late evening Paul Jewell was reported to be the favourite to replace Keane.

'Everyone knew it was going to happen but it was a question of when rather than if,' said Phil Ham. 'The club had reached a stage of the season when they thought it was right to make the change. I don't know that there was a clause in his contract allowing a pay-off six months before his contract expired or anything like that. It was an expensive mistake and a miscalculation and, in hindsight, was not what the club needed at the time. After Jim Magilton they needed an experienced Joe Royle-type figure. Was it the club's biggest mistake? Bobby Ferguson was regarded as a big mistake when he was appointed after Sir Bobby and Jackie Milburn's spell in charge was considered fairly catastrophic.'

7 January 2011. A press conference was called for 11am by the club at which chief executive Simon Clegg said Keane's contract was 'amicably terminated' after 20 months in charge. 'Today is a sad day for me. I have enjoyed working with Roy over the past two seasons and I would like to thank him for his tremendous dedication and professionalism during that period,' added Clegg. 'Regrettably though, we have not made the progress that we had all expected over the last 20 months and this season in particular, with the side slipping to 19th place in the Championship table.' Clegg would admit a few days later that Keane was 'showing the strain' after his run-in with the fans and the time had come to listen to the 'vocal minority and silent majority'.

Keane's response was dignified and was released through the League Managers' Association: 'I'm hugely disappointed to be leaving Portman Road. Results haven't been as good as I'd have hoped so far this season and when results aren't good the manager gets the sack, that's the game. However, I have a genuine belief that we were making progress and that the players have what it takes to turn this season around. We were preparing well for our visit to Chelsea on Sunday and then our Carling Cup semi with Arsenal. Getting to that semi proves what I know the team is capable of. I was also working hard to build the squad during the transfer window, looking at our options to attract new players to the club. I have loved my time at Ipswich, living locally to the club with my family, and have a massive respect for the club, its staff, the fans and the community and I wish them well.'

Coach Ian McParland was put in temporary charge with the FA Cup third round tie at Chelsea looming and Clegg said a new manager would be appointed in the coming days. McParland was then put before the press in what was a whirlwind day at the club as everyone took in the fact Keane was gone, along with the circus which came with him.

'I spoke to Roy this morning,' said a shocked McParland. 'Roy's a professional and a proud man, and he's a human being, let's not forget that, he's going to be upset. If you were to get sacked from a job, you'd be upset. But he's a tough cookie and he'll go on to be a good manager. No, he's a good manager now, he's had success at Sunderland. He'll be fine. I think a lot of people have got the wrong impression of Roy Keane. Roy Keane is a fair, fair man, a fair, honest man. Like any other manager, you have your moments with players, but sometimes they deserve it. There's this persona of Roy Keane, but you couldn't meet a better man than Roy Keane.'

Matt Plummer thought Keane would be given until after the Carling Cup-tie against Arsenal but had no complaints about the timing. 'It could have happened earlier in the week,' he said. 'A lot of people felt a cloud had lifted from over the club. There was a big cloud lingering both on and off the pitch. You sensed that not everyone was happy and people were hankering for the old days. While some wanted to break the shackles and get away from the stereotypical 'friendly, cosy club', I think an awful lot of people felt that was what was special about Ipswich and that the club was no longer special. Since he has gone I have felt it come back.

'Despite all the negativity which surrounded Keane I genuinely liked him. He wanted it to work, he was completely committed to the job and you could see the frustration in him that things were not working. He was fascinating to listen to – I could listen to him talk all day, the way he spoke about his days at Nottingham Forest and Manchester United. However, that was probably part of his problem, you never had faith that he could get it right as Ipswich manager, it was all about what had gone on before in his life.

'He had a charm about him and although there were times when he could be quite intimidating and there were some prickly press conferences, he would happily sit and talk and talk and talk and give people his time. His honesty kept people on his side and I believe a lot of people agreed, deep down, with what he was saying. We are in an age when managers come out with the same tired old rhetoric and all sing from the club hymn sheet. It was refreshing and the local media liked him up until the end.'

Town fan Oliver Procter was unhappy with the way Keane was eventually made a scapegoat both in the media and by the club's supporters for the lack of success on the pitch. 'Keane should not have been sacked before he finally was,' he said. 'We should not cater for the boo boys, and the part-timers [fans] who bring negativity to the club. I think Keane was spot on about the fans, and rather than blame him, all fans need to have a look in the mirror, as we have a job to do too, otherwise the side may as well play behind closed doors. The fans were split on Keane. He had every right to be critical of them and I do not believe he said anything of great offence. I liked his no-nonsense approach and as long as the extra publicity he brought brings finance and improved players, then I have no problem with the way he was portrayed during his time here.'

THE AFTERMATH

Liberation swept over Portman Road when Roy Keane packed up his belongings and left the club, 20 months after he arrived to the loudest managerial fanfare ever heard at Ipswich Town. During those 20 months he took the club from the cusp of the play-offs to relegation candidates, albeit cup semi-finalists as well, having spent millions of pounds on a squad which failed to produce results, entertainment and above all else, pride.

It was a period which left a bad taste; for the extra exposure when the club was at the wrong end of the table, for its expenditure on players branded 'a waste of money' and whom were on wages which insulted the supporters struggling to stay in the black amid the tightening grip of the recession, and for the destruction of its 'friendly club' tag, borne from the family tradition of the Cobbolds but desecrated by all the negative stories in the press.

The fun factor on matchday was gone, replaced by vexation and irritation – at Keane's tactics and the negativity which came from him in his post-match interviews. His honesty was never in doubt, but when the supporters renewed their season tickets in April of the previous two seasons they were under the impression that the good times were going to return – the goal-sprees, the players who could play melodies with their feet and the gratification which came from watching it and being a part of it.

Instead, the club was in a state of paralysis for at least 12 months, building for the future when the present was the promise. This coasting period was endured for only a few months under Jim Magilton but, with Keane given a fair crack, it felt like forever for the fans who travelled the length and breadth of the country to see another 0-1 defeat, another lone striker attempt to battle three defenders under a high ball. And then be told on the way home, via the airwaves, that their side lacked the tools to challenge for a top-six place.

Despite the peaks and troughs of Keane's relationship with the club's supporters, he did not depart as a figure of hate, or a man vilified by his own. The people of Suffolk and surrounding areas took him to their heart, as they had Magilton, and gave him every chance to succeed and instil a sense of hope for the future. Once the vocal minority turned against him it was more a calling aimed at Marcus Evans for change, rather than a personal attack on Keane. As one would expect of a man regarded as one of the finest warriors ever to grace a football pitch, he never hid, he very rarely blamed other people and admitted to his own failures and shortcomings.

It was this human side that the supporters could relate to and trusted. It was the footballing side of Keane which lost respect and trust, for his refusal to buy into the club's ethos of keeping the ball on the ground and for trapping himself in the pitfall of following the crowd with the nation-wide obsession with 4-5-1 and rigid mindsets. At the time of his sacking, former club Manchester United lined up with Dimitar Berbatov up front alongside Wayne Rooney and with Ryan Giggs and Nani marauding down the wings, supported by overlapping full-backs Rafael and Patrice Evra. Other clubs had made a success of 4-5-1 but in doing so had spent exorbitant amounts on specific players who made the system work.

'Fear' was a word used throughout Keane's reign at Town (his mistakes and characteristics were repetitious but I felt they needed repeating in this book to highlight where he went wrong and his failure to change his ways or find a settled side), though rarely was it used in conjunction with himself, except when his future was being called into question. It was the 'fear' of the players which was highlighted, when actually, the manager's fear was the more telling factor. Why was Keane so afraid of giving his players license to express themselves?

He talked of the Championship being a division which was escaped only by those who were 'streetwise' and had the 'character' to prise out results in testing circumstances. There was little doubt the likes of QPR, Norwich, Swansea and Cardiff had the necessary character to see off the division's minnows on cold Tuesday nights, but from just ten minutes viewing it could be grasped that these were sides full of skilful players who were playing on the edge. Be it QPR's Adel Taarabt swaying past opponents in his own half or Swansea putting together 30 passes on the edge of their own penalty area to keep possession and build an attack from deep, they were prepared to take risks and stayed true to their values. Ipswich, on the other hand, were awkward for watching scouts to classify under Keane's management. Was it deliberate long-ball football or just a lack of confidence? Were the players being told not to reach the by-line and instead cross early or again, was it a shortage of confidence? Keane was expected to be a master motivator, a leader of men who would take to the pitch with a never-say-die attitude. Come January 2011, it was his own side fearing themselves and Keane himself fearing the sack.

'I believe there is a good man inside him but it was a major mistake to make him Town manager,' said journalist Dave Allard. 'To do a decent job you have to make friends. Had it been anyone else who was in charge during this period, they would have been gone far earlier.

'When he was manager of Sunderland and brought them to Portman Road, I was in the media centre with Ipswich legend Kevin Beattie who had been asked by a friend if he could try and get a matchday programme signed by Roy. So Roy walked in and heads turned and everyone stiffened up. The Sunderland staff told us that Roy does not sign autographs and would just hand the programme back if we gave it to him. Kevin asked me if I would approach him so I went up to the side of the podium where he was sat and said "sorry Roy, would you mind signing this for Kevin Beattie?" There was a long pause and he asked "*the* Kevin Beattie?" I told him "yes"' and he signed, showing that there is a human side to him. He gave me a big hug, a strange hug, after the Leicester game and I sensed then that the writing was on the wall. I wrote him a letter when he was sacked and we parted on good terms.'

One of the few positive legacies to be left behind by Keane was the continuing presence of Connor Wickham at the club and the fitness of the first-team squad. Wickham filled column-inches in the local and national media every week, even when he was out injured or out of form. For Keane and the club to keep hold of their prize asset was a triumph. While the majority of his transfer dealings were dubbed 'flops', including Lee Martin, Colin Healy and Tamas Priskin, some were a success or might prove to be a success in the coming months and years. The £4 million paid for Grant Leadbitter and Carlos Edwards has looked reasonable value for money at best, as has the £750,000 spent on Jason Scotland, but Damien Delaney improved after a shaky start and Keane should be praised for using so many youngsters, even if his hand was forced due to a lack of other options and funds.

'Some of Keane's signings could go on to do well in the future,' said Phil Ham. 'Jaime Peters would probably be at another club if it wasn't for Keane, as he had been out on loan at places like Gillingham and Yeovil. Luke Hyam came in and was given time and will go on and become a better player for his experiences at this stage of his career under Keane, as will some of the other youngsters. We can also expect more from Carlos

Edwards, Grant Leadbitter, Damien Delaney and Shane O'Connor. I'm not sure Connor Wickham staying at the club was down to Roy Keane as such, I think it was more a case of the club he was at, being in the Championship where he could gain experience, and the club's traditions.'

Few of the players discarded reached greater heights since, although the impact of some, such as Danny Haynes and Pablo Counago, who had scored only twice for Crystal Palace before Christmas, was missed if only for their unpredictability. Jordan Rhodes continued to score regularly for Huddersfield in League One, and David Wright was a regular part of Crystal Palace's side when fit, as was Owen Garvan. Jon Stead had scored six goals for Bristol City by the start of the New Year, as had Jon Walters for Stoke City – three of them in the Premier League.

Defender Gareth McAuley, who after an unsettled start with Keane in charge became a pivotal figure in the Town squad, gave the most interesting view on what went wrong at the club, days after Keane's exit. The softly spoken Northern Irishman said in an interview that some of the players brought to the club 'let the manager down' and that there were some players who were 'not so disappointed' Keane was gone. He said: 'They have not been pulling their weight, and while I've been injured I've been watching games, saying to myself "Is he hiding?", "Is he doing enough?"' He added that he was able to take Keane's criticisms and management style 'on the chin', whereas some of the younger players in the squad did not respond well.

A further example of where Town were at after nearly two years of Keane in charge was on display at Stamford Bridge on 9 January when they were beaten 0-7 by Chelsea in the FA Cup third round. It was the club's worst ever defeat in the competition and would be Ian McParland's only game in charge before coach Tony Loughlan and he left the club. 'It's hard to say whether it would have been any different had Roy still been here,' McParland said. 'I'd like to think it would have been. Who knows?'

There was no time to stew over the manner in which Town crumbled against the Premier League champions as Paul Jewell was appointed as Keane's replacement 24 hours later. The 46-year-old was one of three managers to have won promotion to the Premier League with two different clubs [along with Mick McCarthy and Steve Coppell], having done so with Wigan Athletic and Bradford City, and he signed a two-and-a-half-year deal.

It was a low-key appointment compared to Keane's. Jewell had been out of work for two years and was best remembered for his previous job – a disastrous spell at Derby County where he won 12 out of 58 games.

But low key was what was required at Town to bring back the *status quo* and return the club to its former glories. It was time for Ipswich Town to be Ipswich Town again, not Roy Keane's Ipswich Town. To be the former FA Cup and UEFA Cup winners, champions of England in 1961-62, the club which produced England World Cup-winning manager Sir Alf Ramsey and Sir Bobby Robson, who took England to the semi-finals of the 1990 World Cup. Since April 2009 the club was a one-man band. But, in his own words, no club is bigger than one man.

'The club's history and image goes back further than Roy Keane,' explained Phil Ham. 'When someone mentions Ipswich Town they will think more of Sir Bobby Robson and George Burley than anything else. In a couple of years Roy Keane's spell as manager will seem brief in terms of the club's history and I am sure he will go on and get another job. The manager was bigger than the club while he was here – there was no other Championship club whose press conferences were attended by Sky Sports every week, but traditionally, the club is in a footballing backwater.'

For Ted Phillips, there was the opportunity to change the course of history in dramatic circumstances: 'I was travelling past the training ground one day in the car with my cousin when suddenly Roy Keane stepped out into the road and put his hand up for us to stop. We were doing about 50mph and we could have saved everyone the aggro of the last two years!'